A STUDY OF THE NOVELS OF GEORGE MOORE

A STUDY OF THE NOVELS OF GEORGE MOORE

Richard Allen Cave

Irish Literary Studies 3

COLIN SMYTHE
Gerrards Cross, Bucks
1978

Copyright © 1978 Colin Smythe Ltd.
First published in 1978 by Colin Smythe Ltd., Gerrards Cross,
Buckinghamshire

ISBN 0-901072-58-3

Irish Literary Studies series ISSN 0140-895X

British Library Cataloguing in Publication Data

Cave, Richard
    A study of the novels of George Moore. – (Irish
    literary studies; 3; 0140–895X).
    1. Moore, George – Criticism and interpretation
    I. Title II. Series
    823′.8   PR5043

ISBN 0–901072–58–3

Produced in Great Britain

Set by Watford Typesetters Ltd., and printed and bound by
Billing & Sons Ltd., Guildford, London and Worcester

*For my mother and in memory
of my father*

Contents

Author's Note

When *Héloïse and Abélard* was first published, the critics were warmly appreciative. Surprisingly Moore himself was not content. To Barrett H. Clark he complained: 'So few bother to analyse the book carefully. It would have been very easy to discuss the form, compare my treatment of it with others' treatment of similar themes, and so on, yet apparently no one ever thought of that'. Moore's rueful remark was the starting-point in designing this study. Each of his novels is examined in detail and viewed within the pattern of Moore's total development and the context of his current reading and ideas about technique. The value to him of a wide range of influences is assessed. The novels are reviewed in chronological order though *Esther Waters* is taken slightly out of sequence for the sake of thematic convenience. The volumes of short stories, the tale *Ulick and Soracha* and Moore's translation of *Daphnis and Chloe* are not discussed.

One problem confronts any serious student of Moore's work: the fact that, to use his own words, he was 'a victim of the disease of rewriting'. Few of his novels escaped revision; several underwent wholesale redrafting. In discussing them, therefore, I shall indicate which version I feel to be superior, where more than one text exists. Generally, the Ebury texts are the most accessible. These are exact reprints with identical pagination of the Uniform Edition of 1933, the publishing of which was largely supervised by Moore himself just before his death. This last edition contains the most satisfying version for him of the novels he saw fit to revise and retain in his canon of works. However, as it is a limited and expensive edition, it is not readily available. In the notes to each chapter I give page-references chiefly to the Ebury Edition and to such variants as I have found illuminating. In each instance I give full details of the text I recommend and my reasons for doing so. When a novel was not reprinted in these collections, I have generally used the text of the first edition.

Like all students of Moore's work I am deeply indebted to the bibliographical expertise of Edwin Gilcher in *A Bibliography of George Moore* (Illinois, 1970) and Helmut Gerber in 'George Moore: An Annotated Bibliography of Writings about him' (*English Fiction in Transition (1880-1920)*. Vols. ii-iv. 1959-61). Given their magnificent achievement, it seemed pointless to offer a working bibliography here; instead I have thoroughly annotated my argument.

I wish to thank Mr J. C. Medley, Moore's executor, for his kind permission to quote extensively from the novels. I must express my gratitude to the late Dr T. R. Henn for encouraging my enthusiasm for Moore's work and for supervising the early draft of this study which formed my doctoral dissertation; to Professors A. N. Jeffares and Graham Hough for their advice about reworking that draft for publication; to Colin Smythe for giving far more assistance than one would expect from one's publisher; and above all to my wife for her never-failing help and her useful criticism.

RICHARD ALLEN CAVE

Introduction

Early in 1881 George Moore, now approaching thirty years of age, settled in cheap lodgings off the Strand in London. Not for the first time in his life he had discovered in himself a vocation: he would be a novelist. It was an extraordinary decision for one who till a surprisingly advanced age was virtually illiterate, who had found syntax and spelling a perplexing enigma while at school and who to judge from his letters home in young adulthood had little feeling for the nuances of language and no sense of style whatever. Anyone who knew Moore intimately and who learned of his new decision might well be forgiven for expressing scepticism about the durability of his resolve. Since he came of age Moore had gone to Paris to become a great painter but had failed for want of talent; he had turned to poetry and produced two collections in imitation of Swinburne, Baudelaire and Poe that veered between the silly and the nasty[1]; he had tried drama, but *Martin Luther*[2] was a mechanical performance and no manager, French or English, had expressed any interest in it whatever; and off and on in Paris he had tried to play the roué and the naughty bohemian but had failed again, though this time for want of money rather than of aptitude.[3] For a year he had mouched about England and Ireland and finally came to Cecil Street, the Strand, pinning his hopes for success on the one remaining literary form available to him: the novel.

Fifty years or so later Moore woke on the morning of his eightieth birthday to find in *The Times*[4] a letter of congratulations signed by most of the principal writers and artists of the day, who greeted him as 'a master of English letters' and as one who 'has not ceased to labour with a single mind in the perfecting of his craft'. He was praised for the 'new melodies and rhythms' of his style and for his technique: 'you have taught narrative to flow again and anecdote to illuminate it as the sun a stream'. In 1881

11

Moore had indeed found his true vocation. His progress to success with so many odds against him was remarkable for the sheer effort of discipline, self-criticism and pertinacity required. But for once Moore really was determined and in time he reaped the harvest of patient dedication to an ideal. The eightieth-birthday greetings wrote of the sureness of his place in the tradition of English literature, yet ironically he was an Irishman and most of the strengths of his later work are characteristically Irish. Moreover when he began writing novels in the Eighteen-Eighties he knew virtually nothing of the tradition of the English novel. His reading had been almost exclusively till then in French literature. The models he turned to initially for inspiration and knowledge of the craft of fiction were not his recent English contemporaries, Dickens, Thackeray, Eliot or Meredith, but the French: Balzac, Flaubert, Zola and that francophile Russian, Turgenev.

For all his gaucheness Moore had taken advantage of the ease of French café-society to get acquainted with a whole host of artists and writers in Paris; he was on terms of some intimacy with Zola. Now he set about getting to know the French mind in a different sense through a painstaking study of various French techniques of fiction in direct relation to their power to help him express his own vision of life in a novel. Despite setbacks in his new vocation Moore persisted because writing constantly held for him the challenge of discovery. He only came to understand another writer's principles by imitating them, by testing their capacity to satisfy his own needs as a writer. Their success or failure to do so encouraged him both to revalue the fictional methods he had imitated and to review the experience he wished to communicate through a novel. Writing taught him literary appreciation and it brought him a deep self-awareness too. The rapidity of his development in the course of his first three novels is astonishing. The promptness of his recognition of where his original insights and inspiration lay, the easy sloughing off of styles that failed to enhance these original qualities, the ready willingness to experiment to extend his range, the frank recognition of his own shortcomings are all illustrated by this progress, which could not have happened but for a scrupulous objective assessing of his every effort. There is no doubting the seriousness of Moore's vocation.

The fact of Moore's growth is not in itself unusual; it is a common enough phenomenon in the careers of many novelists. What is of special interest is its actual nature: Moore's appreciating his essentially Anglo-Irish temperament and sensibility through the attempt to shape his particular perception of life to characteristically French forms of expression. What results is a fruitful tension between his recently acquired tastes and his innate instincts that provoked Moore into realising that every fictional method involves selection and compromise; that selection can over-simplify issues; and consequently that, because a novelist is fundamentally concerned with presenting and assessing the quality of life, his mode of selection, his choice of a technique, is in large measure a moral issue. Moore was not choosing his terms loosely when he described the one French novelist to have an enduring appeal for him, Balzac, as 'the great moral influence on my life'.[5] Of the four novelists mentioned, Balzac and Turgenev can be seen in retrospect to have been continuing shapers of Moore's imagination; Flaubert and Zola were powerful but passing enthusiasms. As Moore's first novels are the product of, as well as a demonstration of, his changing estimate of these different styles of contemporary French fiction, the best approach to his early work and aspirations would seem to be through some account of the four writers to whom at the outset of his career he turned for guidance.

What Moore admired in Balzac was his psychological intensity and penetration and that 'sympathy for human life [which] . . . enabled him to surround the humblest objects with awe and crown them with the light of tragedy'.[6] Balzac presents in *La Comédie Humaine* a view of contemporary society as satanic, since it is a world in which the appetite for material acquisition has become the mainspring of human activity. Paris is under the control of Mephistophelean figures like Vautrin, a former convict, who tempts youthful idealists like Rastignac in *Père Goriot* and Lucien de Rubempré in *Les Illusions Perdues* with the joys of social success but exacts their humanity from them in payment for his help in fostering their well-being. Always Balzac's concern is with the slow eroding of men's generous instincts and humane impulses as they become victims of their own material ambitions (whether his subject is the spectacular Faust-like rejections of good made under Vautrin's influence or the various studies of monomania, such as *Eugénie Grandet* or *La Cousine Bette*, where a whole being becomes steadily consumed by the lust to accumulate wealth) and so his vision remains tragic. Balzac's is, as Moore tersely described it, a 'winged realism',[7] for he never loses his sense of the human potential that is invariably and terribly wasted, and this excites his deepest compassion. The degradation both physical and spiritual to which his characters succumb is willed by them, is a deliberate choice from which there is always the possibility of retracting but for the growing strength of their obsessions. With a fastidiously exact attention to detail Balzac charts this process of decay; evil as he presents it is cumulative, ardent, complex, dynamic. But though it is the fate of the individual soul that grips his imagination, because that fate is brought about by social aspirations the way the characters become the architects of their own destruction acts as an exposure of contemporary society, its values and achievement. Balzac's method successfully presents man in his social, psychological and spiritual dimensions in the *Comédie Humaine*. Over the years increasingly it was the third of these aspects, Balzac's spiritual analysis, that aroused Moore's respect: 'with Balzac,' Moore wrote, 'I had descended circle by circle into the nether world of the soul and watched its afflictions'.[8] Moore was right to take the hint from Balzac's title, *La Comédie Humaine*, and imply an analogy here with Dante in whose vision the damned similarly are suffering for a love distorted to its antitheses: lust and hatred. Balzac, like Dante, is confident that there is an alternative pattern of behaviour; Flaubert and Zola by contrast were sceptical of this and questioned whether the whole idea of a spiritual dimension was not misguidedly romantic.

One of Flaubert's characters may define passion as 'the source of all heroism and enthusiasm, poetry, music, art, everything'[9] but that character is Rodolphe, Madame Bovary's seducer, whose words are sophistries: once his lady has succumbed, he is quick to dismiss such attitudes as foolhardy and compromising affectations. A reduction like this of all values to the uniform and the vulgar is the key to Flaubert's method: his characters are the victims of their own mediocrity. Emma Bovary herself yearns to transcend her miserable condition as the wife of a tedious if honest doctor but the motive of her aspirations is only self-satisfaction; there is nothing altruistic or truly creative about her visions of a better life, they are wholly sentimental delusions. Emma strives for some means of expressing her longing for beauty and romance but all her efforts lack true heroism because, being intensely self-centred, they bring about a progressive disruption and exhaustion of feeling. Her consciousness is fated to wither back into the truth.

Flaubert realised that presenting this recurring cycle of disillusionment posed a problem: how were he and the reader to remain detached and escape the lure of Emma's sentimentality. His aim was analysis not empathy; the writing would have to sustain a permanent note of irony: 'the entire value of my book,' he wrote, will consist of my having known how to walk straight ahead on a hair, balanced above the two abysses of lyricism and vulgarity (which I seek to fuse in analytical narrative)'.[10] The satisfaction for himself and the reader would come from preserving this dispassionate objectivity quite inexorably. Reading Flaubert's work for the first time, Moore was 'astonished . . . with the wonderful delicacy and subtlety of his workmanship'.[11] But the very inevitability of the method began to pall. Flaubert's aim may have been to expose the poverty of contemporary material standards yet, Moore realised, the famous method constantly asserts that Flaubert himself accepts those standards as so sure and inviolate as to preclude any alternatives; the method in its pitilessness was far from objective. Moore's second novel, *A Mummer's Wife*, took its initial inspiration from Flaubert but it reaches out for very different psychological and social conclusions. Thereafter Flaubert seemed tiresome to him for his predictability:

> What nonsense has been talked about him! Impersonal! Nonsense, he is the most personal writer I know. That odious pessimism. How sick I am of it, it never ceases, it is lugged in *à tout propos*, and the little lyrical phrase with which he winds up every paragraph, how boring it is.[12]

Moore criticised Flaubert finally because his novels lacked one quality Balzac's had in superabundance and which he deemed indispensable; as Henry James succinctly puts it:

> . . . there was something ungenerous in [Flaubert's] genius. He was cold and he would have given everything he had to be able to glow. . . . Flaubert yearned with all the accumulations of his vocabulary to touch the chord of pathos.[13]

Though his method was of course far less sophisticated than Flaubert's, Moore learned how to touch that note of pathos in

A Mummer's Wife, A Drama in Muslin and *Esther Waters* while avoiding vulgar sentiment. He too evolved through the composition of these three novels a technique of ironic narrative; but it is one where the play of ironies is analytical yet creative and life-enhancing.

Moore had chanced upon Zola's essays, *Le Roman Expérimental*, in *Voltaire*; instantaneously, he claimed, Zola 'inebriated me with theory'.[14] The hangover was of quite a long duration. On the surface Zola's work appears to have much in common with Balzac's: there is the idea of a cycle of interlocking novels creating an autonomous fictional world; there is a similar view of life in society as hell on earth but, even more fiercely than Flaubert, Zola suppresses all pity. The element of choice in committing oneself to the social process that Balzac makes so much of is withheld; inspired by Darwinian theories of heredity, Zola saw man as absolutely destined to fall a prey to his materialistic instincts. Social environment and the family background act like forces of fate. Zola's is a ruthless world where everyone is in quest of money and power as a bid to escape, if only briefly, the determining forces in life by being in a position to mould the lives of others to one's will; and since imagination and sympathy play no part in this world, success is expressed in sadism and destruction. (Saccard, the property magnate coins his wealth from the demolition of Paris for re-development – 'the city was being slashed to pieces with sabre-strokes and he had a finger in every slash, in every wound';[15] and Nana, the great courtesan, humiliates her lovers by making them desport themselves as animals.) The psychological pattern repeats itself remorselessly in its essentials from novel to novel; only the social and environmental circumstances change.

Because he chose to invest environment with such a weight of influence on the individual life, Zola insisted that it should be represented in novels with a painstakingly detailed accuracy; concentrating on the exactness of one's descriptive detail would ensure in the writer a scientific objectivity. 'He has principles,' wrote Flaubert of Zola, 'and they narrow his vision.'[16] The simplification that results can at times make for a mechanical demonstrating of his theories of society; ironically Zola's method tends to be at its best when his vision is most narrow and therefore intensely subjective, when the depth of his obvious hatred of prevailing social conditions generates an extraordinary vituperative energy which releases in his imagination a black poetry, vital though prophetic of despair, the disgust of a latter-day Jeremiah. When this happens the excessive detail ceases to be factual and becomes symbolic; here Zola too, as James said, 'in his way . . . improvises in the grand manner'.[17] His most controlled and thorough performance in this vein is perhaps *L'Assommoir* (which Moore long continued to admire and once considered translating into English[18]): the ever-recurring physical fights establish a basic image for the human condition; the Lorilleux family's little gold factory emblematises Gervaise Coupeau's ambition; the brandy-distillery becomes a haven of security for the Coupeaux once Gervaise and her husband have won some financial success; the danger and the fascination of the brandy-shop are first evoked through the repeated descriptions of the neighbouring dyer's factory which exudes obscene, strangely coloured liquids and then realised in the long accounts of Coupeau's idiot dance while suffering from *delirium tremens* and of Gervaise's brutish death from starvation; throughout the narrative there is the ominous presence of Bazange, the undertaker, a mocking reminder of death. The vision shaping the narrative is poetic and deeply, if narrowly, moral.

Elsewhere, to emphasize the enticing nature of the sins of luxury, Zola supercharges his factual enumerations with psychological images so that, by a fantastic poetic fallacy, objects like food and flowers become symptomatic of the lives of the rich for whose consumption and glorification they are destined. They are endowed by implication with all the trappings of vice[19]; Zola, Moore said tartly, 'embellishes [everything] with erotic arabesques',[20] though he graciously admits to being attracted by the technique: from the first, he continues, Zola 'enchanted me with decoration'.[21] The criticism slyly intimated through the words 'embellish' and 'decoration' here is just. The danger with the technique is that the passion on which it relies will not be sustained throughout a complete work (so that the symbolism is comprehensive and organic as in *L'Assommoir*) but will be intermittent, which will result in stylistic inconsistencies and what James calls 'the fatal break in *tone*, the one unpardonable sin for the novelist'.[22] When this happens the poetic denunciations of vice seem merely a mannerism. To succeed, the poetic impulse must have complete control of the novel but even then, because it derives from dynamic hatred alone, there is a sense of inadequacy. Zola's moral fervour is both his artistic strength and his most serious limitation: there is no fine discrimination (pleasure is always for him synonymous with lust) and the intensity is never relaxed. In rearranging Flaubert's terms to give a different emphasis, Moore came to a closer appraisal of Zola in describing him as 'a man of powerful mind, but singularly narrow vision'.[23] When Moore embarked on his career as a novelist, Zola's technique of simplification held obvious attractions, but he quickly discovered its inflexibility; the style enchanted him for a longer period, but with time that heavy poetic prose came to seem over-indulgent. He had been deceived by externalities.

Though Moore's admiration of Turgenev was of long standing, it was only gradually and in reaction against the determinism of Flaubert and Zola's art that Moore perceived the possible value to him of the Russian's meticulous though unassuming technique. Always Turgenev is conscious of the sheer vulnerability of the individual existence:

> All of us are transgressors, even as we are alive, and there is no thinker so exalted, no human benefactor so great that, by virtue of what he has done for mankind, he may presume that he has the right to live. . . .[24]

Only a nation's culture, the fruit of men's altruistic endeavours, and nature have permanence. Most of Turgenev's novels depict the growth of an acceptance of this and, as a result, the flowering of a special humility in his heroes, which far from being nihilistic and enervating spurs them on to creative exertion. They learn the moral distinction between 'love – the pleasure' and 'love – the sacrifice' and acquire a fine self-sufficiency.[25] Turgenev concentrates on exploring man's sensibility and to define its activity he frequently describes his characters' responses to their natural environment. There is a relevant discussion about this by Shubin, himself an artist, in *On The Eve*. Nature, he argues, 'awakens the need for love, but is not capable of satisfying it'. We must distinguish:

> It drives us gently into other, living arms, but we don't realize this, and expect something from Nature herself. . . . everything around us is lovely, and yet you're grieving. But if at this moment you were holding the hand of a woman you loved, . . . then, Andrei, it wouldn't be grief and anxiety that Nature stirred up

in you, you wouldn't stop to contemplate its beauty; no, you'd find Nature itself would exult and sing, it would echo your own rhapsodies – because you would have given to Nature, dumb Nature, a tongue.[26]

Description is integral to all Turgenev's stories, evoking moods and orchestrating the characters' feelings and psychological predicaments; but this is not pathetic fallacy: nature reflects human emotions only when they are consciously projected on to it by the characters themselves. Nature is beautiful, infinite but impassive; it embodies a life-principle that is unchanging and eternal, that dictates the brevity of the individual life but which if viewed aright (and discovering that perspective is Turgenev's motive for writing) offers its compensations:

> Poetry is the language of the gods. . . . But poetry is not only in poems; it is diffused everywhere, it is around us. Look at those trees, that sky – on all sides there is the breath of beauty, and of life, and where there is life and beauty, there is poetry also.[27]

There is here no sentimental romanticism; as Henry James wrote of Turgenev: 'the element of poetry in him is constant and yet reality stares through it without the loss of a wrinkle'.[28]

It is significant that Moore turned to Turgenev for inspiration when he began a novel about life in Ireland, *A Drama in Muslin*, which examines the ways in which an individual can resist the pressures to conform to social laws. Alice Barton refuses to narrow her vision; the instincts she trusts in do not play her false, rather they initiate a complete revolution in her awareness and endow her with self-sufficiency. The transforming of her sensibility, the maturing of her resilient hopes, is revealed by Moore entirely through her changing reactions to the Irish landscape as she observes it on her lonely walks or seated at the window of her study. In an article about Turgenev that Moore wrote shortly after the completion of this novel he stated that in his view Turgenev's great theme is 'obey nature's laws, be simple and obey; it is the best that you can do'.[29] That evaluation, 'best', did not apparently strike Moore as forcibly in 1888 as it was to do later. It was well over a decade before Moore returned to Ireland and again made Irish life the subject of his fiction. When he did, it was to make Turgenev's great theme his own great theme too, though in a wholly idiosyncratic manner: *The Lake* is at once a portrait of a sensibility and a lyrical evocation of the Irish countryside. In his 1888 article on Turgenev Moore expressed the covert wish that he could draw an Irish Bazaroff in imitation of *Fathers and Sons*;[30] Father Oliver Gogarty of *The Lake* is in many respects that ambition fulfilled. Between the formation of the desire and its satisfaction fell a long period of restless experiment in which Moore had to learn the value of Turgenev's simplicity of expression. Ironically the new influence that in the Nineties beguiled Moore away from a deeper study of the Russian's work was the one who in time led him back by a highly circuitous route to Turgenev with renewed insight: Wagner. By 1904 when *The Lake* was published, Balzac, Turgenev and Wagner had become so deeply fused in Moore's creative consciousness that they formed a wholly original synthesis. Trusting persistently in them, Moore found the means to express his personal vision.

PART ONE:
THE NOVEL OF SOCIAL REALISM

(1) *A Modern Lover*

Although Moore's return to London from Paris in 1880 was dictated principally by the precarious state of his income from Ireland, it at least enabled him to terminate his friendship with, and erstwhile patronage of, the dissolute and unprincipled Weldon Hawkins, the Lewis Marshall of the *Confessions of a Young Man*. Moore was never one to have scruples about turning details of his own or other people's lives to artistic account and in his first novel, *A Modern Lover*, he was inspired by Hawkins's character to devise 'an excellent anecdote'[1] of an artist's rise to popular fame through the aid of three female admirers, Gwynnie Lloyd, a working-class girl; Mrs Bentham, a society hostess; and an aristocrat, Lady Helen Trevor. The text, he wrote later, was concocted 'out of his memories of Balzac, Zola and Goncourt'.[2]

Moore's concern in the novel is with the failure of personality in an artist who makes material and social success his sole aim in life. The worthless nature of Lewis Seymour's character is demonstrated by an analysis of the quality of his art; and his moral viciousness is revealed by the contrasts repeatedly drawn by Moore between Seymour's motives and those of his admirers. Seymour was pampered as a child by his widowed mother, and he has grown up as a dreamer with little sense of the need for the practical and determined application that is necessary to establish a career. His is a sensual not a virile or critical intelligence. He is confronted in his poverty by glimpses of the luxury and the indulgence in pleasure of society life in London, and he lacks the judgement to perceive the social injustice of the contrast between the lives of the rich and the poor. He is enraged; but his rage is not critical, rather it expresses his utter frustration that such a life should not be his; the question of its licentiousness does not trouble him. He cannot accept the reality of his poverty as an incitement to continue in his chosen career as a painter with a greater will than ever to succeed.

Though Moore writes of Balzac's influence on the novel, Moore's hero is quite unlike Balzac's Vautrin or Rastignac: Seymour has none of their dynamic energy, their satanic power of self-assertion. Vautrin and Rastignac acknowledge the moral corruption of society, but they join battle with that society on its own terms, knowing that in such a state of anarchy victory is to the strong. Seymour, however, is overcome with self-pity and dramatises his helplessness and misery by musing on suicide. But even that anxiety is too much for him, and he dispels his fears in consoling day-dreams of success. His tragedy lies in the fact that his anxiety is never sustained sufficiently to evoke in him a creative or self-critical response, for each of his three admirers sacrifices herself that he may continue to bask in the warmth of his illusions. So potent is Seymour's fear of poverty, his memory of life in a garret in Waterloo Road, that all his actions are governed by a moral cowardice, though that cowardice frequently takes the form of a kind of cunning, for he resorts to any amount of hypocrisy, flattery or deceit to solicit the favour of the women who are necessary to sustain the bubble of his self-opinion. He has no real feeling for them except as a means of affirming himself; he is wholly parasitic, as he turns the weakness of their affection for him to his material advantage. The least scruple of conscience in these women he callously dismisses as their selfishness.

Gwynnie Lloyd, a deeply religious working-class girl, sacrifices her modesty to pose nude for a picture by Seymour of a Venus exulting in her nakedness. He is totally insensitive to the mental conflict that underlies her outward resignation and is almost brut-ally indifferent to her need to find some justification for her con-duct as a moral duty.

> 'I do this, Lewis,' she explained . . . , 'because we are nearly starving, because I believe I am saving your life; but you'll not think worse of me; you will respect me, will you not?'[3]

Mrs Bentham compromises her position and shatters her peace of mind to give Seymour social advantages in London and Paris. But his taste for socializing arouses in him a dissoluteness and lethargy that undermine his artistic abilities, the fostering of which was the object of her taking such risks. She is a middle-aged woman separated from her roué of a husband; deprived for so long of any true affection she yearns for an object on which to lavish her sympathy. But the urgency of this desire prevents her from seeing that Seymour might be equally as vicious as her husband. However, the very nature of her affection for him both as an artist and as a man is so maternal in her concern to further his career that ultimately it saves her from the corroding power of his selfishness. Though she is indulgent to his whims, her motive principally derives from an altruistic concern to make his career a success, and this both affords her the strength to face his betrayal of her when he marries Lady Helen Trevor and offers her a consolation for the future, for she continues to encourage Seymour as an artist even when she is deprived of him as a lover.

Lady Helen has no such consoling interest as Mrs Bentham has and so the pathos of her situation is correspondingly more acute. Bored by the narrow-minded ignorance of the men of her social rank, she is attracted by the ardour of Lewis's conversation and ideas. His brilliance disarms her moral judgement and only gradually does she come to appreciate that that brilliance is superficial, that in both his life and his art he lacks the necessary power of will and a real force of emotion to realise his potential. When she meets a true artist, Harding, a novelist, Lady Helen appreciates how slight Seymour's dedication to his work is and how worthless as a result are both his talent and his character. Despite her growing revulsion for her husband, she attempts to preserve her marriage and her family. This is the source of her tragedy, for to do this she allows Seymour to undermine steadily all her own principles of conduct. Flirtation, he argues, is nothing more than 'making oneself agreeable'[4] and she must flirt with men to gain him commissions for designs and portraits. At his instigation she tempts another artist, Holt, whose marriage to a working-class woman prevents his moving in society, with offers of social advancement if he will vote against the friend he has personally nominated to the Royal Academy and aid her husband's election instead. Never having known the virtue of principle in himself, Seymour fails even to perceive, let alone acknowledge its worth in others. When Helen talks of her self-respect he dismisses her scruples lightly as 'one of those little stepping-stones which an admirer lays at the foot of a great man'.[5]

It is a recurring theme in Moore's criticism that art, and particularly painting, is a very revealing indication of the artist's personality.[6] Throughout *A Modern Lover* discussions as to the nature of art and the true artist are included as a means of extending our knowledge of Seymour's psychology. Just as his sensuality is the key to his character so it is the basis of his art. He makes no effort to depict the complex nature of the visible world about him, but attempts to capture a false and mannered atmosphere of total, sensuous licence, by imitating the rococo fantasies of Fragonard, Watteau and Boucher. Harding, the novelist, and Thompson, a painter, who are offered by Moore as types of the true artist, postulate a very different, almost Flaubertian ideal of art as sacerdotal. By a determined self-discipline they have sacrificed for their art everything that Seymour most prizes in life, and their reward is an abundance of inspiration and an ability to persevere until they achieve a satisfying expression of their imagined ideals. Seymour never attempts 'the thorny path leading to some far ideal';[7] when faced with any dilemma whether moral or aesthetic he lacks the necessary resilience to accept the challenge, but gives way to a shallow pessimism from which his dreaming soon rescues him. In his art, his dreams are manifest as an innate *penchant* for the decorative which though popular and technically assured 'ever remained the same, vacant, empty, common-place – he could not create.'[8] For Harding, such fleshly fancies are but 'namby-pamby';[9] he defines art in Zola's terms as based upon the logic of scientific observation: it is to be a moral dissection of contemporary history.[10] Thus the arts 'are the issue of the manners and customs of the day and change with those manners according to a general law'.[11] Seymour absurdly paints Gwynnie as Venus; he does not see the beauty or the pathos of her life as a working-class girl; it is precisely that beauty in daily life which is repeatedly the subject of Thompson's canvasses. The brittle sensuality of the age does not interest Harding, except as material for his analysis and condemnation, though as a result his novels, like Zola's, 'were vigorously denounced by the press as being both immoral and cynical'.[12]

Had Moore chosen merely to develop his initial anecdote about art and patronage he would, no doubt, successfully have achieved his intentions though the result might have been slight. But the discussions on art in relation to contemporary society suggest that the novel has greater pretensions; the exposure of Lewis Seymour's character and art is to mirror the corruption of the society he seeks to emulate, that 'elegant life' which is 'so artistically fashionable'.[13]

These greater pretensions, however, give rise to an uncertainty that to some extent destroys the balance of the novel and mars the force of the original anecdote. The cause of this can, I feel, be traced to Moore's own remark about the novel's conception out of his memories of Balzac and Zola: he has attempted to assimilate what are two conflicting techniques.

The difficulty lies principally in the character of Seymour, in that it is far too simple for the weight of analogy it has to support. Despite the complex incidents of the plot, his character as it is revealed is but an elaboration of a given theme. The central anecdote makes a complex narrative inevitable and sometimes Moore's over-rapid stage-managing leaves in too schematic a form incidents which, given more solid treatment, could have added variety and depth to Seymour's personality. We are merely *told* that 'it was part of Lewis's nature to believe that women were in love with him'[14] and that his conversation wields a hypnotic fascination over Lady Helen. So little is made of this brilliant but malign power of influencing others and so much of the will-less aspects of Seymour's nature that one tends to question the gullibility of his admirers. There is perhaps too strong an intrusion of the personal here as Moore tries to find compensation in the novel to offset his own sense of stupidity in allowing himself to be manipulated by Weldon Hawkins. Most people who met Hawkins at that period of Moore's life, including Moore's own family, were enchanted by his charm and infectious humour.[15] In his various literary dissections of his friend, Moore always expects the reader to take this side of Hawkins's temperament largely on trust; Hawkins's irresponsibility and cunning are dwelt on in far greater detail. What is needed in the portrait of Seymour in *A Modern Lover* is a greater play of irony to clarify the contrast between his admirers' romantic and sentimental illusions about him and Lewis's actual abilities and character. Moore frequently resorts to a kind of women's magazine style in describing Lady Helen and Mrs Bentham's sentimental and 'romantic' feelings for Lewis. Their attitude is in character, but there is a need for a fine sense of irony in the commentary to place morally such adjectives as 'brave' and 'delicious' in these passages. As the accounts stand, they are too like the style they are satirising to be wholly convincing.

The basic deficiency in the characterization of Seymour is that he has no moral complexity. He lacks that capacity for good, the suppression of which becomes, with such of Balzac's characters as Lucien de Rubempré, symbolic of a particular and evil social process. Lucien prostitutes his creative powers for the sake of material success but Seymour never had a truly creative talent and so is confronted with no real moral choice. He is bad 'only because he had not strength to be good.'[16] We are therefore offered no definite *social* causes as an explanation for the moulding of his character. *A Modern Lover* is a deliberate imitation of the French Naturalistic novel but it seems lightweight by comparison with that prototype because it fails to picture society adequately as a fatal determining force.

There is a difficulty too about the use of the discussions on painting as a vehicle for social criticism: as an art, it over-simplifies. Thompson's paintings demonstrate a preoccupation with social themes, but cannot go deeply into causes and effects. Although Harding sees such analysis as the novelist's duty, he is shown only as a theorist and he has a very minor status. Moore does not make Harding a vital positive force in the novel in the way that Balzac, for example, in *Les Illusions Perdues* carefully balances D'Arthez' group of writers, whom Lucien abandons despite their high social ideals, against Vautrin and the Parisian journalists whom Lucien subsequently befriends and who deliberately exploit social wrongs for their own gain.

Because of these shortcomings the view of society that Moore presents in *A Modern Lover* is little more than a literary caricature with no suggestion, as in Dickens or Balzac, that humanity can exist only as a caricature of itself within a repressive society. From the prevailing imagery describing London as a 'siren city' given over to 'a golden nightmare', a carnival of marionettes, in which love and life are reduced to games, to *fêtes galantes*, as artificial as Seymour's rococo decorations, one can see that Moore is attempting also to imitate Zola's poetic improvisations.[17] The echoes of Zola's rhetoric are at times unmistakable and one must say in passing that it is the kind of rhetoric that works better in French prose than in English:

> Carriages came up every minute. All were filled with people who had money, who had come forth to spend it in the night and in his madness he fancied he heard the shower of gold and kisses that fell over the city.[18]

The attempt at poetic simplification is justifiable in itself, though it leads Moore at times into making some ludicrous suggestions that the duration of Lord Beaconsfield's government is famous only as an era of immorality as gross as Zola's Second Empire.[19] As a technique it fails, however, in *A Modern Lover* because it is simply a thin, mannered pastiche of Zola's methods. Moore is attempting to recreate Zola's literary effects without fully appreciating Zola's poetic grasp of certain truths about the social process and the effects of that process on the development of individual psychologies. Licentiousness is not in Moore's characters as it is in Zola's either a final pathetic development of a lust for material possessions or a means of escape from the nagging fear of financial ruin. Seymour's sensual nature lacks the vitality, however frenetic, that animates Zola's characters, impelling them steadily towards damnation.[20] The irony of his career is that despite his worthlessness he succeeds by taking advantage of the good in others, the utter selflessness of that good being his condemnation. Yet is is precisely that force for good in his admirers, and again, though sketchily, in Harding and Thompson, that exposes the weakness of Moore's imitation of Zola. Zola's whole universe is evil, and his vision one of total damnation.[21] To succeed, poetic simplification must be total, it must offer an autonomous world rooted wholly in the artist's personal impression, as it is in Zola at his best.

Interestingly Maupassant, another disciple of Zola's, reworked Moore's basic anecdote in *Bel Ami* and did so in a fashion more deliberately in keeping with Zola's techniques. *Bel Ami* finely offsets the strengths and weaknesses of *A Modern Lover*. Maupassant describes Bel Ami at one point as 'stripping life of the garment of poetry in a kind of ugly rage,'[22] and that is precisely the view of the world that Maupassant himself has chosen to paint. He has developed the anecdote into a novel but retained the narrative simplicity of an anecdote, the technique that he employs to so good an effect in his tales. His novel is consciously schematic: the world is a battle and belongs to the strong; advancement is chiefly possible through the influence of women; 'All women are promiscuous; all one can do is to use them and give them nothing of oneself in return'.[23] This is Zola's technique carried to a stark extreme: the world has been reduced to the proportions of the protagonist's own values and mind; and there is nothing in the novel to suggest that the protagonist's view of that world has its limitations or that he is culpable for his want of insight or sensitivity. Bel Ami indeed mirrors the corruption of the society about him, but only because the world of the novel is as cheap as the man himself: all men are cads and all women are harlots and whatever there is of moral criticism has to be inferred from without by Maupassant deliberately exciting revulsion in the reader.

Bel Ami has a technical perfection and a unity that are lacking in *A Modern Lover*; but the very nature of that perfection raises problems of its own. As Henry James argued: 'the psychological explanation of things here too visibly contracts the problem in order to meet it.'[24] James concludes his demonstration that the technique of reduction injures the irony of the anecdote by suggesting that 'the real force of satire would have come seeing him [Bel Ami] engaged and victorious with natures better than his own'.[25] This, of course, is what Moore attempted with *A Modern Lover* but it is precisely this which prevents the novel succeeding as an imitation of Zola's technique. Moore's need to accommodate a sense of good in human nature and intimations of social injustice in an otherwise evil universe makes for moral complexities in *A Modern Lover* at variance with the psychological simplicity required by Zola's kind of impressionism. The novel fails too as an imitation of Balzac's mode: Seymour's will-power is forever undermined by his innate sensuality and this robs him of that Satanic creative egoism that necessarily animates Balzac's heroes as *exempla* of social wrong.

To have developed his anecdote successfully as a *social* novel Moore would have had to submit more readily to the discipline of either Balzac's or Zola's method of fiction and to accept the necessary limitations of the method he chose. He might also have developed the anecdote as a psychological novel (James's *Roderick Hudson* of 1875 is not so very different in its theme and intentions) but this would have required Moore to abandon his pretensions as a social critic. It would have required too a greater originality of technique and a deeper sense of irony in effecting moral discriminations than Moore yet had in his power. Though it is a flawed performance, *A Modern Lover* is notwithstanding an impressive first novel and that chiefly for the qualities which are the cause of its flaws – for its sheer ambitiousness, for its attempt to be inclusive and encompass all that Moore considered of value in the French tradition of fiction. Though Moore's presentation of his male characters is disappointing the vividness of the strongly contrasting portraits of the three women around whom the novel turns shows a depth of insight into feminine psychology which is to be an enduring strength in his work. Moore remained acutely perceptive of the diverse ways in which women discover in themselves both a need for self-respect and the special personal and emotional qualities on which that respect must be based. As with many first novels by major authors, the principal theme of the book is derivative and disappointing; it is the subsidiary material, in this case the presentation of Gwynnie, Mrs Bentham and Lady Helen, which commands respect and reveals distinctive original powers which are soon to be developed as the real focus of Moore's fiction.

In 1917 Moore revised and largely re-wrote *A Modern Lover* as *Lewis Seymour and Some Women*. This revision is principally in the style of his later novels: simple and direct. To achieve this new stylistic freedom and tighter construction much of the impressionistic landscape description, the finer points in the analysis of psychological motive and the detailed conversations about the relation of art to life have been excised. As a result, greater emphasis than in the original version is thrown on its schematic design. This is borne out by what Moore writes regarding Robert Louis Stevenson in his preface to the revised novel: '. . . it's the story that counts. . . . Style and presentation of character and a fine taste in the selection of words are secondary gifts'.[26] Moore seems to be attempting to overcome the technical imbalance of the first version by pursuing in his revision a method and tone not dissimilar to that of *Bel Ami*. While many of the narrative complications of *A Modern Lover* are avoided, so too are many of its finer concerns. Less is made of Mrs Bentham's maternal and protective attitude to Seymour and more of her flaunting of convention in becoming his mistress. Lady Helen's character is altered completely: she is now a New Woman, whose liberty and frankness are imperilled by a husband who prefers covert liaisons and a hypocritical kow-towing to propriety for the sake of his social position and material success. She no longer becomes gradually aware of his moral and intellectual poverty by his attempts to pervert her self-respect, but is awakened rapidly and less subtly to the nature of his character by his resemblance to a social climber, a 'money-kisser' that she encounters at a party.[27] The sense of self-sacrifice in both women is much under-played.

By 1917 Moore no longer considered himself a disciple of Zola and so he heavily cut the passages in *A Modern Lover* in which he debated the relative value of Realism and Naturalism in art. Instead a new theme is introduced concerning the morality of the nude. Seymour talks of freedom from restraint, poses as a model both for his life-class and for Mrs Bentham and submits a nude portrait of Lady Helen to the Academy exhibition, all of which provokes salacious gossip and a lengthy discussion on morality and art. Not only are these irrelevant to the issue of the novel, even as an attack on Victorian prudery, but the 'fie-fie', precocious tone of the passages concerned suggests that Moore is indulging in a sensualism for which he elsewhere criticises Seymour. One feels the need for a sense of irony to clarify his ambiguous position.[28] Both these major revisions distort the moral perspective which it was Moore's original intention to depict. Neither version of the novel is thus wholly satisfactory; but the greater technical perfection of the second has been achieved only at the expense of most of the thematic virtues of the first.

(2) *A Mummer's Wife*

The subject of Moore's second novel, *A Mummer's Wife*, is a sustained examination of the theme he touched on in the opening chapters of *A Modern Lover*, when he described the relationship between Lewis Seymour and Gwynnie Lloyd, his neighbour in the Waterloo Road slum. Seymour's, Moore writes 'was a soft, sensuous nature, and instinctively took the easiest road to walk in, without a thought whether it was the right or the wrong one'.[1] Gwynnie, by contrast, acts entirely out of carefully nurtured principles:

> Religion has been laid so carefully about her early life that it was the soil to which tended the roots of all her thoughts. If her father had not taught her his faith, there was one word he had engraven on her mind, which was *Duty*. . . .'[2]

The opposition of Lewis's easy amorality with Gwynnie's earnest pursuit of right has pathos because neither can really understand the other. Lewis, as we have seen, is a thoughtless cad, who takes advantage of Gwynnie's scruples. The predicament in *A Mummer's Wife* has considerably greater pathos since the man in question, an actor, Dick Lennox, though he is as free of conscience as Lewis, acts always with generous intentions towards his lover, Kate.

The plot of *A Mummer's Wife* is simple. Kate Ede elopes with Dick Lennox to escape a life of working-class drudgery, a loveless marriage to an invalid and a household dominated by her mother-in-law, a woman with a callous puritan mentality. Kate's strict evangelical upbringing prevents her finding peace in her relationship with Dick; she takes to drink to escape her conscience, loses her baby through her own negligence, steadily alienates Dick's affections and dies sordidly, a victim of the guilt she cannot allay. The novel is a tragedy about the evil of a perverse kind of con-

33

science that compels a terrible isolation on its possessor. Kate is desperately alone even with the one man who loves her and wishes to bring joy to her life. Obviously there are analogies in this theme with French fiction and particularly with Flaubert's *Madame Bovary*. Where Moore's fiction differs most pointedly from Flaubert's is in the character of Lennox, who is a richer, more complex creation than Emma's seducer Rodolphe. The effect of this is to turn the focus of the analysis away from the woman's psychological predicament to a detailed dramatic appraisal of how her temperament affects the people who form relationships with her. *A Mummer's Wife* draws much of its inspiration from Flaubert for its overall scheme of ideas and subject-matter, but in the detail of its setting and narrative incidents and in its emotional and psychological analysis, especially of the conflict in love between Kate and Lennox, it is wholly original.

Kate has spent a lifetime in Hanley; she has never journeyed beyond the limits of the potteries except in her imagination. From a certain prospect in the town an immense vista of Staffordshire is visible: there appears to be nothing but 'desolate plains full of pits, brick and smoke', until in the far distance one sees the outline of the Wever Hills.[3] For Kate as a child these hills were the gates of fairyland and throughout much of her subsequent life they had been the stimulus for romantic dreaming. With her marriage 'dreams had gone out of her life, everything was a hard reality; her life was like a colliery, every wheel was turning, no respite day or night; her life would be always the same, a burden and a misery.'[4] She visits the prospect with Dick Lennox and ironically it is precisely in the terms of that landscape and of its associations in Kate's mind with her youth that her lover tempts her to escape:

'There is no doubt that the view is very grand, but it is tantalizing to have those hills before your eyes when you are shut up in a red brick oven. How fresh and cool they look! What wouldn't you give to be straying about in those fresh woods far away?'[5]

Some weeks later Kate succumbs and agrees to elope with Lennox. They walk by night to the same spot. Nothing is now distinguishable in the darkness but the furnace fires:

It seemed to Kate like a hearth of pleasure and comfort . . .
and all her fancies were centred in this distant light . . . and she
deemed that it would be in or about this light that she would
find happiness.[6]

This vision of Hanley plain, as 'an immense sea of fire, and
beyond nothing but unfathomable grey',[7] comes to symbolize much
of Kate's life and tragedy. She desperately seeks some outlet for her
emotions and her imagination, some escape from a life that her
environment, physically and mentally, makes an 'unfathomable
grey' by condemning all that is imaginative and instinctive within
it as vicious. But so innate are the values of that society in Kate
that when she does succeed in kindling the fires of instinct within
herself she has no power to control the blaze and is consumed in
the hell that she makes of her own mind. Her imagination is not
for her a blessing but a curse. Kate's tragedy is one of arrested
development and the sins of her immaturity expose the intellectual
and imaginative poverty of the particular attitudes in society that
have educated her.

Kate has been brought up in that evangelical tradition that
deems the world a fallen place in which salvation lies only in unceasing toil as a kind of penance. Diligence is the cardinal virtue
and life a round of duties fulfilled: *laborare est orare*. Leisure,
being inactive, contemplative, is equated with self-indulgence, the
sin of the Prodigal; and to delight in the beauty of the visible
world is to honour the vain works of the Devil. Kate's desire for
ease, for some imaginative relief from manual work, and her
normal curiosity about the nature of love and the relation of the
sexes (a curiosity which she partly satisfies through covertly reading fiction) are condemned by her mother as immoral:

She thought it 'a sinful waste of time, not to speak of the way
it turned people's heads from God'; and when one day she found
Kate's scrapbook made up of poems cut from the *Family Herald*
she began to despair of her daughter's salvation.[8]

Marriage to Ralph Ede is defined for Kate as a matter of duties
and responsibilities to be honoured:

Of love small mention was made. The bridegroom spoke of his
prospects of improving the business, the bride listened, interested
for the while in his enthusiasm.[9]

Finding in her consumptive husband no release for the tenderness, sympathy and affection welling within her, Kate comes to consider that her instincts for love must be a delusion and so she submits to her mother-in-law's pious authority and becomes for the most part indifferent to the world about her.

The quality of Kate's life in Hanley is powerfully evoked in the opening chapters. Sleepless nights spent nursing her husband through his attacks of asthma follow days spent scrupulously supervising Ralph's drapery shop and her own dress-making business, where she is forever in the grip of a sense of urgency to complete her orders by specific times. It is a life where all too brief moments of rest are the only luxury, where a pause for tea or ale is a really sensual pleasure. What makes these scenes so impressive is not so much the accuracy of Moore's description of Hanley itself and the pottery factories (true to his Naturalist principles Moore had visited Staffordshire on a fact-finding expedition while preparing to write the novel) as his imaginative involvement with the physical nature of Kate's existence. Her efforts of will that are necessary to stifle her nausea as she administers Ralph's ether; the confidence of her movements about the sick-room that reveal her long familiarity with his illness; her terror when he is wracked with pain even though she knows from past experience that the attack will pass; her careful enumeration in her mind of the stages of the attack and her hurried preparation of new medicines or fresh arrangements of the bedding in an attempt to forestall or stave off the worst excesses of its violence; all this is conveyed with a vivid dramatic immediacy. Just as vividly portrayed is Kate's mental state with the total concentring of all her energies in her husband's need which is a real act of love:

. . . till at last, grasping the back of a chair, he breathed by jerks, each inspiration being accompanied by a violent spasmodic wrench, violent enough to break open his chest. She watched, expecting every moment to see him roll over, a corpse, but knowing from past experiences that he would recover somehow. His recoveries always seemed to her like miracles, and she watched the long pallid face crushed under a shock of dark matted hair, a dirty nightshirt, a pair of thin legs; but for the moment the grandeur of human suffering covered him, lifting him beyond the pale of loving or loathing, investing and clothing him in the pity of tragic things. The room, too, seemed transfigured. The bare wide floor, the gaunt bed, the poor walls plastered with religious prints cut from journals, even the ordinary furniture of everyday use – the little washhandstand with the common delf ewer, the chest of drawers that might have been bought for thirty shillings – lost their coarseness; their triviality disappeared, until nothing was seen or felt but this one suffering man.[10]

The poignancy of Kate's response arouses sympathy in the reader because Ralph himself takes her help so much for granted. Embarrassed by his dependence on her, he treats Kate with wilful peevishness, constantly searching for grounds on which to accuse her of being unfeeling. The quality of their life together is exactly caught in their brief exchanges of conversation between Ralph's spasms: she ever placating, rarely admitting how his attitude hurts her; he petty, using his frailty as his weapon against her:

'Better! If I'm better, it's no thanks to you,' he said. 'You must have been mad to leave the window open so long.'
'You wanted it open; you know very well that when you're very bad like that you must have change of air. The room was so close.'
'Yes, but that is no reason for leaving it open half an hour.'
'I offered to shut it, and you wouldn't let me.'
'I dare say you're sick of nursing me, and would like to get rid of me. The window wasn't a bad dodge.'[11]

In Kate's life the only compensations for all her toiling are her weariness and an arid sense of duty accomplished. In her mother-in-law's view, this is all she should expect of life as a Christian.

Mrs Ede senior embodies typical working-class Puritan values and as such she is the ideal to which Kate's upbringing has encouraged her to aspire. She is a kind woman in her way but she lacks the true Christian virtue of a selfless humility, a consciousness of her own shortcomings in the face of Divine Perfection. The incongruity gives Moore an opportunity for some humorous irony:

The tall figure knelt upright. It was not a movement of cringing humility, but of stalwart belief, and as she handed her the Bible, Kate could not help thinking that there was pride in her mother-in-law's very knees.[12]

Out of pride in her own rigidly held principles Mrs Ede condemns the belief that the instincts and the imagination have a part to play in life, and she does so with an assurance of her own infallibility as a Christian. For human weakness or sin she has no compassion: 'If I had my way I'd whip such people [actors] until I slashed all the wickedness out of them'.[13] She is trying to reduce the complexity of human experience to the simple pattern of what in her opinion is respectable behaviour and so she rejects with sectarian hatred just that concern for the instinctive life that makes Christianity so humanitarian. By simplifying it, she has perverted her creed and denied it any relevance as an active force for good in this world. The humour of Moore's portrait of Mrs Ede and the care he takes to establish her kindliness towards people whom she can see are genuinely suffering prevent her becoming a caricature of the values that the novel is questioning.

Unlike Mrs Ede, Kate cannot find consolation in the Puritan faith; work for her is not a piety and it leaves her too drained of energy and too frustrated to believe seriously in the prospect of heavenly rewards hereafter. She wishes to do good to others because of her innate kindness and she nurses her husband through no sense of duty but because she cannot witness his suffering without pity. For the sake of easy relations in the household she submits, however, to Mrs Ede's authority and in that submission lie the seeds of her tragedy. Kate has chosen to live within Mrs Ede's principles; she has not educed her own sanctions for her conduct out of her innate sense of what is right and developed and strengthened them through her experience of the world. Mrs Ede's attitudes constantly frustrate her but she lacks the courage to assert her own convictions, and so her imaginative, moral and emotional growth as an individual has been stunted. Kate is dangerously incapable of a detached critical response to her experience of life.

It is at this point that Dick Lennox, an actor and the manager of a touring opera company, comes to lodge at their house. He is kind, polite, human, expansively huge in person and in manner without being gross and, above all, disarmingly good-humoured. Therein lies the danger, for this humour is not benign; it disguises a total want of moral sense. His humanity lacks a genuine concern for others, his patience is but indifference, and his kindness is exerted only as a means of preserving the calm of his private world. His self-sufficiency is perfect.

As the portrait of a sensualist, Lennox has far greater solidity than the characterization of Lewis Seymour. Moreover it has a dramatic interest for the reader that the portrait of Seymour lacked in that the complexity of the study is only gradually apprehended as Kate herself discovers the paradoxical make-up of his personality. The more she comes to rely on him as a protection and a refuge, the more elusive he becomes and withdrawn into himself. Though he gives her love and a degree of sympathy, these are qualities set apart from his quintessential self. His independence which he so meticulously conserves has both its strengths and its weaknesses. The subtlety of Moore's discriminations between independence and indifference shows a considerable advance on his first novel in psychological analysis.

As the novel progresses, one gradually appreciates that Dick Lennox is being presented as a contrast with Mrs Ede; but his world is not the obverse of hers, for the two are subtly and viciously linked. Mrs Ede condemns any form of imaginative and emotional activity as escapist and therefore wicked; she makes no attempt to distinguish: all pleasure is to be condemned as undermining the will to duty; the imagination can never be a creative force. Lennox turns this very attitude to material advantage by offering in his operettas a wholly sensual form of art, for they are tawdry fictions designed to satisfy the emotionally starved and pander to their desire for wish-fulfilment. Its attraction for its largely working-class audience, like the attraction of romantic verse and stories for Kate in her adolescence, lies precisely in its want of any involvement, imaginative or otherwise, with the rigours of daily life.

Dick Lennox complements Mrs Ede: he too is a study in self-interest. Just as Kate undervalues Mrs Ede's essential kindliness and cannot perceive the despair at the human condition that motivates her mother-in-law's beliefs, so she over-values Lennox's warmth. Again this is a failure of insight; she interprets his nature as essentially romantic, when in fact his blatant sensualism is utterly prosaic. Passion, for him, is not of this world; it is confined to the world of operetta which is but a parody of fine feeling. Lennox can conceive of no expression of deep emotion, however sincere, as anything but theatrical, for the simple reason that he experiences no such depth of feeling in himself. He seeks for nothing more in life than the satisfaction of his appetites. Another character, Mrs Forest, admirably criticises him:

'You're always in the same mood, never rising above your-self or sinking below yourself, finding it difficult to understand the pain that those who live mostly in the spiritual plane experience lest they fall into a lower plane.'[14]

This is the reason why he never fully understands Kate's dilemma. In the ensuing tragedy, Kate fails for want of insight, Dick fails for want of imagination. He remains to the end 'kind, huge and indifferent'.[15]

Moore's evocation of the way of life of the theatre company is as gripping as his depiction of life in the Edes' household. Once again in careful imitation of Balzac and Zola, Moore studied the background meticulously to gain an accurate verisimilitude. Moore's younger brother, Augustus, who was a journalist with the *Pink 'Un*, introduced him to Jimmy Glover, the conductor with an operetta company that was touring a production of *Les Cloches de Corneville* in an English translation by the two Moore brothers. Moore joined the company for a short period, befriended Glover and incorporated many of his stories of theatre life directly into the novel. (Over the years, Moore made quite a practice of using his friends' ideas and expressions in this way.[16]) These authentic touches apart, the vividness of the scenes with the theatre folk derives from Moore's ability to capture the right tones for the dialogue: that easy familiarity partly affectionate, partly malicious that develops amongst such an enclosed, specialised community; the freedom from any hint of moral judgement despite a relish for gossip; the delight in pursuing endless chains of nostalgic or comic stories or in earnestly analysing minute details concerning the act-ing of particular roles to gain particular effects, especially when there are more pressing financial matters to discuss. It is because Moore makes his characters live with such panache through the dialogue that he succeeds in his larger aim of creating a social group that live entirely in and for the moment, which allows them to rise completely above personal sorrows. They never trouble today about tomorrow's security. The actors' self-sufficiency and indifference have their admirable sides. To communicate as Moore does the moral and emotional limitations of these characters, while showing how these limitations are in a sense necessary for their survival in their profession, is a remarkable achievement. The sheer warmth and geniality of the actors ensure that they never lose the reader's sympathy.

These then are the two ways of life between which Kate must play out her tragedy. Having convinced herself since her marriage to Ralph that love is a fiction, Kate is dazzled by Lennox's kindness and show of attention. Unlike Emma Bovary, Kate seeks no Byronic tempests of the emotions but only tenderness, comfort and security. Hers is a need to feel less a drudge and more a woman; and for the woman in her Dick shows a keen respect. But in her longing Kate, like Madame Bovary, confuses a sensuality gilded over with an elegant manner with delicacy of feeling; she poeticizes Lennox's vulgarity. After his first visit to her house, Kate begins to re-read the sentimental literature she abandoned in her youth and indulges in fantasies of herself as a romantic heroine, trying to live more intensely in her imagination than in reality. Her need had been for both an imaginative and an emotional release and the power of her novels to satisfy both needs leads her dangerously to identify the two instincts as the same in reality. When Kate first hears one of Lennox's operettas she is overwhelmed by the surging power of the music. Because his art leaves her so satisfied she assumes he will be as dynamic. Quite without knowledge of his real character she imagines she can build an ideal relationship with him. Perhaps she could do so, were she to accept him for what he is and modify her idealization. Though Kate feels humiliated when she discovers her paragon usually plays the clown-roles in his productions rather than 'have another salary on the list', the experience does not provoke her into taking a fresh look either at him or at herself.[17] At his first gesture of affection she loses her self-possession completely. Lennox's rapid courtship of Kate is, however, one of the two weak sections of the novel. His attempt to seduce her while she is accompanying him on a tour round a pottery factory is clumsily plotted and crudely expressed:

'What a pretty child you must have been! I can fancy you with your black hair falling about your shoulders. Had I known you then, I should have taken you in my arms and kissed you. Do you think you would have liked me to have kissed you?'
She raised her eyes again, and a vague feeling of how nice, how kind he was, rushed through her, and perceiving still more clearly that this moment was his moment, Lennox affected to examine a ring on her finger. . . .

'Ah!' he said, 'had I known you then, I should have been in love with you.'

Kate closed her eyes, and abandoned herself to an ineffable sentiment of weakness, of ravishment; and then, imagining that she was his, Lennox took her in his arms and kissed her rudely. But quick, angry thoughts rushed to her head at the first movement of his arms, and obeying an impulse in contradiction to her desire, she shook herself free, and looked at him vexed and humiliated.

'Oh, how very cross we are; and about a kiss, just a tiny, wee kiss! . . . I'm sure I didn't mean to offend you . . . I love you too well . . . I loved you the first moment; I assure you I did. . . . I think you a deuced pretty woman, and I'm sure I could love you very much,' and recognizing this, Kate remained silent.

And thus encouraged, Mr Lennox attempted to renew his intentions. . . . The guide would be back in a few minutes, and, inspired by Kate's pale face, he came to the conclusion that it would be absurd to let her go without kissing her properly.

He was a strong man, but Kate had now really lost her temper, and struggled vigorously, determined he should not gain his end. Three times his lips had rested on her cheek, once he managed to kiss her on the chin, but he could not reach her mouth: she always succeeded in twisting her face away, and not liking to be beaten he put forth all his strength. She staggered backwards and placed one hand on his throat, . . . now he was pinioning her; she could see his big face approaching, and summoning up all her strength she strove to get away, but that moment, happening to tread on her skirt, her feet slipped. He made a desperate effort to sustain her, but her legs had gone between his.

The crash was tremendous. A pile of plates three feet high was sent spinning, a row of salad-bowls was over, and then with a heavy stagger Mr Lennox went down into a dinner-service, sending the soup-tureen rolling gravely into the next room.[18]

We are not far here at times from the tone and style of just those novels that Moore has been criticising Kate for reading. The clumsiness and crudity might have had a point if Moore had more richly exploited the farcical possibilities of the episode, humorously offsetting Kate's romanticism with a grotesque physical reality. But farce is quite out of keeping with the tone of the rest of the novel. Moreover though Lennox has a certain vulgarity he is suave too; he's not the kind of oaf to go in for all this fumbling and leering amidst the crockery. Funny though it is, the scene marks a failure on Moore's part in taste and in characterization. Moore is on much safer ground in the passages which were quoted earlier in this chapter, where the lovers visit by night the place which has been the scene for so much of Kate's romantic dreaming throughout her life. There is a poetic justice in this and Moore can reveal both the danger to Kate of succumbing to Dick and yet the urgent necessity of her whole being to submit to his, in terms which are not crude, bathetic or sentimental.

When she elopes from Hanley with Lennox, Kate rejects, though not at first consciously, its ordered if imperfect world for a chaotic bohemian existence, devoid of any sense of values above a common humanity. Kate's insecurity is both physical and mental. Through sheer force of will, Arnold Bennett's Sophia Baines in very similar circumstances builds a Hanley in miniature within and about herself to survive the deceptions played on her by her lover Gerald Scales and, after he has abandoned her, to protect herself from the tide of licentiousness that sweeps over Paris during the days of the Commune, though in doing so Sophia isolates herself emotionally from that world. Kate has neither such will-power nor such self-possession. She joins a way of life that is by its very nature rootless, and absurdly tries to build a respectable family life with Lennox who is oblivious to both her designs and her motives for them. He can in no way respect the fact of her eloping with him as a sacrifice, because he has no respect for the values she has thus rejected, and hence has no sense of moral responsibility towards her. When she calls herself wicked, he is just bewildered. Her scruples and modesty, the last vestiges of her former life which constitute for her a kind of self-respect, he proceeds to undermine by training her to be an actress and singer and by requiring her on stage to play the coquette and play it successfully.

The fundamental opposition between Kate and Lennox quickly takes on new forms, until it becomes total. He sees love as a matter of sexual gratification and finds her cold. Kate wants understanding and companionship and sees love despite her romantic tendencies as a flowering of the sensibility. Though she is grateful to Dick for giving her a kind of freedom, she realises too late that she has been betrayed by her own confusion into accepting the first sentimental substitute for her ideal that she has encountered. Finding herself now in a world of flux, having forfeited everything that constitutes her self-respect, she unjustly assumes that life in the theatre is licentious. Dick now becomes for her, absurdly, not only an emotional but a moral refuge, whom she guards jealously as her own. Though ridiculous, Kate remains a figure of pathos, because her ambitions in life are sound ones: she wants emotional maturity but the steps she takes to achieve it make her a victim of her own conscience. The life that remains to her is spent in making desperate efforts to escape her sense of shame.

Moore's account of Kate's collapse is masterly as he traces the stages of her addiction to drink, its consequences for her marriage to Dick and the gradual shrinking of her consciousness till her whole being is concentrated finally in a raw mental anguish that she cannot stifle:

> For her the world seemed to have ended, and she saw the streets and passers-by with the same vague, irresponsible gaze as a solitary figure would the universal ruin caused by an earthquake. She had no friends, no occupation, no interest of any kind in life; everything had slipped from her, and she shivered with a sense of nakedness, of moral destitution. Nothing was left to her, and yet she felt, she lived, she was conscious.[19]

The account is powerful because of Moore's refusal to intrude with any kind of commentary. This is the great strength of the last half of the novel. Moore has prepared the ground so well with his depiction of the contrasting ways of life of Hanley and the theatre that commentary becomes unnecessary as Kate and Dick pass beyond the psychological *impasse* between them to open conflict, physical violence and an inevitable separation.

The power and the horror of it all emerges through the dialogue with its controlled but mounting tension as Kate tries regularly in their battles to provoke Dick with accusations of infidelity to hit her so that the pain may act as a kind of penance for her own deep-rooted guilt, while he aims always to conciliate her but only goads her as a result to even greater fury. The tension breaks finally in a burst of violent activity which Moore describes in a flat, precise style which works actively on the reader's imagination because of its very starkness.

> He might easily have felled her to the ground with one stroke, but he contented himself with merely warding off the blows she aimed at him. From his great height and strength, he was easily

able to do this, and she struck at him with her little womanish arms as she might against a door.

'Take down your hands,' she screamed, exasperated to a last degree. 'You would strike me, would you? You beast! I know you would.'

Her rage had now reached its height. Showing her clenched teeth, she foamed at the mouth, the bloodshot eyes protruded from their sockets, and her voice grew more and more harsh and discordant. But, although the excited brain gave strength to the muscles and energy to the will, unarmed she could do nothing against Dick, and suddenly becoming conscious of this she rushed to the fireplace and seized the poker. With one sweep of the arm she cleared the mantelboard, and the mirror came in for a tremendous blow as she advanced round the table brandishing her weapon; but, heedless of the shattered glass, she followed in pursuit of Dick, who continued to defend himself dextrously with a chair. And it is difficult to say how long this combat might have lasted if Dick's attention had not been interrupted by the view of the landlady's face at the door; and so touched was he by the woman's dismay when she looked upon her broken furniture, that he forgot to guard himself from the poker. Kate took advantage of the occasion and whirled the weapon round her head. He saw it descending in time, and half warded off the blow; but it came down with awful force on the forearm, and glancing off, inflicted a severe scalp wound. The landlady screamed 'Murder!' and Dick seeing that matters had come to a crisis, closed in upon his wife, and undeterred by yells and struggles, pinioned her and forced her into a chair.

'Oh, dear! Oh, dear! You're all bleeding, sir,' cried the landlady: 'she has nearly killed you.'

'Never mind me. But what are we to do? I think she has gone mad this time.'

'That's what I think,' said the landlady, trying to make herself heard above Kate's shrieks.

'Well, then, go and fetch a doctor, and let's hear what he has to say.' . . .

'Yes, yes, I'll run at once.'

'You'd better,' yelled the mad woman after her. 'I'll give it to you! Let me go! Let me go, will you?'

But Dick never ceased his hold of her, and the blood, dripping upon her, trickled in large drops into her ears, and down into her neck and bosom.

'You're spitting on me, you beast! You filthy beast! I'll pay you out for this.' Then, she perceived that it was blood; the intonation of her voice changed, and in terror she screamed, 'Murder! murder! He's murdering me! Is there no one here to save me?'[20]

Moore's early reviewers found the style here repulsive[21], presumably because Moore refuses to make any overt moral or emotional analysis. Such comment would of course be quite redundant. Pathos is so inherent in the whole situation that it requires no heightening through the style. To have given the writing an emotional charge of that kind would not only have made the details of Kate's decline unbearably painful, even nauseating, but it would also have destroyed the finely balanced response to both Kate and Dick that Moore has carefully invited throughout from the reader. What is remarkable is that Moore can sustain this degree of control in the writing through a long portion of the novel and through a variety of situations: the round of fights in their various lodging houses; Kate's disruption of one of Dick's rehearsals with the company; their crawl together round the taverns of the Strand and Soho, while Dick waits for Kate to become so insensible that he can get her into a cab to take her home.

Apart from the occasional redundant and infelicitous use of imagery, the only moment where this dramatic power fails Moore is in the final sequence of Kate's death, where Moore eschews the somewhat bald, straightforward style and tone with which he formerly presented her and resorts to a tasteless poeticism. The final, Beckett-like situation of a body collapsed and exhausted while the manic consciousness rages on is the fitting end to Kate's tragedy with its implications that there can never be peace for this tormented soul even in death. The conception is right, the manner and tone are at fault, for the crude imagery of a carnival for vices and virtues introduces a grotesque humour which dissipates the pathos.

The most diverse scenes were heaped together in the complex confusion of Kate's nightmare; the most opposed ideas were intermingled. At one moment she told the little girls, Annie and Lizzie, of the immorality of the conversations in the dressing-rooms of theatres; at another she stopped the rehearsal of an *opéra bouffe* to preach to the mummers – in phrases that were remembrances of the extemporaneous prayers in the Wesleyan Church – of the advantages of an earnest, working religious life.

It was like a costume ball, where chastity grinned from behind a mask that vice was looking for, while vice hid his nakedness in some of the robes that chastity had let fall. Thus up and down, like dice thrown by demon players, were rattled the two lives, the double life that this weak woman had lived, and a point was reached where the two became one, when she began to sing her famous song . . . alternately with the Wesleyan Hymns. Sometimes in her delirium she even fitted the words of one on to the tune of the other.[22]

This fails because the account is too rushed in the telling. The reporting of the situation rather than the presenting of it is perhaps what is to blame here. Moore's command of dialogue in the novel is one of its impressive features and it would not have been beyond his powers to have evoked Kate's breakdown in more direct terms. The failure here does however substantiate the achievement of Moore's style and technique elsewhere in the novel.

In her state of spiritual sterility, Kate loses all power to distinguish even kindness for the virtue that it is in Dick and his fellow actors and later among the socially outcast, the prostitutes who help her in her drunken poverty. Kate's emotions make her a prey to sentimentality but not, as Flaubert would suggest in Emma Bovary's fate, because the world itself is totally mediocre and insensitive. Whatever the stage of Kate's degradation, there is always someone near to offer her help, even though that kindness can never really penetrate deeply enough into her consciousness to ease her isolation.

That Kate's tragedy is born of immaturity of mind, of a failure of any sense of perspective, is emphasized in the novel by the presence and character of Dick's friend, Mrs Forest, whose function is more than that of an adulteress to attract Lennox finally away from Kate. She is a poet and lives intensely in her imagination, but she has the power to distinguish the heroes of art from those of life's mould. She is convinced that man is far from divine but is nonetheless aware of his potential nobility. The heroes of her imagination reveal to her the short-comings of men, an insight that fosters in her a wealth of sympathy. She recognises the limitations in Lennox but accepts them. Though of a contemplative nature, she has a commonsense practicality when the occasion demands: she refuses to comply in a 'lewd', adulterous relationship with Dick and so can nurse the dying Kate with a clear conscience. She has a flexibility that gives her a true appreciation of the relative worth of others, the lack of which is essentially the cause of the breakdown of Kate and Dick's marriage: they failed, as she rightly observes, to achieve 'a psychological union'.[23] Deep feeling, for Mrs Forest, is not a fantasy, but she knows that it is attendant only on those who, through sympathy and moral perspective, can connect the passion in us with the prose. There are depths of feeling for example in Ralph Ede that Kate never appreciates until they meet again by chance in London some years after their divorce, when she is deeply moved by his willingness to forgive her and freely admit his own share of responsibility for their separation. The vista of a wholly different life opens up before Kate; the potential to achieve it lay all along in her real pity for Ralph and might have grown into a true union with him, had she only been able to free that sentiment of pity from its associations with 'duty'.[24]

To see Mrs Forest's character and function in the novel in these terms is very much to take the will for the deed. The values Moore intended her to establish are evident in her portrayal, but as a character in the plot she fails to convince and does so for reasons that relate to a particular, though not serious, weakness in the book as a whole. Once again, as with *A Modern Lover*, this relates to Moore's ambitions to write a *social* novel.

A Mummer's Wife offers much satire of sentimental fiction and of escapist operetta; to consider Mrs Forest's exotic meditations in a Celtic twilight, as Moore would have us do, as an emotionally educative, and therefore a truly creative art is absurd. She had to be an artist of some kind, or at least artistic, in order to draw together successfully, and carry her full weight in, all three themes of the book – imaginative, emotional and moral – but this female member of the Rhymers' Club, who lectures improbably at Working Men's Clubs on chastity in the married state, is scarcely the type required. Why moreover does she form a relationship with Lennox? and what could persuade a woman of her intelligence to commence writing *opéra bouffe* for the popular stage in collaboration with him? Such questions are not irrelevant to a work so consciously realistic as this and so concerned elsewhere for the niceties of motive. The answer lies partly in her perfunctory introduction into the narrative,[25] but the matter does not rest there.

The basic difficulty is that in what is essentially a working-class tragedy she, an aristocrat (though a Bohemian and therefore a classless one), is offered as a positive force with the conscious implication that her sanity and her sense of proportion are the fruit of her cultivated sensibility. As such, she introduces into the novel a concern for wider social issues that the novel elsewhere fails to support. In one of her moments of practical commonsense she argues with the doctor concerning Kate that 'if the human race is to be evolved into a higher degree of perfection, no weak half-measures will avail to effect the change; there must, on the contrary, be a radical change in hereditary environment'.[26] This suggests that she and Moore are of the opinion that maturity of mind is a question of education, from which she has benefited, but which will be possible for such as Kate only through social reform. On the strength of the book as it stands, such a position must surely be described as patronizing. It would bear weight only if Kate were seen as the helpless victim of a social process, but the moral and psychological analysis of the novel reaches out for much more subtle and complex explanations than this for her tragedy. Kate, Lennox and Mrs Forest cannot be described as representative of particular social forces or conditions. Moore's principal interest is in the condition of their private beings, in their emotional, imaginative and moral needs as individuals. Mrs Ede indeed expresses puritanical moral attitudes which became in the nineteenth century a part of the psychology of the industrial revolution, but Moore makes no wholehearted effort to draw a parallel between Mrs Ede's values and the industrial life of Hanley. She is not representative as, say, Gradgrind is. The view from Hanley over the industrial landscape of Staffordshire with its red-brick ugliness and its sea of fire is used by Moore as an image of Kate's spiritual condition; the visit to the Potteries arouses in her only a sentimental nostalgia for her childhood, which weakens her resistance to Lennox's advances: neither incident is turned to account for any urgent social comment. Moore's true attitude to the social background and the shallow depth of his concern for reform are revealed at that moment in the novel when the touring company is forced to disband because of political and social unrest in the industrial towns they are visiting:

> In many of the towns they visited strikes were on, and the
> people were convulsed with discussions, projects for resistance,

and hopes of bettering their condition. Great social problems, the tyranny of capital, and such-like, occupied the minds of men. . . .[27]

The casualness of 'and such-like' shows that the matter is merely incidental to the narrative; there is no attempt to relate the unrest constructively to Kate's predicament. The evidence of this early part of the novel emphasizes the utter inadequacy of Mrs Forest's position. To succeed as social criticism the novel would have to be completely overhauled, and that to the detriment of much that constitutes its success as a psychological novel. One can appreciate Moore's need to include such a character as Mrs Forest: without a balancing positive force, the novel with a psychological thesis like *A Mummer's Wife* always runs the risk of suggesting that *all* life is like this, and must of necessity have a tragic outcome. One finds such a tendency at times in Flaubert, for example, and in Arnold Bennett. The confusion of *A Mummer's Wife* derives from Moore's belief that the inadequacies of certain moral attitudes prevalent in society would be bettered through social reform. That two of the aims of education should be to teach an ability to discriminate and to induce a creative approach to leisure, one cannot deny. But the maturity of mind which Kate so tragically lacks is not of necessity dependent on that kind of education; this is what makes Mrs Forest so incongruous as a social reformer. A mature temperament is not synonymous with eccentricity, and, what is more to the point, it can exist untutored within the working class, as Moore's own *Esther Waters* admirably testifies.

The writing of *A Mummer's Wife* confirmed for Moore what he had begun to discover with *A Modern Lover:* that a social novel written in imitation of Zola's or Balzac's formula would succeed only if the novelist was prepared to make certain reductions and simplifications in the moral and psychological life of his characters. This discovery was complementary to a growing awareness that his personal interest and own best aptitude as a novelist lay in depicting the precise mental, emotional and imaginative qualities that define an individual's unique personality. The success or failure of a character both to discover his potential personality and to define it to his own satisfaction was to become Moore's central theme. *A Mummer's Wife* has its flaws, but in the last analysis they are far outweighed by its strengths. What remains in the memory after reading the novel is a vivid sense of the distinctive personalities of Kate and Dick Lennox, of Ralph and Mrs Ede. What continues to impress one on re-reading it is Moore's power to make these distinctions through dialogue and through a narrative line of precisely described episodes which dramatize the fluctuating psychological oppositions and sympathies between his characters. This is an imaginative conception of no mean order.

(3) *A Drama in Muslin*

In the careers of Kate Ede and Lewis Seymour, Moore presents a justification of his central theme – that there can be no development of personality without a self-imposed discipline – in negative terms; both lack integrity. The strength of *A Mummer's Wife* lay in Moore's portrayal of the slow dessication of Kate's consciousness; the weaknesses of the novel derived from Moore's attempt to relate his psychological and moral analysis in some way to prevailing conditions in society. In *A Drama in Muslin*, Moore offers something like a personal definition of what he understood as a *social* novel:

> The history of a nation as often lies hidden in social wrongs and domestic griefs as in the story of revolution, and if it be for the historian to narrate the one, it is for the novelist to dissect and explain the other; and who would say which is of the most vital importance – the thunder of the people against the oppression of the Castle, or the unnatural sterility, the cruel idleness of mind and body of the muslin martyrs, who cover with their white skirts the shames of Cork Hill?[1]

The argument is couched in the terms of his immediate theme (the plight of the Irish gentry and particularly of their debutante daughters), but the distinction it tries to draw is a false one, for a novelist as a historian of manners cannot afford to make so facile a division. A historical perspective, a feeling for the change in social conditions and in people's response to them is essential if a novel as a record of one's daily life in time is to be complete, that is as a *social* novel. Whatever other virtues they possess, Moore's first two works fail ultimately in this genre because of his inability to trace any adequate sociological correlation for his characters' psychological dilemmas. But Moore's attempt to deny the value of

52

such correlation is something of a pose, for, ironically, in *A Drama in Muslin*, the two issues are effectively united.

The characters of *A Mummer's Wife* were representative of moral attitudes and the resulting drama was symbolic of Kate's mental strife; the characters of *A Drama in Muslin* are also contrasting psychological studies but they demonstrate the moral inadequacies of a specific social condition which they all share and which is linked to a national and historical process by economic ties. The principal theme – the education of the young person – is one traditional in the novel; the related situation – the dangers of the awkward age when girls are admitted into fashionable adult society – is recurrent in late Victorian fiction. In *A Drama in Muslin*, theme and situation are made precisely social issues by Moore's decision to set his novel in Ireland in the contemporary present, the Eighteen Eighties, when the status and power of the gentry were being challenged by the Land League and the political movements seeking Ireland's independence.

In the opening chapter five young ladies, Alice and Olive Barton, May Gould, Cecilia Cullen and Violet Scully, are leaving their convent school; their ambitions in life, the adult identities they would like to assume, are revealed. Their different chances in fulfilling themselves are the subject of the novel. Alice Barton alone refuses to accommodate herself to the way of life that is offered her; with immense courage she chooses rather to find independence in England but is ostracized by her family and class. The characters of the five girls are not simply representative of mental and moral attitudes but also of social effects: by analysing the factors that are shaping the girls' consciousnesses, Moore is able to evaluate the society to which they are being introduced. The quality of life in a particular society, as Marx suggested, can be measured exactly by the social and intellectual status accorded to women. These girls of the Irish aristocracy have no position whatever unless they are married; without marriage, they are virtually without identity.[2] As Mrs Barton advises her two daughters:

'A woman can do nothing until she is married. . . . A husband is better than talent, better even than fortune – without a husband, a woman is nothing; with a husband she may rise to any height. Marriage gives a girl liberty, gives her admiration, gives her success, a woman's whole position depends upon it.'[3]

All a woman's ideas should be set, as a matter of duty to herself, on making a desirable match; this for Mrs Barton is what propriety demands; it is what propriety means. The condition of Irish society is such however that the number of marriageable girls vastly exceeds that of eligible consorts, and so propriety can be acknowledged only at some cost. What the girls quickly discover is that if they are to succeed in their ambitions in the given social situation they must take account of no value other than expediency. They must devote themselves to attracting men and before that their intellectual, moral or religious scruples must give way. The older single women they meet at their first levée at the Castle are a poignant threat of what their own future might be. All cannot succeed in finding a husband and each season adds to the host of tragic failures. As the years go by, with repeated failure their arrogance and youthful optimism will give place to overt manhunting, until in middle age they will become objects of pity, giving vent to their frustrations in bitter, malignant criticism of the young hopefuls who are taking their place. To succeed is virtually to consign oneself to a lifetime as an animated doll, an object to gratify the male sense; to fail is to become a shrew. As Alice Barton observes of either fate: are such women *ladies*? Many are so stimulated by their lessons in wanton flirtation that rather than face such a future they succumb to covert prostitution, like May Gould, or attempt an elopement, as does Olive Barton. The matriarchs who defend the system have no concern for the tragic humiliation and the depravity they enforce on their daughters in the name of duty.[4]

No one is stronger in voicing her defence of the system than the heroine's mother, Mrs Barton, and she is herself the type of womanhood which the code of propriety offers as ideal. In her view woman is to be a summary of all that is sensuously attractive to men; she is to cultivate the art of amusing, to make artificiality her charm, and with that art is to tempt others, especially men, to look on life as lightly as she does. In Mrs Barton herself the bewitching charm of youth has hardened to a deadly but elegant harlotry; the glittering, coaxing manner now gilds over a hard disposition to turn men's sensual weaknesses to her advantage. Cunningly she infatuates her elderly admirer, Lord Dungory, and satisfies his desire to appear a young roué; in return she exacts his financial support in securing a good match for her daughter. She tyrannically controls her household; her husband is an amiable bore, a mere cypher who provides her with an income from his estate out of which she finances his hobbies of music and painting simply to rid herself of his presence. Mrs Barton is not an unsympathetic character; she abuses men's tendencies to sentimentality, but they are gullible fools and the deceptions she practises are designed to secure her a position from which she can best do her duty, as she sees it, by her daughters. All the qualities which in the course of the novel we come to admire in her daughter, Alice, are quite characteristic of the mother. She has intelligence and a power of self-assertion in the face of failure or defeat (all her ambitions to make Olive a marchioness are frustrated); these are good qualities in themselves but in her misplaced in being directed to such worthless ends. Like Shaw's Mrs Warren she has great energy and a capacity for good but her potential is dissipated when it is put to the service of a mind that confounds conscience with expediency and morality with custom. She genuinely wishes for her daughters' happiness, but can conceive of none except on her own terms of propriety and of material and social advantage. She sets Olive to flirt with an officer to gain experience in handling men but forbids the young man the house when she realises Olive is becoming emotionally involved with him. The only consolation Olive receives from her mother is the assertion that it enhances a girl's reputation at the Castle if she has previously dismissed an admirer. When Alice chooses to marry a man she loves but who is beneath her socially, her mother refuses to acknowledge him or to attend the wedding.

For all her style, Mrs Barton is essentially vulgar, a fact which Moore reveals through her frequent lapses in tone. Her charm is not so persuasive to the reader as to her admirers because of disconcerting touches of slang and idioms that intimate that her manner is bogus. In the company of men her politeness is excessive; when alone with other women, especially her daughters, she wastes no effort on keeping up such a pretence of brilliance. Her coarse pragmatism shows how shallow her sensibility actually is and the new tone rings true to her real personality:

'Oh! we are very late; we shan't be there before ten. The thing to do is to get there about half-past nine; the Drawing-room does not begin before eleven; but if you can get into the first lot you can stand at the entrance of Patrick's Hall and have the pick of the men as they come through. That's the place to stand; all the Dublin girls know that trick.'[5]

Henry James would no doubt have relished the challenge of revealing the depths of evil and low cunning to which a mind like Mrs Barton's can reach without ever dispelling the reader's sense of her fascination. (Mrs Brookenham in *The Awkward Age* is almost her exact counterpart and Mrs Brook's genius constantly beggars all moral description.) It is however the shoddiness, the desperation, the precariousness of Mrs Barton's way of life that Moore wishes to stress, for it is through this aspect of the novel that he can introduce the wider social implications of his narrative.

Mrs Barton's moral indifference is but a single manifestation of a greater national indifference that underlies the position of her class, the Irish landlords. For generations they have trusted in land as a security that could not fail, but their concern for their property does not extend beyond the matter of their immediate financial returns.[6] Alice Barton realises this and begins to question whether there is not 'something wrong in each big house being surrounded by a hundred small ones, all working to keep it in sloth and luxury'.[7] The peasants slave to provide the income by which the landlords purchase the means of gratifying their sensual pleasures; and the debutantes, their charms fully cultivated, are the objects purchased to gratify them. The thematic parallel is finely substantiated in a scene where, by a process of *montage*, Mr Barton's bargaining with his peasants over their rents is integrated into his wife's refusal on financial grounds of Captain Hibbert's proposal for Olive's hand.[8] The technique is borrowed from *Madame Bovary* where Flaubert punctuates Rodolphe's seduction of Emma with an account of the prize-giving at a local agricultural fair; Flaubert's intention is comically to deflate the pretensions of human sentiment. Moore uses the device more seriously to integrate the principal themes of his novel by showing how material calculation triumphs over fellow-feeling in both encounters.

Moore presents the historical facts of the situation – the increasing power of the Land League, the evictions and the Fenians' incitement to violence both against the landlords and in support of Home Rule, which culminated in the Phoenix Park Murders – through the response of the landlords, as the ones whose livelihood was to be most crucially affected. Over dinner the news is debated and the weakness of the conservative position established simultaneously with the actual contemporary details. Landed property has meant security for generations; there has never ben any question of the gentry's protecting their interest before and so, in the face of rebellion, they are oblivious of the need for concerted action if they are to withstand the unified attack promoted by the Land League. Self-interest conflicts with self-interest and they are easily overwhelmed and left strengthless to resist.[9] Their response reveals not only their inadequacy in the face of opposition but also the shallow nature of whatever values control their motives. Lord Dungory seeks to distance himself from the crisis by making it the subject of one of his facile epigrams: 'L'âme du paysan se vautre dans la boue comme la mienne se plaît dans la soie'.[10] The murders instigated by the League are covertly welcomed by the men as a means of forcing the Government's hand; while the women can scarcely disguise their pleasure that, as a result of so many deaths, the new inheritors of lands and titles augment the number of eligible matches. They all profess religion; but the Catholics among them question why the Pope fails to protect their interests by condemning the involvement of the clergy in the nationalist movements, while the Protestants become proselytes to defend their interests by trying to persuade the peasants to change their faith and become biddable with bribes of food and education.

But Moore's attitude is not damning: the position of this class was after all his own and he evokes a profound sympathy for them. Their whole lives are directed, as Yeats observed, to 'too much business with the passing hour', to 'too much play, or marriage with a fool',[11] so much so that they have no genuine concern other than for sustaining their own artifice, to the cultivating of which all their education has been directed. They hold to propriety and custom, but these are merely the superstructure of that artifice and so are devoid of any true value. So complete is the world of illusion they inhabit, their aestheticism is so divorced from life, that they show but blank incomprehension that the conditions of that life should be subject to change. They arouse our sympathy, as do the landed gentry in Tchekov, for their frantic clinging to all that they recognise as permanent even to the brink of moral, spiritual and financial chaos. Lord Dungory advises Alice Barton: 'Gardez bien vos illusions, mon enfant, car les illusions sont le

miroir de l'amour'.[12] The illusion is more than that, it is a whole
way of life that induces, particularly in the women, a death of the
spirit and the intellect, of all those qualities in fact that are essential if they are to adapt themselves to a struggle for existence.
Historical change is about to compel a new way of life on them
and yet how can they begin to cope? ' "What could they do with
their empty brains? . . . with their feeble hands?" '[13] The threat
that they may have to emigrate to America following countless of
their own former tenants there paralyses them.

The peasant-tenantry are viewed as impartially as the gentry:
they are not idealised as victims of the social process. Indeed Moore
presents the wretchedness of their condition and the grossness of
their manners with a frankness that shocked his first readers:

> The peasantry filled the body of the church. They prayed
> coarsely, ignorantly, with the same brutality as they lived. Just
> behind Alice a man groaned. He cleared his throat with loud
> guffaws: she listened to hear the saliva fall: it splashed on the
> earthen floor. . . . One man bent double, beat a ragged shirt with
> a clenched fist; the women of forty with cloaks drawn over their
> foreheads and trailing on the ground in long black folds,
> crouched until only the lean hard-worked hands that held the
> rosary were seen over the bench-rail. The young men stared
> arrogantly, wearied by the length of the service.[14]

Under cover of their church-going the peasants promote League
activities; they rack-rent and treat evictions as a field-day; and
they take advantage of the state of anarchy to settle personal
grievances:

> A dastardly outrage was committed last night in the neigh-
> bourhood of Mullingar. A woman named Mary —— had some
> differences with her sister Bridget ——. One day, after some
> angry words, it appears that she left the house, and seeing a man
> working in a potato-field, she asked him if he could do anything
> to help her. He scratched his head, and, after a moment's reflec-
> tion, he said he was going to meet a 'party', and he would see
> what could be done: on the following day he suggested that
> Bridget might be removed for the sum of one pound. Mary ——
> could not, however, procure more than fifteen shillings, and a
> bargain was struck. On the night arranged for the assassination
> Mary wished to leave the house, not caring to see her sister

shot in her presence, but Pat declared that her absence would excite suspicion. In the words of one of the murderers, the deed was accomplished 'nately and without unnecessary fuss'.[15]

While social reformers debate an ideal justice for the peasants' protection, they are 'but weasels fighting in a hole'.[16] But indifference on the part of the landlords has brought them to this state of deprivation; they are part of a web of national corruption and injustice; and their condition is a subject for profound pity and concern. They appear only briefly throughout the novel but always in dramatic contrast to the socializing of the gentry; their abject, near-naked figures, seen staring through the windows of the country ballroom or caught in the glare of the headlights of carriages bound for dinner parties at the Castle, act as a constant reminder of the extortion on which those festivities depend:

> In the broad glare of the carriage lights the shape of every feature, even the colour of the eyes, every glance, every detail of dress, every stain of misery were revealed to the silken exquisites who, a little frightened, strove to hide themselves within the scented shadows of their broughams: and in like manner the bloom on every aristocratic cheek, the glitter of every diamond, the richness of every plume were visible to the avid eyes of those who stood without in the wet and the cold.
> 'I wish they would not stare so,' said Mrs Barton; 'one would think they were a lot of hungry children looking into a sweet-meat shop. The police ought really to prevent it.'[17]

Though they are threatening presences, the writing does not become melodramatic or histrionic since Moore does not write out of fear of the imminent crisis. He knew that change must come and like his father welcomed it.[18]

Moore is helped in preserving the impartial tone by his decision to present his view of life in Ireland largely through the perceptions of his heroine, Alice Barton, a daughter of the gentry yet one increasingly critical of its way of life. Moore does not present the whole novel from her single point of view but shifts between an objectively recorded narrative and Alice's private meditations on those scenes in which she has been personally involved. By using Alice in this way Moore preserves the right balance between sympathy and insight and ensures that the social criticism he offers is given in an incisive and dramatic form. As the facts about the life of her class impinge on Alice's sensibility they are pondered over and judged by her as she experiences the moral, emotional and psychological repercussions on herself. She tests everything against what she calls her conscience. Moore adapts the theme of the education of the young person so that it becomes a process of discovery for Alice and the reader of the condition of Ireland. As a result the critical stances advocated grow out of Alice's experience and are known and felt to be just by the reader. The society is judged by the quality of life, both material and spiritual, that it creates for itself.

This is the first time Moore has used a mediating consciousness in his fiction. The difficulty with this technique lies in creating a consciousness which the reader can find interest in and learn to respect. As Moore had previously failed to write a convincing study of a sensitive intellectual, his achievement with Alice Barton is a significant advance in his development.

Alice's intelligence, which she inherits from her mother, is her most treasured possession, although it endows her with a detachment that is the cause of much mental torment. Early in life she has perceived the discrepancy between the professed creed and the practice of her class, its hypocritical 'Sunday mummery' based on the belief that 'society could not hold together a moment without religion'.[19] She no longer believes in the necessity of divine sanctions for her conduct and has come, like so many of Turgenev's characters, to appreciate that both the power of her own conscience and the joy that is born of her truth to her own sense of right are the true gauge of reality:

I do not know that I found the world very different from what I expected to find it. Of course there is evil – and a great deal of evil; and if you will fix your eyes upon it, and brood over it, of course life seems only a black and hideous thing; but there is much good – yes, there is good even in things evil; and if we only think of the goodness we become happier even if we do not become better; and I cannot but think that the best and the most feasible mode of life is to try to live up to the ordinary and simple laws of nature of which we are but a part. . . . and the ideal life should, it seems to me, lie in the reconciliation . . . in making the two ends meet – in making the ends of nature the ends also of what we call our conscience.[20]

Alice's rectitude of mind expresses itself in her complete unselfishness and her sympathy with suffering humanity. Out of her unwillingness to hurt her parents she at first places her duty to them before that to her own self-respect and outwardly conforms to their way of life. Entertaining such deceit betrays her mind to a sense of insult and she becomes increasingly critical of her parents, especially of her mother, and suspicious of her relations with Lord Dungory. Following her mother's instructions in the art of pleasing men leaves her feeling spiritually unclean. When she tries to assert her own principles and opinions she merely rouses her mother's petulance: 'I don't know how it is, you always contradict me and you seem to take pleasure in holding opinions that no one else does'.[21]

Alice's own values are established at the beginning of the novel in the play that she has written for her school-friends; it is a dramatization of Tennyson's *King Cophetua*. Her aim is to demonstrate the nobleness of mind that moves a king to refuse a princess and marry a beggar-maid, confident of finding in her a more consoling sympathy. Her vision has all the idealism of youth, but that does not depreciate its eloquent plea for honesty of motive. However, such scruples are naive and sentimental in the opinion of Alice's socially conscious friends and her sister Olive; they respond merely to the superficial fact of the beggar's having done well for herself, and see in her success the fulfilment of their own objectives in life:

'I don't see, Alice, why you couldn't have made King Cophetua marry the Princess. Who ever heard of a King marrying a beggar-maid? It seems to me most unnatural. Besides I hear that lots of people are going to be present, and to be jilted before them all is not very pleasant. I am sure mamma wouldn't like it.'
'But you are not jilted, my dear Olive; you do not like the King, and you show your nobleness of mind by refusing him.'
'I don't see that; who ever refused a king?'[22]

Alice's frustration deepens with her more intimate acquaintance with the society that promotes such values. Critical of her home-life and of her class's attitude to poverty, to money and to the peasantry, bored with the idleness of her existence and nauseated by the acid gossip of her contemporaries, she retreats more and more within herself to escape her growing sense of moral degradation. This withdrawal brings no lasting peace for it aggravates her fear of extreme loneliness. She longs for some show of sympathy, but cannot submit to the dictates of society, as Olive, Violet and May do, in order to find satisfaction. Marriage on her mother's terms would cost her her integrity while spinsterhood, the only socially acceptable alternative, would leave her an object for derision or pity. Alice has not even the consolation of religion, like her friend Cecilia, who accepts such dreariness as her Christian lot. Painstakingly Alice must carve her sanctions out of the granite of her misery. Like Henry James's Nanda Brookenham and Ibsen's Nora, Alice has the intelligence to question the amorality of accepted social standards. To criticise that state of matrimony which reduces the woman's role to nothing more than a brainless but pleasurable gratifying of the senses is also to imply a condemnation of the husband who accepts such trite qualities as essential in his partner. Intelligence, women find, is not safe for them; it is 'unladylike'. Their tragedy is to be despised for what is best in them.

It requires an enormous effort of that intelligence in Alice to save her from black despair but once she trusts to it she finds it brings its own rewards. Reading poetry encourages her to explore and cultivate her sensibility; writing about her needs and experiences helps her to come to terms with her predicament and in time gives her the means of making a modest independent income out of journalism. The strength to preserve her mental balance comes too from her innate compassion for others. She finds in her criticism of society a reason not for indulging in self-pity but for bestowing compassion on the countless others who are subject to that fate. That she shares their fate is sufficient to free her of a wish to patronize; her understanding affords her rather a sense of duty towards them, to succour them in their distress. Her journalism allows her secretly to support May Gould when she becomes pregnant and Alice works with an attitude almost of martyrdom, as if seeking a penance for her own sins against her self-respect in acquiescing in her mother's schemes; nor is her compassion stifled by any suggestion of repugnance when May returns unrepentant to the same way of life. Alice's objective moral sense never blinds her to the relative good in others. The fine integrity of her intelligence is admirably demonstrated in her relations with the writer, Harding, whom she meets at the Shelbourne Hotel during her first Dublin season. She is moved by his kindness in helping her to publish her writing; she is delighted to find a mind responsive to the things which interest her but, in contrast with Kate Ede, Alice has enough insight into herself not to idolize him instantly but to wait, observe, consider. His attitude to society is sympathetic with her own, but his constant, cynical analysis reveals to her his want of any permanent values; he has no personality, only an inhuman mask of contempt and a cruel wit that belittles even his own achievements. She is eventually attracted to Doctor Reed because of his fearless endeavour. He has risen by his own efforts from being a child of the peasantry and so is deeply critical of the prevailing social injustice, but as a doctor is not without sympathy for suffering humanity of whatever class. In loving Reed she finds the strength finally to stand up to her mother; in marrying him she fulfils her ideal of marriage as interdependence, a mutual sharing of the burden of maintaining a home and family. Moore takes care in the final sequence to mark that this is in no way a fairy-tale solution: Reed is poor and they must both work to support their household; they will live in a shabby terraced house in a London suburb, but their happiness will be honestly earned, not the fruit of extortion; and their children will know the true meaning of home. This last chapter is a necessary adjusting of the perspective to stress how completely Alice and her husband are sustained by values that lie within themselves and not by social appearances.

Few, of course, will follow her example: though Alice knows her husband is what is truly a gentleman by temperament, he is not so in the eyes of the world by birth or income, and they are ostracized and derided by her family and the other gentry. Knowing that society morally for what it is, they are readily able to rise above its pettiness through confidence in each other and in their self-respect.

Alice's enormous effort of intelligence and the healing power of her altruism are emphasized within the structure of the novel through contrast with her friend, Cecilia Cullen. She has been a cripple from birth and so leads a life apart, retreating within herself, but without Alice's power of self-criticism. Nauseated by the prevailing code of values she condemns with Zolaesque loathing all joy and love as a bestial degradation:

'. . . like the rest you demand the joys and satisfactions of the flesh; but, unlike May and Violet, you shall not live and be satisfied with them. They shall become loathsome in your eyes, they shall sicken in your sight and mind, and when the first fever of curiosity and desire has passed, you shall drink the draught in horror; you shall long to dash down the brutal cup, your lips and mouth shall burn as with poison, and your heart shall wither within you, and your yearning soul shall call to be delivered of its uncleanness.'[23]

True beauty, Cecilia argues, lies only in the unattainable mystic ideals of Christianity, but her ecstasy, her longing to take the veil as a nun is in reality sensual hysteria. The world in her view is to be suffered only as a temptation to be resisted, so that she welcomes her nausea with life as a kind of chastening penance. As Alice quickly realises, her nausea is essentially self-pity for her deformed condition. The real and the ideal can indeed, as Cecilia argues, rarely be one, but that to a Christian is the source of his strength, his humility and his compassion. Alice, though an agnostic, comes closer to such strength and tranquillity of mind than Cecilia's mysticism does, for Cecilia is capable only of despising life; she cannot read into it as God's creation any of His beauty. Hers is a tragic perversion of a fine ideal; she has simplified her vision to the verge of intolerance and so fails in the one great commandment of her faith: she cannot love her neighbour, for she abhors her living self. Alice finds life good in spite of its evil and evil often, as in Cecilia's own case, in spite of its good. That knowledge in Alice acts as a discipline to check her imagination's inherent tendency to the sentimental and the egotistical; Cecilia, however, creates an imaginative order that is stripped of all that is infinite, but thereby it is robbed of all that is dynamic or meaningful beyond the sphere of her own egocentric values.

Cecilia's kind of life-denying hysteria frequently passes for piety amongst Irish catholics; and Moore was fascinated by the type. During his work for the Irish Literary Theatre and the Gaelic League later in his life, he was frequently to be the victim of such people's vociferous, socially inflammatory criticism. Inaccurately (though understandably) Moore came to see the type as representative of Irish Catholicism and it led him to make some foolish attacks on Irish bigotry. He was however to treat the type seriously and sympathetically once more with his character Father Gogarty. Interestingly that novel, *The Lake*, explores the awakening of a young priest's consciousness from a mindless repression like Cecilia's to a joyous humanism like Alice's.

A Drama in Muslin has a more complex form than Moore's previous novels but this was necessary if he was to integrate as successfully as he does his range of themes. Alice Barton at once reveals the way of life of a particular society and is the means of criticising it; the valid objectivity of her judgement is stressed by the parallel study of Cecilia's hysteria, which is produced by the same moral and social factors. The one weakness in the novel's structure lies in the presentation of Dr Reed. One can appreciate Moore's need in view of his subject-matter to push his male characters somewhat into the background; that Mr Barton, Lord Dungory and the rest never rise above the status of caricatures is a just comment on their worth as individuals. Dr Reed plays a vital role, however, in Alice's decisions, for his is the hand that guides her through the most painful stages of her progress to maturity and independence. His characterization is sketchily done and his worth is never objectively established. Moore presumes that by this stage of the book the reader values Alice's opinion as sound commonsense and so simply expects Reed to be taken on trust.

There is, however, a more important problem with the novel, and interestingly Moore himself draws critical attention to it in his preface to his later revised version, *Muslin*. It is not a question of structure or thematic integration as with his first two novels but of inconsistency now in the actual writing with its 'headlong, eager, uncertain style (a young hound yelping at every trace of scent.)'[24] The lack of a unity of style is not, however, quite as drastic in its effect as Moore and some reviewers have suggested. The chapters of omniscient narrative are given largely in an easy descriptive style and his characterization developed as in a *A Mummer's Wife* by some fine dialogue. The problem arises with his attempt to portray Alice's consciousness or, as Moore calls it, her 'heart'.[25] He does this in a number of ways: by straightforward authorial comment as in the previous novels – a kind of indirect reporting of her thought-processes; by her recollection of incidents or her response to Cecilia's letters that have offered a particular smart or challenge to her self-respect; and by her reflections which are given in passages of sustained lyrical prose. Confronted by the desolate winter landscape, Alice muses on her own spiritual isolation; she responds to the mood of the landscape which, as in Turgenev, becomes a means of orchestrating her feelings: it affords her a means of articulating her unconscious feelings and responses. The inter-relation of these three methods anticipates Moore's later style in portraying consciousness, although here the effect is cruder, less technically assured than in *The Lake* or *Héloise and Abélard* because the transitions are too abrupt. The shifts between objective and private narrative worlds are also awkward but inevitable given the actual structure of the novel. The changes in style and tone are not confusing and the reader quickly adjusts to the pattern. Homogeneity would have been possible, of course, only if the novel had been cast entirely from Alice's point of view.

The specially mannered style Moore adopts for Cecilia is justifiable on the grounds of dramatic characterization. Hers is a consciousness heightened to hysteria; that the tone of her utterance is melodramatic and obsessive is not, therefore, in itself a fault. The Biblical cadences and tortuous rhetoric are wholly in character with her evangelical attitude and it is a particularly felicitous irony that, despite her repudiation of this world, the poetic symbols that define her vision of heavenly love are invariably expressions of the beauty of nature. She echoes the Psalms and the Song of Solomon, yet in an attempt to deny that the worship of God begins in a glad worship of the visible world. The only valid criticism is perhaps one of length here; the hysterical tone becomes repetitive and tedious; but the loss to the structure of the novel is considerable in the revised *Muslin* where most of her scenes are omitted.

Both these attempts at presenting consciousness with a lyrical or heightened and poetic prose-style are effective. Unfortunately Moore does not restrict the passages of prose-poetry to the portrayal of consciousness but indulges in a number of set-piece descriptions where he seeks to imitate either the 'passionate prodigality' of Zola's denunciations of luxury (such as the description of materials in the Court Dress-Maker's shop, or the way that women's bare shoulders at a ball remind him of exotic flowers) or Huysmans' *images forcées*[26] (such as the references to the debutantes' presentation with its excitement like that of a first communion, or the opening description of the friends' last evening at school, where the sunset, in a development of Baudelaire's *Recueillement*, is likened to the death and burial of a young girl). The first two passages cited demonstrate what Susan Mitchell described as Moore's 'tiresome preoccupation with . . . millinery and confectionery'.[27] They are too indulgent, too conscious of producing an artistic effect to succeed as Zolaesque condemnations:

> Shoulders were there of all tints and shapes. Indeed it was like a vast rosary, alive with white, pink and cream-coloured flowers: of Maréchal Niels, Souvenir de Malmaisons, Mademoiselle Eugène Verdiers, Aimée Vibert Scandens. Sweetly turned, adolescent shoulders blush white, smooth and even as the petals of a Marquise Mortemarle; the strong, commonly turned shoulders, abundant and free as the fresh rosy pink of the Anna Alinuff; the drooping white shoulders, full of falling contours as a pale Madame Lacharme; the chlorotic shoulders, deadly white, of the almost greenish shade that is found in a Princess Clementine. . . .[28]

And so the list continues, while Moore forgets his narrative and enjoys himself. The effect is at first comic and subsequently as Susan Mitchell says 'tiresome'. In a novel concerned with depicting varying degrees of consciousness in terms of poetry and symbol such additional descriptive impressionism can only be intrusive as it is in no way integral to the theme. Considering that the description of Alice's response is frequently used as a vehicle for criticising other characters and for directing the reader's sympathies, some of these purple passages could in a modified form have been presented more successfully as part of her evaluation of the life about her; or again as exemplary of the novelist Harding's cynical approach to the Castle season. As it stands there are too many layers of consciousness. Even so, the novel does not merit Moore's harsh dismissal of it in 1902 as 'perhaps the best subject I have ever had excepting *Esther Waters* and . . . the worst written'.[29]

In revising the novel as *Muslin*, in 1915, Moore attempted to overcome this problem of style by heavily cutting all the lyrical passages, but the loss was greater than the gain. Without a full depiction of Alice's growth to maturity of mind *Muslin* appears as merely an interesting document in social history, for it is precisely that development, as I have demonstrated, that gives the first version its organic unity. Through a careful self-discipline, Alice Barton found the means of acknowledging the necessities of her life in society and as a woman without prostituting her self-respect. She became the prototype of Moore's humanism:

Alice Barton is a creature of conventions and prejudices, not her mother's but her own; so far she had freed herself, and it may well be that none obtains a wider liberty.[30]

The qualification – 'it may well be' – evident in this final judgement is the key to the real strength of the novel: Moore's capacity for a dualistic response to his subject, his ability to sympathize with Alice's point of view without losing a larger social perspective that allows him to depict the limitations of that view. The attitude controlling the fiction is one of creative scepticism. Moore was right to compare his first Irish novel with Turgenev's work, even though the comparison shows up the technical crudity with which his dualistic response is presented in contrast with the Russian's. With *Esther Waters*, written nearly a decade later, the technique is more accomplished and closer to Turgenev's, because the dualism is not apparent simply in the structure and organisation of the novel, rather it has become the whole creative impulse behind the book, giving it a remarkable imaginative unity. It is this which secures its status as Moore's first masterpiece and which explains its surprisingly modern tone.

(4) *Esther Waters*

(i)

> . . . poor talkers and poor livers are in all ways poor people to
> read about. . . . Mean manners and mean vices are unfit for
> prolonged delineation; the everyday pressure of narrow neces-
> sities is too petty a pain and too anxious a reality to be dwelt
> upon.[1]

Bagehot's dismissal of the poor as a fit subject for the novel comes
from his criticism of Dickens but it is worth pondering over since
the terms he uses and the attitudes that lie behind them are not
peculiar to him alone. They recur later in the century in the attacks
on Zola and other attempts at treating the working class seriously
with forthright realism. There is, of course, no such thing as a 'fit
subject' for art; any material can stimulate an artist to creativity;
'fitness' is solely a criterion for evaluating his *treatment* of the
chosen subject. But the implications of Bagehot's remarks are
more wide-ranging than this. It is noticeable how quickly he moves
from the word 'poor' to the more emotive term 'mean' and from
'mean manners', implying a lack of gentility and education, to
'mean vices' with its suggestion of the abject, the sordid, the offensive. 'Mean' is a dangerous word to conjure with in this context,
for it rapidly shifts its nuances from the purely descriptive (where
'mean' is a synonym for 'poor', 'shabby') to the evaluative, socially
and morally (where 'mean' suggests inferiority of rank, weakness
of ability or understanding, pettiness of mind and spirit and a
lack of moral dignity). From being an objective comment on an
individual's financial state, the term has come to be a subjective
appraisal of that individual's worth as a human being. The effort-
lessness of the shift in meaning shows that the writer feels the
second condition is an inevitable consequence of the first. Such
an assumption exposes the writer's essential indifference and lack
of discrimination. How can anyone's suffering or anxiety be dis-

missed as 'petty' if it affects the quality of his life? While such assumptions can be made, the writing of novels about the working class, like *Esther Waters*, is a social and moral necessity. The true condition of 'meanness' needs to be carefully defined and understood; and it is here that fitness of treatment rather than fitness of subject becomes the crucial issue.

Bagehot's indifference to the working class derives from an implicit sense of his own superiority. Such condescension can at times, however, pass itself off as a kind of concern for the distressed condition of the poor, but it is in truth merely curiosity about lives which are *different*; the unusualness is the appeal. The aesthetic young narrator of the *Confessions of a Young Man* envisages writing a novel about the English servant class and he begins collecting suitable material:

> I used to ask you [the housemaid, Emma,] all sorts of cruel questions; I was curious to know the depth of animalism you had sunk to, or rather out of which you had never been raised. And generally you answered innocently and naively enough.
> . . . you were very nearly, oh, very nearly an animal, your temperament and intelligence were just those of a dog that has picked up a master, not a real master, but a makeshift master who may turn it out at any moment.[2]

The young man is no doubt trying to achieve a degree of clinical detachment in imitation of the de Goncourts' spirit of enquiry in which they composed their novel of working-class life, *Germinie Lacerteux*,[3] but the effect is insufferably cruel in taking advantage of the maid's naivety. The narrator questions Emma in a way that serves only to substantiate his assumptions that she is 'mean' in the worst senses of the word. That she cannot appreciate how he is humiliating her is no excuse for his treatment. The author's spirit of enquiry is merely a snobbish and sensational curiosity that is both morally and artistically dishonest.

It is worth pointing out the nastiness of the tone and attitude here in order to show by contrast how remarkable Moore's achievement is with the completed novel *Esther Waters*, where his detachment in presenting the grim reality of his heroine's condition does not exclude a sensitive and compassionate understanding of her predicament. There is true heroism in Esther's fight 'against all the forces that civilisation arrays against the lowly and the illegiti-

mate'.[4] *Esther Waters* is a genuine social novel in its treatment of
the fact of poverty and it well deserved those contemporary reviews
which wrote warmly not only of a 'beauty of moral effort' but also
of Moore's 'respect for common life'.[5]

On one level Moore's novel is about the desperate quest of the
poor for security, for a home and for subsistence in a society that
sees them as 'mean' in the condemnatory senses of the word.
'Money, Money! oh, the want of a little money – of a very little
money!'[6] Esther's cry is echoed by most of the characters in the
novel. 'A little money' constitutes a certain status and with that
comes a modicum of self-respect; and with respectability one is
saved from the ranks of the benighted. But the right to be free of
the opprobrium attendant on 'meanness' has to be earned; to be
industrious is to chasten the soul and one must work for one's
'good'. It is Moore's object to criticise the enormity of this confusion of moral and social values, by showing the tragic consequences that it promotes. There is of course nothing new in this:
condemnation of the hypocrisy, cant, exploitation and ruthlessness
attendant on a class system that justifies itself on ethical grounds
is a constant theme in Victorian fiction that has any social and
philanthropical intentions. However, even if this criticism was by
now something of a convention, it was well worth reiterating for
its object was still a verifiable social fact. The particular force and
originality of Moore's approach to the subject lies in his choice
of a fallen woman, an unmarried mother, as his heroine, whose
suffering is to expose the grim realities of city life. Having trans-
gressed accepted moral canons, her need for security for herself
and her child is particularly acute and her chances of achieving
it are slight.

(ii)

For the Victorians, chastity was perhaps the cardinal virtue; it
suggested a rigid observation of propriety and it was frequently
cherished as a redeeming feature in otherwise vicious characters.
As Professor Dalziel has shown in her study of popular fiction of
the early Victorian age: 'Chastity outweighs avarice, envy and
wrath.'[7] That women fell into two moral categories seems to have
been the attitude common to all classes:

'There's only two kinds of women (high or low) and that's those as respects themselves and those as doesn't. Them as does, I respects; those as doesn't, no one respects – and I despises.'[8]

The fallen woman is a recurrent theme in fiction but invariably as a quarry for the chase. Authors who attempted to treat her at all sympathetically found themselves at the last conciliating public opinion by arranging either for her death or her emigration as did Dickens with Nancy, Lady Dedlock and Little Em'ly; and George Eliot with Hetty Sorrel. The one early Victorian novel that attempts to treat the subject at all differently and in depth is *Ruth* and Mrs Gaskell's theme and her attitude in many ways anticipate Moore's:

'If her life has hitherto been self-seeking and wickedly thoughtless, here is the very instrument to make her forget herself, and be thoughtful for another. Teach her (and God will teach her, if man does not come between) to reverence her child; and this reverence will shut out sin, – will be purification.'[9]

Ruth is a very courageous work; but Mrs Gaskell knows her audience, and, more importantly, the limits beyond which she may not go: enormous rhetorical resources are called into play to control the reader's values and the direction of his sympathy by creating an almost exaggerated sense of Ruth's self-effacing innocence and naivety and later by melodramatically exposing to humiliation Mr Bradshaw, the man who torments her and sets himself up as her judge and accuser. Moreover, Ruth has throughout her trials the protection and support of the Bensons who take her into their home out of pity. By presenting much of the action through their response to their charge, Mrs Gaskell subtly educates the reader himself into a more responsible attitude that thwarts convention, for 'the world's way of treatment is too apt to harden the mother's natural love into something like hatred'.[10] Even so, Mrs Gaskell finally baulked at the conclusion her novel demanded and, much to Charlotte Bronte's disapproval, subjected Ruth to martyrdom as a nurse during a fever epidemic. In her conclusion Mrs Gaskell asserts that Ruth's robes have now been washed and made white in the blood of the Lamb. Only in God's, not in Man's house, could the fallen one be restored as a ministering angel.[11]

Moore also takes as his principal theme the moral restoration of
an unmarried mother despite her treatment at the hands of society.
Like Mrs Gaskell, he explores the possibility that her 'sin' will
initiate in his heroine a growth in moral awareness by arousing
within her a reverence for life. Unlike Ruth, Esther has no protection; of low birth and with an illegitimate child, she is an outcast, a
pariah, and her predicament exposes all that is inhuman and hypocritical in a world that damns her in the name of religion. The
form of the novel owes much to the picaresque tradition, but the
sequence of 'adventures' provides here a cross-section of society
from Mayfair to Soho and has a complex and cumulative purpose.
The scenes demonstrate simultaneously by concrete, dramatic
examples Moore's criticism of society and its unchristian attitudes;
the quality of working-class life; and the gradual maturing of
Esther's character in response to the growing difficulty of fulfilling
her responsibility to her child. Moore offers little commentary or
rhetoric to control or educate the reader's response, instead his
whole meaning and intention are presented as dramatic incidents.
    'Esther Waters,' Moore wrote, 'is Alice Barton in another
form.'[12] Alice's career is a quest for honest personal values in
despite of the ethos of her class, who survive by the exploitation of
the poor; Esther's is more simply a quest for self-respect despite the
circumstances of being exploited. With the people of her own
class, Esther like Alice is the yardstick for critical judgement: her
stepfather and his family, Esther's fellow-servants, the customers
at the King's Head tavern, all illustrate in a succession of related
vignettes the power of an inhuman social process to blunt, distort
or annihilate all the essential values that constitute a fully
developed humanity. Myriad details, incidents and characters of
varying degrees of importance shade in a demonstration of the
contemporary social scene not in abstract terms but as an active
process in human affairs; and thus highlight the central portrait
of Esther herself, who is at once a focus and the means of placing
morally every detail in the total canvas.

(iii)

Esther's labour as a servant allows her employers to live in
pleasurable comfort. Her life is one of enforced drudgery; all
pleasure is denied her lest she should fall into temptation:

. . . Mrs Bingley continued:

'It is my duty to know what you do with your money, and to see that you do not spend it in any wrong way. I am responsible for your moral welfare.'

'Then, ma'am, I think I had better leave you.'

'Leave me, because I don't wish you to spend your money wrongfully, because I know the temptations that a young girl's life is beset with?'

'There ain't much chance of temptation for them who work seventeen hours a day.'[13]

Esther must make herself a slave in order to achieve a meagre degree of security, a pittance, and even that is dependent on her health and physical strength. Esther's lot is symptomatic of her class. Drink for many, such as her step-father, Jim Saunders, is one means of escape from its relentlessness and that brutalizes an already rough existence. Large families are usually the outcome, and a round of beatings, starvation and visits to the pawn-shop ensue, in order to keep father supplied with money to satisfy his growing addiction.

Of course, the more hands there are in a family capable of work, the larger the income. Saunders makes no pretence of having a responsible attitude to his children; they work for his benefit. The older ones mould paper animals on piece-work and the younger ones prepare their materials to speed their production.

. . . I'm tired of making dogs; we have to work that 'ard, and it nearly all goes to the public; father drinks worse than ever.[14]

The enormity of the conditions under which they work seems more poignant for the children's innocent acceptance of the fact: one ill-made object and 'if the manager'd seen it he'd have found something wrong with I don't know 'ow many more, and docked us maybe a shilling or more on the week's work'.[15] That would mean a reduction in Saunders' beer-money and he would terrorize the family out of spite: when Esther buys him steak and porter on the night she returns home the children 'remarked significantly that they were now quite sure of a pleasant evening'.[16] Later, he is prepared to turn Esther out on to the street when he learns of her pregnancy, until 'softened' by her offer to pay for her food and lodging:

Why didn't yer tell me that afore? Of course I don't wish to be 'ard on the girl, as yer 'ave just heard me say. Ten shillings a week for her board and the parlour – that seems fair enough . . . I'm sure we'll be glad to 'ave 'er. I'll say right glad too. . . . There's a lot of us 'ere, and I've to think of the interests of my own. But for all that I should be main sorry to see yer take yer money among strangers where you wouldn't get no value for it.[17]

Saunders' parental disregard is not an isolated case. Through want of security, many in Esther's position turn to regular prostitution, but the rich as Esther discovers are prepared to countenance even that abuse of marriage and motherhood and turn it to their account. Wealthy mothers employ wetnurses to free them of their full responsibilities, and many working-class girls gain a lucrative income from a life spent alternately as a prostitute and wetnurse; their own children cost merely the nominal charge of farming them out to a child-murderer: 'so, instead of them a-costing 'er money, they brings, 'er money'.[18] This is a social fact and a genuine instance of the rich being fed with the life-blood of the poor:

Lord, it is the best that could 'appen to 'em; who's to care for 'em? and there is 'undreds and 'undreds of them . . . and they all dies like the early flies. It is 'ard, very 'ard, poor little dears, but they're best out of the way – they're only an expense and a disgrace.[19]

In the context of the novel this is a powerful nightmare symbol of the condition of the poor generally with its patterns of extortion and victimization that result in a severing of all human ties and responsibilities. The absence of real affection is felt the more strongly for the bogus sentimentality, 'poor little dears', with which the nurse assigns the children to their fate. Behind the baby-farmer's words lies the unspoken but firm injunction to Esther that she should be sensible and think only of herself, for children are merely 'an expense and a disgrace'.

Drink offers one way of escape for the working class from the need to earn a subsistence and is a means of forgetting the only conditions under which that is possible. An alternative for those weary of the scant livelihood work brings is the illusion of hope and release excited by gambling: 'A bet on a race brings hope into lives which otherwise would be hopeless.'[20] A win at the races is the equivalent of more than three months' wages for Mr Saunders.[21] All bet in the hope of winning the security of a new kind of life away from the sweat and toil; for the rich can buy anything, they can even materialise that utopian dream of the industrially oppressed, a life in the country. The success of the Barfields' horse, Silver Braid, in the Stewards Cup transforms the town of Shoreham; the glint of gold evokes magical illusions:

> Lives pressed with toil lifted up and began to dream again. The dear gold was like an opiate; it wiped away memories of hardship and sorrow, it showed life in a lighter and merrier guise, and the folk laughed at their fears for the morrow and wondered how they could have thought life so hard and relentless.[22]

Few remember the cost of the success; for to strengthen the horse's legs with exercise over muddy terrain the Barfields prayed for rain and sacrificed a whole year's crop of hay and wheat. 'Let ever ear of wheat be destroyed so long as those delicate forelegs remained sound. These were the ethics at Woodview.'[23] Once the fever has died and the money been spent, the hardship and misery become the more unbearable.

Gradually betting seems the only hope worth living for. The gambler is consumed as his addiction takes a hold like a disease on his blood and brain; his single-minded passion is pursued to the neglect of the real demands upon him. When Esther visits the butler Randal's home at Shoreham she is surprised by the utter destitution of his wife and family and his hypocrisy in disguising this life from his fellow-servants:

> Esther . . . remembered the little man whom she saw every day so orderly, so precise, so sedate, so methodical, into whose life she thought no faintest emotion had ever entered – and this was the truth.[24]

To Mrs Latch, Randal is the 'Prince of Liars'.[25] His subsequent brief appearances throughout the novel mark the stages of his degrading mania: his every possession is pawned and his livery too, so he is unable to seek employment; his family are reduced to begging; and his own scruples would be farcical were it nor for his age and pathetic condition:

> 'What do you mean? You didn't use to mind coming round for half a quid.'
> 'That was to back a horse; but I didn't like coming to ask for food. . .'[26]

Similarly, amongst the frequenters of the King's Head tavern, Ketley sells a flourishing business only to fail as a professional punter; Sarah Tucker steals from her employers to finance bets that her lover feels to be a 'moral certainty' for the Cesarewitch; she is convicted and imprisoned; even children in the neighbourhood lie, deceive and rob; all for the want of money to breed more money. Conscience and self-respect are the first things expended as the addiction gains a hold. But the cherished hopes are invariably delusions; the losses greater than the gains. As the dreams pale to extinction the longing for the safety of illusion becomes a threat to reason: Randal attempts, and Ketley commits suicide; others lust for drink while their impoverished families suffer the final degradation of entering the Workhouse. The need for money, for a little pleasure, has betrayed them to a passion that devours all that constitutes their humanity until finally, as William's slow death by consumption symbolizes, they gamble away their very life-blood.

A Drama in Muslin had shown how the landed gentry seek to perpetuate a valueless and tawdry dream-existence at the expense of the Irish peasantry. They fought against the social and political aspirations of the poor, for fear that they themselves should be forced to awaken to reality. *Esther Waters* also poses questions about social justice:

> Then the betting that's done at Tattersall's and the Albert Club, what is the difference? The Stock Exchange, too, where thousands and thousands is betted every day. It is the old story – one law for the rich and another for the poor. Why shouldn't the poor man 'ave his 'alf-crown's worth of excitement?[27]

Financial speculation is a form of gambling through bargain and barter with the marketable value of labour. The judge condemning Sarah for theft is right to define gambling as a desire to obtain wealth dishonestly and not as a just reward for endeavour; but he neither consults his own conscience nor attempts to consider whether that reward is always a fair return for the labour that is exacted or why the condition of the working class should provoke them to seek relief or a means of escape.

> His Lordship, whose gallantries had been prolonged over half a century, and whose betting transactions were matters of public comment pursed up his ancient lips and fixed his dead glassy eyes on the prisoner. . . . 'For my part I fail to perceive any romantic element in the vice of gambling. . . . Drink, too is gambling's firmest ally.' . . . And lordship's losses on the horse whose name he could hardly recall helped to a forcible illustration of the theory that drink and gambling mutually uphold and enforce each other.[28]

This is one instance where Moore is resorting to obvious caricature and an unsubtle, ponderous rhetoric to expose the judge's hypocrisy. It lacks the dramatic force and complex irony of the episode quoted above from William's trial, where William is right to complain as he does, though the reader's response to the truth of his opinion is tempered by an awareness of William's own character and the knowledge that he is speaking there chiefly out of pique that the law protects the interests of a part of the community to which he does not belong. Technically, Moore's commentary on the judge at Sarah's trial fails because it is too contrived; but it does serve to show the effectiveness of Moore's use of dramatized narrative situations elsewhere. Even here, though the means are heavy-handed, Moore makes his point felt: exploitation is a crime, an all-consuming disease that breeds of itself till the corruption is total, and ethical values are robbed of active, specific meaning. This is, of course, a necessary simplification; but gambling is an irrefutable social fact while, as a symbol, it is loose enough to be all-embracing in its sphere of reference.

Some of the force and purpose behind the wealth of incident and character will now be apparent. The variety of pace and texture in these episodes is finely controlled such that each is developed to a length proportionate to its moral and social significance. Moore's polemic is, with minor exceptions, successfully converted into the material of the novelist's art.

Katherine Mansfield, writing about *Esther Waters* in *Novels and Novelists*, objected to the detail and factual accuracy of these scenes; they were to her merely an excuse for journalistic reportage that lacked creative relevance and so were detrimental to the over-all design.[29] Moore, with his painter's training, had a retentive memory for observed detail so cumulative that control became a difficult but necessary aspect of the creative process for him. There are places where matters get out of hand (particularly in the long bar-room conversations building up an 'atmosphere' about horses and racing, where even Moore's otherwise spirited dialogue cannot sustain the tension) but elsewhere the massing of detail has an important and relevant function as a setting for Esther's personality. Esther passes through varied *milieux* in the social scale as her fortune fluctuates, but in spite of her difficulties and precarious financial position everything that is vital to her and her purpose remains constant. Whenever for a brief period she is established in security there is no relaxing of the principles that governed her quest for it. What Miss Mansfield fails to appreciate is that the significance of the descriptive detail lies in its power to evoke the *quality* of life that accompanies various degrees of social security. That this is in turn a deliberate setting for Esther's character is emphasized by the fact that so much of the description is presented through Esther's eyes and in the terms of her response to it.

A good example of this is offered in Chapter XX[30] in the account of Esther's brief stay as a servant first with the Bingleys and then with the Trubners. Moore records her seeming good luck in gaining a position at sixteen pounds a year. The Bingleys' house and shop are described; the several members of the family introduced in turn and their beliefs as Dissenters established as a tendency to exact 'the uttermost farthing from their customers and their work-people'[31] on weekdays, and to sing hymns fervently on Sundays in a drawing-room which is never otherwise used. Esther's situation is then bluntly contrasted in all its relentless monotony:

> And it was into this house that Esther entered as general servant, with wages fixed at sixteen pounds a year; and for seventeen long hours every day, for two hundred and thirty hours every fortnight, she washed, she scrubbed, she cooked, she ran errands, with never a moment that she might call her own. She was allowed every second Sunday out of four, perhaps for four and a half hours. . . .[32]

The irony of Esther's initial enthusiasm at finding a 'good place' is all too apparent. The stark catalogue of her hours and duties and later her thrifty calculations over spending her wages emphasize the enormity of her hand-to-mouth existence. To see her child, she must pawn her dress. Then there is the ceaseless drudgery, taxing strength and will:

> Even the rest that awaited her at eleven o'clock was blighted by the knowledge of the day that was coming; and she was often too tired to rest, and rolled over and over in her garret bed, her whole body aching, all that was human crushed out of her. . .[33]

The moral significance of these contrasting standards of living is pointed further by two short dramatized incidents. While cleaning one morning, Esther finds a half-crown and is tempted to take it to pay for her monthly visit to her son, Jack, but refrains through shame at her dishonesty. She leaves the room hastily to discover one of the Bingley sons spying on her and is shocked to realise that he has arranged this trap to test her honesty. Later, Mrs Bingley, unaware of Jack's existence, demands as her moral right to know how Esther spends her wages.[34] Esther is to have no identity, no individuality, no personal life; she is to be merely of the type of featureless servant. The biblical text commending the laying up of incorruptible treasure in Heaven (ironically, a condemnation of materialism) provides in this household an excuse for forcing the lower classes to accept any amount of toil as an object-lesson in humility. When Esther refuses to accept that burden with gratitude she is treated to a torrent of abuse and condemnation; and later when Esther's next employers, the Trubners, hear of Jack, she is again immediately categorized as a 'loose woman' and dismissed. The Trubners talk of Christianity but ignore its practical concern for contrition and forgiveness; and, in the interests of piety and modesty, would prevent transgressors of the moral or social law from earning even their daily bread. Their piety is uncharitable, unfeeling, hypocritical; but it conforms to their delicate sense of the socially acceptable.

In both these episodes, after a brief authorial description of the property, the nature of the household and its inhabitants is communicated almost wholly through dialogue and Esther's thoughts while pursuing the arduous duties of her working day. *Esther Waters* went through many editions during Moore's lifetime but he revised it far less intensively than many of his other novels. He attempted no major adaptations of the structure or the characterization; the revisions were interestingly all local, textual ones, and, as R. A. Gettman has demonstrated,[35] these show Moore steadily converting authorial material (straight comment and description) into a style of *oratio obliqua*, so that it becomes not Moore's but Esther's response to the world about her. This gives such material greater vitality and a constructive function in being now an organic part of Moore's depiction of his heroine's consciousness. Increasingly Moore found stylistic means of focussing the reader's attention on Esther.

(iv)

Esther's dilemma of moral choice, like Kate Ede's, is between two contrasting ways of life. But the later novel marks a considerable advance both technically and in social awareness. The Edes and Dick Lennox were representative of opposing moral attitudes; so too are William Latch and Fred Parsons, but they are more closely integrated in the total social process. Their opposition is a means of dramatising Esther's psychological conflict, while their typicality affords Moore an opportunity for a more detailed analysis of crucial aspects of his social theme.

William, like Dick Lennox, lives by exploiting the weakness of a desire for pleasure in the poor. He voices all the delights and advantages of gambling with the false logic of the materialist, and is as much a parasite on the backs of the poor as the wealthy masters he criticises. 'I don't know what's your taste, but I likes something out of which I can make a bit.'[36] Nonetheless, William is attractive, kind, scrupulous to make Esther's life secure and to make amends for his former desertion; he wants to act honestly with her and with his customers; and his ambition is for a home and contented family life. But such admirable qualities are limited by the conditions necessary for his success as a publican and bookie. His aspirations for a greater security for his family are unquestionably fine ends; but he builds his house on sand in interpreting 'security' as his right to imitate the Barfields' way of life without questioning whether that life is in every way full or honest. Styling himself on the squire is particularly absurd since William as well as Esther knows that, shortly after both left Shoreham, the Barfields were declared bankrupt and had been forced to sell their stock and all but a fraction of their estate. Both Woodview, the Barfield's house, and William's pub, the King's Head, are denounced as immoral centres of their respective neighbourhoods. Will's betting chatter, like the butler Randal's 'erudition', is littered with anecdotes of the aristocracy and the golden age of racing, which are savoured almost as self-dramatizations. William's elopement and marriage with the Squire's niece, Peggy, and their subsequent way of life also develops this theme: to Esther, he 'had gone where the grand folk lived in idleness, in the sinfulness of the world and the flesh'.[37] The failure of his first marriage does not arouse any understanding or critical response in William. His family had once been gentry and had owned the Barfields' estate:

> 'Yes, the Latches were once big swells; in the time of my great-grandfather the Barfields couldn't hold their heads as high as the Latches. My great-grandfather had a pot of money, but it all went.'
> 'Racing?'
> 'A good bit, I've no doubt. A rare 'ard liver, cockfighting, 'unting, 'orse-racing from one year's end to the other.'[38]

'A rare 'ard liver' has more than a hint of wish-fulfilment, it is totally devoid of moral perspective, but then William's moral sense is never brought to play critically on matters that further his own interests – 'Bet I must, if I'm to get my living'[39] is always his excuse and his justification. When Esther encourages him to help Sarah Tucker when she is arrested for theft, he does so simply as an expression of his love for his wife, not out of any sense of responsibility for having introduced Sarah to the man who has encouraged her to rob to finance his gambling.

William's virtues and ambitions are but promises to be fulfilled in the event of his financial success; but he can never give Esther the contentment he wishes, because he himself is a victim of the gambler's dissatisfied longing for better and greater gain, which is possible only by attracting more customers to his illegal business. The wealth he does acquire is put to no constructive end and he dies penniless of consumption caught while betting on the course during an inclement winter. He has made gambling the condition of his existence: it is mechanistic, destructive.

The virtue of Moore's characterization lies in his avoiding the temptation to simplify and make William wholly vicious. Mrs Gaskell leaves the reader in no doubt about the selfish and shallow value of Ruth's seducer, Bellingham. As Esther rightly observes of William: 'He ain't no more wicked than another; he's just one of the ordinary sort – not much better nor worse'.[40] The warmth of his ideals is sincere enough, and he is wholly unconscious of committing evil because his knowledge of the world (by which he means the Squire and his first wife, Peggy) has persuaded him that such methods are an acceptable social convention. William is no stage-villain; the knowledge of his self-betrayal and his bewildered questioning why there should seemingly be one law for the rich and another for the poor has pathos. The irony of his blindness to his own moral predicament gives his dialogue a wonderful vitality:

Them hypocritical folk. Betting! Isn't everything betting? How can they put down betting? Hasn't it been going on since the world began? . . . We are ruined and the rich goes scot-free. Hypocritical, mealy-mouthed lot. 'Let's say our prayers and sand the sugar'; that's about it.[41]

As the novel shows, there is an element of truth in this: social values are confused, biased, unjust. William fails in honesty, because he lacks a sufficient self-awareness and discipline to appreciate that the grounds on which he accuses his superiors apply equally to himself. He simultaneously exposes and identifies himself with the persuasive sophistry with which society veils its true motives. His career is at once a demonstration of a prevailing social ethos and a critique of its inadequacy. Moore's success in defining character through dialogue is particularly fine. It is precisely because he is 'just one of the ordinary sort' that William is typical and effective as a vehicle for Moore's criticism. That William's disappointments in life never educate his understanding is tragic, for while chance rules his life so completely he cannot achieve and sustain a rich identity. Esther's intuitive and compassionate understanding kindles the reader's own.

Fred Parsons' life is styled according to his belief in Calvinism which celebrates conformity and acceptance; his sermons picture the hell-fire and damnation that await the transgressor. Like the Trubners, he believes that the outrages of this world must be suffered at God's command if peace is to be attained in heaven, and that to seek to escape or to alleviate that suffering through drink or gambling is a temptation of the Devil's. Fred cannot appreciate that his attitude is essentially negative in that it is really an acquiescing in moral and social injustice. Worse still, it is a self-satisfied expression of pride in his own purity of motive and conduct.

Again Moore does not simplify – Fred is not an unsympathetic character. He too is tragic in that his purity is not the creative force it should be if truly Christian. The pathos of this inner sterility is admirably communicated through his dialogue, where a certain dryness of tone is apparent throughout. Sexual sin is the one most abhorrent to him and his life's preaching has been directed against it. He genuinely wishes to forgive Esther for her past as her future husband and to accept her illegitimate child into his home; but this requires of him a wholehearted opposition to his former principles. The necessary effort to oppose in practice his professed doctrine is too heavy a demand even for his love. He prevaricates and seeks safety in generalisation:

> It may not be a woman's fault if she falls, but it is always a man's. . . . Those who transgress the moral law may not kneel at the table for a time, until they have repented. . . . A sinner that reproach – I will speak about this at our next meeting. . . . I love you, Esther, and it is easy to forgive those we love.[42]

There is more than a hint of condescension in this reply. The words have an almost homiletic cast of phrase and rhythm that robs them of any deep sense of personal conviction or involvement; the strongly abstract quality is the measure of how far his religion is divorced from any felt social obligation. His actual words never quite ring true to the intention that lies behind them; but one can appreciate the metal strife that blocks the sincere expression, 'I forgive'. Even then, however, one questions his presumption that he *has* the right to forgive; as he judges, so is he judged and condemned for sexual snobbery.

Fred lacks his mother's compassionate understanding of human error that comes from a ready acknowledgement that 'We're all sinners, the best of us'.[43] The same is true of Mrs Barfield; she is honoured as 'the Saint' by her servants, because 'like all the real good ones, she is kind enough to the faults of others'.[44] When she learns of Esther's pregnancy, she blames her own lack of vigilance and forethought, her weakness in not counteracting more strongly the lax moral tenor that her husband, the Squire, encourages in his household. Fred is too militant to perceive the value of such a sense of shared responsibility. Even his actual deeds of charity are vitiated by an inherent wish to be thought of as good in word and deed: when he warns Esther of the Salvation Army's legal proceedings against William he cannot resist telling her of the risk he runs in doing so, just as he responds earlier to her frank confession about Jack's illegitimacy by an avowal of his own purity. It is a pity that Moore underestimated the dramatic power of his dialogue to illustrate Fred's psychology; his detachment is in places marred by authorial reference to the icy tones of Fred's voice and to his high falsetto, which intimates an unwarranted caricature of Puritan zeal.[45]

It is Fred's personal failure, his inability to recognise his true duty relative to his creed, that ultimately makes his protest against betting and drinking ineffectual. His faith is essentially a glorying in his own powers of self-discipline and the damned are all those who fail to measure up to his own standards of excellence. Even his joy in Esther reflects back on himself:

> He pressed her hand, and thanked her with a look in which appeared all his soul; she was his for ever and ever; nothing could wholly disassociate them, for he had saved her.[46]

Betting is, as he suggests, a desire to obtain wealth without work; crime and prostitution are possible results; but betting, drunkenness, and prostitution are the effects, not the root-causes of corruption. In condemning merely those effects, religion and the law are sanctioning, however unwittingly, the greater social evil. Fred, like the judge at Sarah's trial for theft, has not sufficient critical detachment to effect true justice or mercy. By an act of choice, Fred has committed himself to Calvinism as a means of coming to terms with the world he lives in; the rigour of his creed demands the sacrifice of much of his humanity as is evident in the struggles between his conscience and his intuitions whenever he tries to help Esther.

Both William and Fred have identified in their respective ways too closely with the material values of the community to have more than a slender knowledge of themselves: the forms their self-deceptions take, to the detriment of their better qualities, exemplify the fraud, hypocrisy and injustice upon which their society is founded and to the protecting of which every social, religious and legal force is directed. William devotes his life to chance, Fred to an inflexible commitment; both men fail to understand Esther's attitude to life and to her child and that failure in understanding is a measure of their inability to achieve full human stature. In fictional terms, Will and Fred remain merely types, while Esther through her quest for self-respect becomes a fully realised character.

(v)

The simplest human sentiments were abiding principles in Esther – love of God, and love of God in the home. But above this Protestantism was human nature.[47]

Esther cherishes not only the holiness of the heart's affections but also the maintaining of her self-respect, as her Christian duty. Her seduction seems to her an abuse of both these values: she tries to compel William to marry her as a means of regaining her equanimity, but he deserts her. She has sinned against herself, and her pregnancy is for her the cross she must bear as punishment. She comes to accept her sin by acknowledging the child that is the consequence as her future responsibility in life. There is no crying out against fate: Esther accepts the pattern of the future as a duty, the fulfilling of which will be a progress towards a renewed self-respect and her path to God's forgiveness. Her desperation finds relief in that purpose: 'You must wait until it is a symbol of living faith in the Lord!'[48] Her devotion to her child is more than the mother animal's instinct to protect her young: Jack is a symbol of 'her good', her sense of principle, her honour; as the flesh of her flesh he symbolises her very life:

Her personal self seemed entirely withdrawn; she existed like an atmosphere about the babe and lay absorbed in this life of her life. . . . She touched this pulp of life, and was thrilled, and once more her senses swooned with love; it was still there. . . . She could not sleep. She could not sleep for thinking of him, and the night passed in long adoration.[49]

Formerly, she was a doggedly obstinate girl but her temper is now transformed into a dedicated and resolute determination to succeed for the child's security, despite the inevitable hardship. Always thoughts of the child's love for his mother and his future pride in her calm Esther's flashes of anger and quieten her fears that fulfilling her duty might be beyond the capacity of her physical strength. Her sheer resilience is monumental. Esther values her independence, however hard it is to win, more than the easy security sought by most of her class. Not 'everyone for herself' but 'everyone for her own' is Esther's axiom, despite the stigma of Jack's illegitimacy.

It is from a sense of doing right by her child that she chooses William as her husband rather than Fred, although Fred's sectarian background and attitude offer potentially a more satisfying life for herself. William has money to give the child security and a good education and he is Jack's real father, as the child himself innocently argues. Her own misery at the hands of a biased step-father makes her fear to take such a risk with Jack's future happiness. She is critical of the origins of William's wealth and fears the ability his wealth gives him to entice the child away from her. She alone can give Jack a sense of principle and shield him from the attraction of his father's way of life. William gives ample proof of his power to ingratiate his way into the child's affections by a display of his wealth and the gift of a few toys and clothes. Fred argues that the dictates of her faith should mean more to her than her duty to Jack. But his creed is too rigidly simple and, as a result, too exclusive of the factual problems of living, in Esther's opinion, for him to appreciate her predicament. Fred feels that she holds her family in greater esteem than her reverence for God, because Esther refuses to condemn William's affluence, but she counters his accusation frankly: 'Ah, religion is easy enough at times, but there is other times when it don't seem to fit in with a body's duty.'[50] Her duty, as she sees it, is to honour and obey William as her husband, not to plague his life with discord. She will be neither priggish nor a shrew. Her duty to her neighbour is as important to her as her duty to God; and that is Esther's path to grace:

A woman can't do the good that she would like to in the world; she has to do the good that comes to her to do. I've my husband and my boy to look to. Them's my good. At least, that's how I sees things.[51]

The Victorian wife was expected to honour the marriage-vow of obedience, but Esther maintains a mind of her own and William respects her individuality and her right to her own opinion. This is his finest quality; Fred, however, remains utterly bewildered that she is not contaminated by her husband and the environment of the King's Head. Her defence is simple and direct: '. . . we don't choose our lives, we just makes the best of them.'[52] Her life with William is not ideal but circumstance has made it a necessity and she enters into it, fully awake to the consequences of what she is doing. Marriage with Will is not a submission to chance but a compromise and one for which Esther accepts partial responsibility; seeing it so dispassionately she can work to make good come of it. The pattern of her life is thus an expression of her faith. This affords her the strength to resist the escapist illusions that tempt her class; and because that pattern is founded on a humble acceptance of her original 'sin' with Will, she is free of the zeal and egocentric pride that beset Fred. She is confident of the efficacy of prayer and of divine forgiveness for human error, provided that man acts what he feels to be right as his duty in the given circumstances. Here is the source of her courage to face the vicissitudes of life with undaunted determination; to keep the knowledge secret from Jack of her deep grief at William's slow death from consumption; and, immediately after his funeral, to turn resolutely once more to the task of earning a living for herself and her son:

> She must live for him; though for herself she had had enough of life. But, thank God, she had her darling boy, and whatever unhappiness there might be in store for her she would bear it for his sake.[53]

There is a significant, almost Laurentian passage near the beginning of the novel, when Esther, after many years of life in the London slums, responds instinctively and intensely to the beauty and healthy vitality of life in the country on the Barfield's estate and the Sussex Downs:

> It was a pleasure to touch anything, especially anything alive. She even noticed that the elm-trees were strangely tall and still against the calm sky, and the rich odour of some carnations, which came through the bushes from the pleasure-ground,

excited her; the scent of earth and leaves tingled in her, the cawing of the rooks coming home took her soul away skyward in an exquisite longing; and she was, at the same time, full of a romantic love for the earth, and of a desire to mix herself with the innermost essence of things.[54]

This is notable as one of the few moments in the novel when Esther knows rest. She has already impressed us in the opening chapters as a girl with a natural piety and intuitive moral sense and this passage reveals to us the source of her inner security in her profound instinct for life. The joy and wonder she feels here return again after the birth of her child when all her fears for the future are dispelled by a radiant delight in the child's very being – an instinctive delight that totally suffuses her personality and constitutes her only experience of passion. Stylistically, these passages mark Moore's first attempt to depict the lyrical nature of personal response; thematically, it is the gradual renascence of this mood in the concluding chapters that rounds to completion the pattern of Esther's life and reveals Moore's psychological purpose.

The memory of her youthful but instinctive response to the beauty of Woodview 'had become the most precise and distinct vision she had gathered from life'.[55] Esther lost her purity of heart and body both in her own and, consequently for her, in God's sight. 'He had not forgiven because she could not forgive herself.'[56] Her conscience forces her out into the world but the memory of her Eden endures, and that romantic impulse of her sensibility relieves the tedium, the 'meanness' of her physical condition. Her 'vision' now centres entirely on her child; Jack becomes a symbol of the life-force that Esther is determined to cherish, an emblem of the values by which she lives. 'Helping others,' as Mrs Barfield remarks of Esther's life, 'that is the only happiness.'[57] In her resilience and her selfless devotion to the child, she too is at one with the mystery, 'that unconscious resignation, which like the twilight hallows and transforms. In such moments the humblest hearts are at one with nature and speak of the eternal wisdom of things'.[58]

The opening paragraph of Chapter XLIV[59] subtly repeats that of the first chapter describing Esther's arrival at Woodview; now, an ageing woman, she is returning to Shoreham. Though stripped of all her possessions and bereft of her husband, she has never been daunted by the fact of her poverty; rather it has inspired her and augmented her instinct and gratitude for life itself. Jack, now a young man, has become a soldier; his life will be in constant danger but Esther has achieved her aim and brought him to adulthood. Her life has known sorrow, loneliness and humiliation, but, as the pattern of her duty is fulfilled, her faith is rewarded with a recovery of the inner unity that was her youthful innocence. Esther's life has been blessed with a lyrical instinct for faith, unknown in William's grim materialism and denied by the society at whose hands she has suffered. Like the proud estate of the Barfields, the fruit of man's egoism is subject to death and decay, but life in nature is unceasing. The wild life of the Downs is encroaching on the ruins at Woodview and, despite the wintry desolation that is the setting of the final chapters, the rooks are building their nests again in promise of the spring. The cyclic pattern of the novel is not simply a technical masterstroke; it is an essential development in the fulfilling of Moore's psychological theme, for in the very pattern lies the significance, a pattern that is not deterministic but a creative development of the heroine's inner truth.

Esther achieves fullness in the life that is the portion allowed to her by society. The psychological theme is triumphantly resolved in her vindication; but, within the total social context, Moore is not blind to the tragic limitations of her achievement, of which Esther herself is mercifully all too unconscious. Her culture is limited simply to her faith; her achievement is her power to accept and make a virtue of necessity. The limitation imposed by her simplicity of mind is in no way Esther's failure; it is wholly to the blame of society. The particular achievement of the novel lies in Moore's mature social awareness: he honours Esther's nobility of motive, but that feeling is tempered with compassion, for her success is relative when seen in implied comparison with the fullness of life that should have been her right as a human being. Her bringing of Jack to man's estate is at once a triumph of her personal integrity and a criticism of society for attempting to deny and suppress the values she seeks to maintain, thereby depriving her of the opportunity for a more plentiful flowering of all her faculties. Conversely, it is the sheer weight of opposition that makes her success, however relative, the more notable. She is the controlling sanity in which Moore's critical insights take root. The compassion of the novel springs from Moore's ironic awareness of the predicament of the working class: that what God hath given as every man's

right, man or at least society has to a large extent taken away, and
done so often in the name of religion.

The assured technical subtlety of this response to his subject is
an enormous advance on the final sequence of *A Drama in Muslin*,
where he similarly attempted to place Alice's moral achievement
in its accurate social context. There is detachment here; but a
detachment that is understanding and compassionate in its concern for human potential: it does not activate a progressive reduction of life to the mediocre, as it so frequently does in Flaubert;
nor does it disguise a pathological curiosity as in *Germinie
Lacerteux* by the de Goncourts. If the novel develops by implication a basic irony, that irony is neither ubiquitously destructive nor
is it the tactic of one seeking to defend his own uncertainty, as in
many of Huxley's social novels. Moore's technical success is the
more notable for its almost classical simplicity. Esther is a working-
class girl with little education, and any deep analysis of the nature
of motive and of possible alternative courses of action, on Moore's
part, would be unacceptable as realism. To guide her conduct she
has only a sense of the sanctity of her duty to her neighbour and
her child and an innate will to live. Her psychology is presented, as
we have seen, wholly in terms of action as response to her dilemma:
the tight consecutiveness of the narrative is the pattern not only
of her life but of her mind and personality: 'You was the father
of my child and it all dates from that.'[60] When we consider the
complexity of Moore's response to his subject, this simplicity is
all the more creditable. What Katherine Mansfield has criticised
adversely as an 'even flow of narrative' is a surprising technical
virtue rather than, as she sees it, a failure of creativity or imagination.[61]

(vi)

Esther Waters was Moore's first financial as well as artistic success and it has come to be the novel by which he is best known. It
has not however found favour with all critics. The novel has
certain flaws in its composition and these must be appraised before
the justness of some adverse criticisms can be properly assessed.

Most of the characters in the novel are shown to be conditioned
by social pressures such that their progressive degradation is an
exposure of the moral depths to which society in general has fallen.

William and his gambling circle, Sarah Tucker, even Fred Parsons, are presented effectively in this way. Esther however is different; she is decidedly not 'one of the ordinary sort':

> Was her love of her child such love as would enable her to put up with all hardships for its sake; or was it the fleeting affection of the ordinary young mother, which, though ardent at first, gives way under difficulties? Mrs Spires had heard many mothers talk as Esther talked, but when the real strain of life was put upon them they had yielded to the temptation of ridding themselves of their burdens.[62]

This 'difference' presents Moore with two problems concerning Esther's motivation. Why, one may ask, is she gifted with a sensitivity towards her instinctual self, when none of the other characters have this intuitive insight? Nothing in her background explains this quality; indeed the rather puritanical tenor of her upbringing makes it the more surprising. Moore obviously intends Esther's responsiveness to the Sussex landscape to be in the nature of an epiphany affecting her to the core of her being and exciting in her a new awareness of herself. He certainly achieves this aim, though it is rather in retrospect that the pattern of events in the rest of the novel endows this passage with the necessary weight of significance. The style of the passage might have been heightened to advantage to impress on the reader more immediately than it does the unique and special nature of the experience.

A more important problem and one less happily solved concerns Esther's seduction. The plot demands that Esther be an outcast in order to demonstrate the hypocrisy of accepted *mores*. Once again Esther has to be both a contrast with, and yet acceptably representative of, the working class. Why does a girl with her moral scruples fall? Moore treats the issue in a vague way, both terse yet confused that leaves the impression that the seduction is somehow determined: Esther 'knew that her fate depended on resistence'[63] but she finds herself powerless to fend Will off. The outcome is inevitable as the very term 'fate' foreshadowed; but Moore does not attempt to explain why physical lassitude overpowered her moral scruples. Esther's part-excuse: 'I shouldn't have touched the second glass of ale'[64] is ludicrous as an explanation. It is part of Moore's purpose to show how most of the other characters in the novel are the victims of pressures within society but to suggest as he does that Esther's loss of virginity and innocence is also 'fated' as part of that process, conditioned by the lax moral tone of the Barfields' household, is absurd. In his keenness to develop his central theme of Esther's role as a mother, Moore has given this crucial episode too loose and cavalier a treatment, which raises unnecessary questions of consistency in motivation. This is particularly lamentable in that a perfectly acceptable emotional 'cause' lies close to hand and is several times stressed in the narrative. Esther questions herself about the life at Woodview:

> I know very well indeed that it is not right to bet; but what can a girl do? If it hadn't been for William I never would have taken a number in that sweepstakes.[65]

To have developed this theme of Esther's infatuation for William and the way he unthinkingly exploits her love and undermines her scruples would have been truer psychologically to the circumstances. Moreover this would have afforded a good parallel later in the narrative with her friend Sarah's desperate passion for Bill Evans, about which Esther herself is so understanding. It would conform too to the pattern of Moore's final novels which are concerned to show how true values are discovered through an awareness of a personal moral failure. By including unwarranted and unnecessary apostrophes to fate, Moore seems to be trying to free Esther of responsibility and this may be an act of caution on Moore's part, an unwillingness, such as lies behind Mrs Gaskell's rhetoric in *Ruth*, to challenge conventional standards too forcefully.

Unfortunately, the matter does not rest there: the references to fate persist. Esther's moral difficulty in choosing between William or Fred as a husband is to a large extent conditioned by the facts of her seduction but she resolves her dilemma in the child's interests, not her own. Again Moore partly veils over the moral complexities of the issue:

> She sighed and felt once again that her will was overborne by a force which she could not control or understand. . . . She stopped thinking, for she had never thought like that before, and it seemed as if some other woman whom she hardly knew was thinking for her.[66]

Such commentary tends to belittle the courage of Esther's decision and her true motive and is perhaps pointless anyway, as Esther usually has a choice of actions, even if that choice is limited to the lesser of two evils. One might however argue in Moore's defence that what he is trying to do here is to define within the obvious limits of Esther's vocabulary her sense at times of overwhelming impulses to act in particular ways that rise from her subconscious, a kind of autonomous will which she cannot understand adequately enough to explain but which experience has taught her to trust in her confrontation with a morally confused and confusing world. The novel shows how through this trust Esther transcends her social predicament; she is not a trapped animal. If she sometimes sees herself in these terms, as when she discovers that Mrs Spires' trade is in baby-farming, it is always as a first frantic reaction to a particular dilemma. This mood of dejection quickly passes as the deeper reaches of her mind suggest to her a course of action that allows her to preserve her integrity. Admittedly Moore might have made this opposition of conscious and subconscious responses clearer to the reader than he does through his commentary.

It has been necessary to dwell at length on these passages as they have been criticised as detrimental to the novel by Ian Gregor and Brian Nicholas in their study, *The Moral and the Story*.[67] *Esther Waters* is on their showing a sickly product of the decadence, 'melodramatic' in its theme of the good girl beset by a wicked society, uncertain in its moral attitudes and its social analysis, and prone to what they consider to be an Aesthetic religiosity. A false note is struck in William's death-bed repentance; but the general movement of the novel is not guilty in this last respect. Moore's quest for a compassionate and less rigid approach to morality is not wanton, as we have seen, nor is his attitude to faith. If Esther is 'religious', she is so in no narrow sense but because she has a need to reverence certain values and relationships in her life. One of the achievements of the novel is the careful distinction it draws between life-denying and life-enhancing forms of piety.

The morality propounded in Moore's final novels is healthily related both to specific humane and social values and to a feeling for natural vitality and organic growth. His attitude in *Esther Waters* is the same. Gregor and Nicholas's thesis is concerned with the transitions that moral analysis in the novel underwent at the turn of the century, from George Eliot to Lawrence. Had they approached Moore's work as a whole with more sympathy, they would have found him to be a more valuable and instructive example than they appear to have done. The references to fate are certainly the cause of some confusions but the real power of the novel lies elsewhere and is such that these lapses of judgement in Moore's commentary are minor and local.

At one point in their analysis, Gregor and Nicholas remark that 'the presentation of Esther's duty to her son and her husband *suggests* a more subjective appraisal of personal fulfilment, of the life well-lived'.[68] To argue that this theme is 'a suggestion only at variance with the main tendency'[69] of the fiction which they see as struggling to remain faithful to the scheme of French naturalism is to get the whole novel out of focus. They place undue emphasis on brief passages like those examined above about Esther supposedly being fated; and ignore Moore's stated intention that with *Esther Waters* he was trying to break away from the restraints imposed by the deterministic, linear structure of naturalism and its conventions, which he found morally and psychologically limiting because they took little account of the inner lives of characters and, particularly with Zola, reduced instinct to merely animal urges. Moore wished for a structure and method that would give him room for more subtle discriminations. He does not deny that there are forces that condition the individual's life in society (his awareness of these forces is responsible for that irony that has been shown to lie at the heart of the novel's conception); but what he is questioning is whether they need affect more than the material facts of existence. Their power is such that some types of personality succumb to their influence completely; and tragically futile lives like Will's result. Moore believed man could find the strength to resist these pressures within his private moral being. Lena Milman, who read *Esther Waters* in draft-form, was alarmed by the psychological innovations of the novel and Moore wrote her the following defence of his work:

Nothing seems to you 'more despicable than the following of one's inclinations'! If one does not follow one's inclinations the result seems to me to be complete sterilization. It is only those who are wanting in strength who do not follow them – will you allow me to substitute the word instincts? We must dis-

criminate between what is mere inclination and what is instinct.
All my sympathies are with instincts and their development.
Instinct alone may lead us aright.[70]

Far from being merely a 'suggestion', 'the subjective appraisal
of personal fulfilment'[71] is Moore's primary theme and for this he
had to create a wholly new kind of narrative structure. The cyclic
pattern with its psychological and moral implications concerning
man's need to trust his instincts to achieve psychic health is a profoundly original creation. *Esther Waters* marks Moore's discovery
of what was to be the principal philosophical theme of his later
work. If there are some minor uncertainties of definition, it is
because this is a first assay into territory previously uncharted in
the landscape of the mind.

Far from finding the novel 'melodramatic' as Gregor and
Nicholas do, many critics, including Katherine Mansfield and H.
G. Wells, have been disturbed by the fact that the climaxes are
all in the minor key and that the tone is unified throughout. There
is, they argue, a want of 'warmth' and of 'emotion', and decide
that this is because the work is without humour.[72] Moore's detachment is not without sympathy and understanding; but the kind of
humour and warmth such critics demand has been deliberately
eschewed by Moore in the interests of psychological verisimilitude.
To demand it is to misunderstand the nature of Moore's intention
and achievement. Esther's life is hard, monotonous, grim; a life in
which there is little humour; and the novel seeks to communicate
the exact quality of that life. Esther herself is not without warmth,
as her scenes with the child illustrate, and she responds with a
burst of affection when genuine kindness is shown her by Mrs
Barfield, Miss Rice, William or Fred; elsewhere, she meets with
so little kindness that she is forced to suppress what is her finest
quality. It remains to her credit that so naturally effusive a desire
is not distorted or warped in the repressing. Except in the minds
of the most intelligent of novelists, the comedy of the human situation can easily become cynical and belittling. Moore's particular
humour is very much in this satirical vein; and he was, after all,
consciously writing against the literary tradition of a comic working class. Also, humour, warmth and a feeling for the poetry of
life, when directed towards the poor, often betray the author into
a condescending tone, or, worse, into sentimentality, as Forster's

treatment of Leonard Bast exemplifies. Esther, by contrast, has 'all the natural prose of the Saxon'; she is a 'plain girl' with 'a plain way of putting things'.[73] Her brusqueness and temper can develop into cruel spitefulness when her possession of the child is threatened by William's return. Moore softens none of the coarseness of her existence, for it is the contrast of this with her inner beauty of temperament which elicits his compassion and justifies his indictment of society. Here is all the cruelty of life, but no hint of pessimism. Moore was right to avoid the risk of sentimentalizing Esther; to have done so would really have been an insult to the reader's intelligence. Creative emotion can be expressed as much in technical control and restraint as in imaginative exuberance. Moore's detached control in *Esther Waters* is never relaxed; there is little false rhetoric, no romantic over-emphasis for the sake of 'artistic' effect; and the reward is an utter fidelity to his subject. Moore himself in the final moments of the novel actually precludes this type of criticism as tending to sentimentality and offers a directive for the true interpretation of his aim and attitude:

One thing led to another, and Esther gradually told Mrs Barfield the story of her life from the day they bade each other goodbye in the room they were now sitting in.
'It is quite a romance, Esther.'
'It was a hard fight. . .'[74]

PART TWO:
A PHASE OF EXPERIMENT

(5) New Influences — New Problems

Alice Barton is a creature of conventions and prejudices, not her mother's but her own; so far she had freed herself and it may well be that none obtains a wider liberty.[1]

After the publication of *A Drama in Muslin* Moore directed his creative sympathies for the next fifteen years to an attempt to find a solution to the problems posed by that final clause: could one attain an even wider liberty? were there other sanctions for conduct than a moral conscience and a perception of one's duty to one's neighbour? what was the proper relation between culture and morality? Moore's ultimate ambition was to find a place in life for the cultured sensibility, intellectual aspiration and religious ritual that would enrich the subjective self without corrupting in any way one's moral and social obligations. His new preoccupation was how to render in terms of fiction the fashion in which an individual shapes his own consciousness, his private mind-life. Moore's own terms for this, as he stated them in *Mike Fletcher*, were:

Among those whose brain plays a part in their existence there is a life idea, and this idea governs them and leads them to a certain and predestined end. . . . A life idea in the higher classes of mind, a life-instinct in the lower.[2]

Significantly, only one of Moore's novels of this period, *Esther Waters*, examined the theme of the life-instinct of the working-class; it was his one assured success. The remaining six novels for a variety of reasons were all failures and Moore to his credit was not blind to their weaknesses although, as he afterwards wrote in the preface to *The Lake*[3], these novels served his purpose, for without his awareness of their thematic and technical inadequacies *The Lake* and *The Book Kerith* would not have been the accomplished and, to Moore, satisfying achievements they were. The six novels mark a difficult, taxing, but necessary transitional phase in Moore's work during which he was steadily to discover his own unique fictional tone and method; it was a period too which saw Moore, even as he wrote these novels, becoming increasingly mistrustful of the very concept of a life-idea as encouraging a dangerous limiting if not actual failure of personality, a kind of mental strait-jacket stultifying one's potential for growth. His disillusionment with cerebral 'philosophies of life' of the contemporary fashionable kind that he explores, for example, in *A Mere Accident* and *Mike Fletcher*, contributed in a large measure to his vigorous celebrating of the instinctive life in his later works. This period of relative failure as a novelist proved in the long term a remarkable time of self-discovery.

Moore's initial and principal mistake in composing these novels of intellectual life was in the model he chose to imitate in both style and form: Huysmans. Most of Huysmans' novels, after he abandoned Zola's Médan circle, focus on a quest for a way of living, aesthetic or monastic, which will afford some protection to his heroes, who are thinly disguised portraits of himself, from the mutability and sordidness of physical reality. His is the recurring Romantic hope of finding in the imagination or the intellect a still point in an otherwise changing world; Huysmans' originality in treating this theme lies in his belief that to present a poetic interpretation of the details of the environment with which a character chooses to surround himself and then to study in detail his refined pursuits and intellectual interests will reveal precisely what constitutes his unique individuality. 'Reality' is circumscribed by one's egocentricity in Huysmans' view so for the reader to appreciate what books Des Esseintes reads in *A Rebours*, what pictures or plants he collects, what precise shade of paint he chooses to decorate the walls of his study is to understand Des Esseintes's psychology; the impulses which compel Durtal in *La Cathédrale* to embrace the Catholic faith are to be inferred by the reader largely from Huysmans' elaborately impressionistic guide to Chartres, its architecture, art, stained glass and vestments. Nothing is seen by Huysmans as its natural self but is charged with symbolic intimations; in his work, description and representation are taken to an absolute extreme. The actual prose style as well as the form and content of Huysmans' novels has an important function in evoking for the reader the nature of each hero's particular consciousness, for it is through the style that Huysmans conveys his character's personal modes of perception. For this purpose he evolved a poetic, mannered prose using what he termed *images forcées*, in which obsolete, slang and professional terms jostle alongside accurately observed facts and a Zola-like brand of impressionism to stimulate a complex play of allusions and sensations in the reader's mind. The term *forcées* carries, however, its own criticism; and beyond having an initial power to shock, the result is rarely the beauty-laden prose intended but rather one labouring for effect and monotonously insistent in tone.

With Huysmans, French fiction ceased to be concerned as in Balzac, Flaubert and Zola with acted moral truths but attempted to paint by analogy and symbol the mind's play with abstractions as it seeks for a gratuitous, wholly private, self-centred perfection. Though Huysmans' intention is to communicate the intensity of the life within, the actual effect on the reader because of the methods he uses to present that life is rather one of sterility, inhuman decadence, imaginative and emotional atrophy and nausea. In part this is because he chooses to write about exotic fantasy-characters rather than representative figures so that one tends to associate uniqueness of perception with pathological eccentricity; later writers examining the nature of consciousness learnt partly through his example not to underestimate so drastically the possible uniqueness of the common man's inner experience. The other major problem posed by Huysmans' method of giving the experience of the novel from an exclusively subjective viewpoint is that the author inevitably loses moral perspective and with that any certain and effective control over the reader's response to the material. How is one to respond to Des Esseintes? With mere curiosity, scepticism, sympathy, disgust? Is he to be seen as tragic or absurd? Far from encouraging the reader to enlarge his imaginative insights, confronting such a fictional method may well cause him to cling to his existing values as the only certain basis for interpreting the novel.

When *A Rebours* appeared in 1884, Moore reviewed it enthusiastically in the *St James's Gazette*[4]; his excitement was prompted not simply by the content of the book but by the possibilities for future fiction that Huysmans had revealed. Just what these possibilities were is ably summarized by Arthur Symons in his essay on Huysmans in *The Symbolist Movement in Literature*:

Here, then, purged of the distraction of incident, liberated from the bondage of a too realistic conversation, in which the aim had been to convey the very gesture of breathing life, internalised to a complete liberty, in which just because it is so absolutely free, art is able to accept, without limiting itself, the expressive medium of a convention, we have in the novel a new form, which may be at once a confession and a decoration, the soul and a pattern.[5]

Symons, of course, composed this in the late Nineties, by which time Moore's enthusiasm for Huysmans, kindled over a decade earlier, was quite exhausted. But Symons' excellence as a critic lay in his ability to define the precise nature of his fellow-authors' response to continental writing and art, better usually than they could do themselves. Moore at first merely imitated superficial aspects of Huysmans' style in some of the descriptive passages in *A Drama in Muslin* but with *A Mere Accident* and *Confessions of a Young Man* the influence went deeper as Moore attempted to reveal the innermost soul of two types of Aesthete. As the third title here suggests (and Symons seems to be deliberately echoing Moore's term) Huysmans' technique does not afford the clinical analysis of the hero favoured by Flaubert and Zola but creates a context in which the hero subtly confesses himself to the reader. The overriding limitation of the technique, though, is that it allows the author no means of suggesting growth or change in the hero's personality. Huysmans' character Durtal passes from being a Satanist to being an oblate in a monastery; his spiritual progress occupies four separate novels but though the four stages of his progress are given in detail there is little opportunity for Huysmans to explore the periods of transition between these stages, when Durtal through the technique of 'confession' comes to know himself and wish for a new way of living.

With the exception of Esther Waters and Evelyn Innes, Moore's characters in the novels of this period are all 'trapped' both within their own mentalities and within Moore's fictional technique: John Norton becomes more and more a recluse; Mike Fletcher finds himself compelled to commit suicide; Hubert Price learns to live with the knowledge that he is an utter failure. *Evelyn Innes* and *Sister Teresa* show Moore battling against the limitations of his chosen method, struggling to find an alternative and satisfying way of life for his heroine and discovering in the process that he must radically alter the whole form of his fiction in order to do so. Esther alone amongst his characters at this time has the capacity for development, and the method of her story owes nothing whatever to Huysmans. By the time Symons wrote his article on Huysmans, Moore was talking of his disillusionment with the novel as a form; poetic prose was a 'dead' style and English generally a 'dead' language for literature, being self-conscious, cloyingly literary and incapable of fresh, pristine statement.[6] By 1896, Moore had found a new enthusiasm: his future as an artist lay in a rediscovery of his native Ireland; here was truly virgin soil.[7]

Esther triumphs in her modest way because she shares some of her author's own staunch resilience. Moore delighted in his own capacity for change and renewal and in his confidence in himself that allowed him to make a decisive break with the past as he did on numerous occasions, to dismiss it as his dead life and begin afresh. In the novels of this transitional period Moore examined various aspects of contemporary culture – Pater's aestheticism; the fashionable cult of religiosity that followed in the wake of the growing enthusiasm for Wagner's operas and particularly *Tannhäuser* and *Parsifal*; Schopenhauer's pessimism; the delight amongst intellectuals for assuming attitudes merely to shock the conventionally-minded. His aim was to determine how sustaining and creative a life these 'life-ideas' offered the 'soul'. As he explored these interests in his fiction, many of them cherished enthusiasms of his own, and imaginatively assessed the quality of life they brought to the individual, so Moore came to understand contemporary culture more deeply and knowing it he found it increasingly necessary to criticise and reject it. His writing slowly revealed to him that much of what the age called civilised was in truth decadent. This, I think, explains the lassitude that overtakes most of these novels making for an increasingly flat, pedestrian expression as Moore becomes again and again disillusioned with his subject, feels a duty to complete his narrative and yet is unwilling totally to revise the novel in its progress so that it offers a more critical perspective on the material. Ever conscious himself of the conventionally-minded and their tyrannic influence through the lending libraries on the art of fiction in England,[8] Moore could not bring himself for all his disillusionment to take a high moral tone. Inevitably, some confusion results over Moore's intention with these works.

The most serious consequence of this confusion of intent relates to a recurring view among critics, fostered chiefly by William Gaunt in *The Aesthetic Adventure*,[9] that Moore is the quintessential English Aesthete along with Wilde. Not only is this a misrepresentation of Moore's art but it has also led to a certain unwillingness in some critical circles to view his work seriously. Certainly Moore was, as we have seen, influenced by many of the continental figures whose work moulded English Aesthetic taste in the late Eighties and Nineties; he also at this time was living in the Temple near Yeats and Symons to whom *Evelyn Innes* is dedicated, and so would seem, particularly through friendship with Symons, to be at the hub of the Aesthetic movement. But Moore was a generation older than most of the English writers associated with that movement; he was now well into his middle-age and the London of the Nineties was a pale Anglicised imitation of the Paris of his youth; Moore had known personally many of the authors and artists who were known to the writers of the English movement only from the printed page. The respect Moore accorded to French literature and art of the time is not matched by unstinting praise of his English associates; and by the time he left England for Ireland in 1901 his ardour even for French literature had decidedly cooled and significantly only his love of French painting remained a lasting pleasure.

Even *The Confessions of a Young Man* is not really the Aesthete's bible it is often said to be. Admittedly the central character is one "George Moore" but this is the author's younger self, the self-conscious Bohemian at loose in Paris in the Eighteen-Seventies. Many of the incidents in the book and the descriptions of "Moore's" interests echo Huysmans' *A Rebours* but the pastiche has an ironic edge to it; the imitation is not exactly adulatory. As in *Hail and Farewell*, Moore's finer fictionalised autobiography, an older, wiser self is amused by his young self's antics, his attitudinizing, his flamboyance: amused, not condemnatory, but nonetheless detached. The book achieved some notoriety amongst his English readers, many of whom saw it as a gospel for the New Life but only because they chose to ignore the mocking satirical tone. 'I am feminine, morbid, perverse. Above all perverse,'[10] claims the young "George Moore" but the very reptition shows how far removed he is from really shocking us: pretentious and naughty, perhaps, even at times annoying; but his exaggerations do

not disturb us, they move us merely to laughter. Gaunt may con-
clude his discussion of Moore with the quotation from the *Con-*
fessions 'Oh! for excess! for crime!'[11] but it is not *characteristic*
of Moore's outlook for where else in his work do we find further
evidence that this was a settled taste? That Moore enjoyed writing
the book one cannot deny, and much of the literary criticism it
contains is consistent with what he wrote later in this *genre*; but the
grandiose, ebullient rhetoric, the bombastic inversions and con-
tradictions, the very excessiveness of the autobiographical sections,
all suggest that Moore's intentions are playfully satiric. Writing to
Dujardin about the French translation of the book, Moore
shows particular concern that the translator capture the right
tone:

> If my translator is a young man you may tell him that the irony
> of the English disappears somewhat in the French. I achieve I
> think a lighter and more spirited phrase, and there is always the
> touch of exaggeration which the French fails to convey. In
> English, I have my tongue in my cheek; in French, I am deadly
> serious. [Here follow several examples of mistranslation] . . . he
> misses, you see, the slight exaggeration. My book is a *satire*.[12]
> (Moore's italics.)

Pater's reference to Moore's 'Aristophanic joy'[13] is more perceptive of the tone of the *Confessions* than Gaunt's account of 'one
brought up in the principles of art for art's sake.'[14] As Holbrook
Jackson wrote: Moore merely 'played at decadence'.[15] Humour
and irony are perhaps difficult qualities to gauge; many of Moore's
contemporaries chose to overlook them certainly, but the modern
critic must distinguish: a comparison of the *Confessions* with
Moore's later autobiographies, with his more serious critical judgements and with Hone's *Life* makes one readily perceive the degree
of exaggeration which is the essence of the comedy.

Understandably Moore expresses a certain warmth and nostalgia
for his youthful follies in Paris and his laughter at his own expense
disarms our judgement. His aim with the *Confessions* was, as he
wrote to Lena Milman: '. . . to fix the ephemeral and sometimes
almost involuntary passing of emotions, that is all';[16] but to anyone
who accepts the *Confessions* as literal autobiography the recurrence
of similar ideas, situations and intellectual attitudes in novels like
A Mere Accident, Mike Fletcher and *Evelyn Innes* would seem to

suggest that Moore was upholding settled values and opinions in these works which in point of fact he was beginning to question and even repudiate; the fact that the novels end not in a state of mental equilibrium but with the frustration, collapse or suicide of the protagonists must deeply perplex such a reader. The problem is essentially that caused by the limitations of the Huysmanesque method. It needs absolute assurance in one's values to be able to voyage into a soul that one wishes to show as negative or 'evil', especially in a way that will be illuminating and constructive in its power to evoke compassion for the character's tragic waste of potential; Moore's attitude to his subject was too ambivalent, too exploratory for him to sustain the confident moral control over it that is required in a novel of this kind. The only really successful portrayal in the contemporary novel of the type of Oscar Wilde is in James's *The Tragic Muse*, where Gabriel Nash is presented to the reader through his own eloquence and, more importantly, through his friend, Nick Dormer's reactions to him. Dormer is at first attracted, almost mesmerized by Nash's conversational brilliance, but as his sense of responsibility to his own talent as a painter, to his family and to his patroness-lover, Mrs Dallow, matures so he penetrates Nash's façade and sees the inner triviality of the man. James does not dictate how the reader should respond to Nash; rather he actively quickens the reader's understanding through Dormer's changing perceptions and, because of the friendship of the two men, he ensures that knowledge of Nash's limitations is not accompanied by any loss of the reader's sympathy. This kind of technical complexity was, of course, beyond Moore's abilities; the Huysmanesque presentation of character simply leaves the reader to infer his own and the author's viewpoint, giving us no intermediary like Dormer (at least not an adequately developed one[17]) to act as a yardstick for judgement.

The confusion the reader feels on completing one of Moore's novels of this period is not unlike that he will experience with some of Aldous Huxley's early satires, such as *Antic Hay* or *Point Counter Point*. Like Moore, Huxley is here intent on criticising a society that is so proud of its *sapientia* that it strives to intellectualise all its passions and dismisses those instincts that it cannot master in this way as necessary but boring or nauseating physical functions. Huxley's own attitude is carefully veiled and in default of better guidance the reader imagines Huxley suffers the same mental *impasse* as that which is afflicting his novelist-character, Philip Quarles:

> The problem for me is to transform a detached intellectual scepticism into a way of harmonious all-round living.[18]

Both Moore and Huxley seem in these instances to be using the novel as a means of convincing themselves that too exclusive a personal philosophy or one wholly of negative definition can never be satisfying or harmonious. A 'life-idea' alone is not enough; yet neither writer can break free of his scepticism to create and endorse a positive vision. The writing of these novels was for both authors self-purging; in embracing indulgence and reproach, they mark a necessary stage for each man in his progress towards a maturer view of life. If one views Moore's novels of this transitional period out of the context of his overall development, however, one must admit that there is more than a degree of truth in one contemporary review of *Vain Fortune* that described these works as 'unsavoury subjects clumsily presented'.[19]

Moore makes one notable adaptation of Huysmans' method. Huysmans presents the psychological life of characters who are recluses or contemplatives by patiently cataloguing the objects with which they surround themselves as images of their taste and intellectual interests so that 'plot' is replaced by a kind of art-criticism. Moore imitates this way of revealing his characters' inner selves but offers the material not as impressionistic description but in the form of lengthy conversations. Dialogue is one of the particular strengths of Moore's early social novels where it has a tense energy and is psychologically allusive; but now Moore began to elaborate on the subjects for discussion at the expense of the characters of the speakers. Norton, Mike Fletcher, Evelyn Innes and her father all have unusual intellectual pursuits which required a certain amount of research on Moore's part: medieval Latin poetry, ecclesiology, Schopenhauer, Palestrina, Renaissance musical instruments, Wagner's operas. Not content with creating an acceptable verisimilitude, Moore positively flaunts his new-found knowledge, and the effect is tedious. Even when literary and musical analogues are introduced into the dialogue as a symbolic or ironic commentary on the speaker, the effect is more pretentious than illuminating, for the equations are not usually fair ones and are often preposterous, as when Owen Asher likens Evelyn to Balzac's Lucien de Rubempré at some length. Moore attempts to give us profound intimations about Evelyn's consciousness by including imaginary reviews of her operatic performances and her own detailed analyses of how she interprets Wagner's heroines which she discusses bar by bar with her friend, Ulick Dean. It may be that Moore is attempting here to conflate Huysmans' technique described above with an aspect of Turgenev's work which he had come increasingly to admire, namely Turgenev's ability to transform the traditional *conte d'amour* into a more complex creation by infusing it with a weight of philosophical and political discussion.

Writing in 1888 about Turgenev's novels for the *Fortnightly Review*,[20] Moore commented on the Russian master's power to communicate a 'picture tense with emotion, a fabulous and yet unimagined photograph of the mind'. Referring to *Virgin Soil* as Turgenev's 'most complete work; the best synthesis of his talents', Moore argues rightly that the power in communicating 'subtle and soul-revealing touches' derives from the triangular conflict that generates the plot, where the hero, Nejdanof, is caught between the sexual attraction of Marianne and the intellectual attraction of the revolutionary, Markelof. This is in fact a recurring pattern in Turgenev's novels: his strength lies fundamentally in his concern with the nature of love, both as manifested in a personal relationship between the sexes and as a social impulse for charitable reform. The first kind of love freely enables one character to reveal his most intimate thoughts, ideals and emotions to another; that there is usually some discrepancy of social standing between the lovers leads to a consideration and judgement of contemporary social values, so that the traditional love story calls into play many facets of the lovers' psychology, intellect and idealism. There is consequently a remarkable completeness about Turgenev's characters despite the seeming simplicity of his novel-structures. Discussion is essential in his tales because through it his lovers seek seriously for a compatibility, a united purpose in life, profounder than physical attraction.

Moore fails to exploit the technique to its proper advantage for his characters are recluses and their intellectual interests amount to monomanias; there is no emotional or social conflict in their lives which a frank exposition of their intimate beliefs might resolve. Evelyn Innes' long discussions with her two lovers, Asher and Dean, about her Wagnerian interpretations, which come closest to Turgenev's manner, do not reveal her deep motives for loving them. Moore's discussions remain obstinately the exposition of ideas for their own sake: he does not take care to mould the attitude and tone of expression of each viewpoint in a way that illuminates the character of the particular speaker, as Gissing, for example, does in *Born in Exile* and *New Grub Street*. Moore of course composes his dialogues out of acquired knowledge for the most part rather than longstanding experience of particular intellectual positions, so is not capable of imagining the different approaches to a subject and contrasting shades of opinion which are necessary for creating a proper debate; ideas must be more than expounded, they must be dramatically rendered. Moore's imaginative failure here is not helped by the fact that he is constantly making his characters relish their own conversational skill and their facility in coining brilliant epigrams, usually just when they have been particularly long-winded or inane.[21] Since Moore's purpose is, as we have seen, to expose the monotony and triviality of a life devoted to mere cerebration, such remarks are particularly unfortunate; as Robert Liddell remarks, 'seldom can an author have made a worse gaffe'.[22] Moore, conscious of his efforts in studying the background for these novels, temporarily becomes blind to taste and discretion; as Dormer says of Gabriel Nash:

> That was one's penalty with persons whose main gift was for talk, however irrigating; talk engendered a sense of sameness much sooner than action.[23]

Moore's characters' daily life in time exists merely to give substance to their wit; they are mere talkers in a way that Turgenev's or Gissing's characters never are. Moore's method is adequate for his critical works such as the debate with Gosse on the novel in *Avowals*,[24] but it is woefully out of place in fiction.

One final weakness that recurs throughout these six novels concerns a kind of intellectual symbolism. At its most localised, it takes the form of such slovenly aids to characterization as the following:

> John raised his eyes – it was a look that Balzac would have understood and would have known how to interpret in some admirable pages of human suffering.[25]

This is cheap and meaningless. Intellectual symbolism is notoriously difficult to use in commentary and description without its appearing self-conscious and obtrusive.

To take this kind of symbolism a stage further and make it an integral part of the exposition can be highly rewarding; but again there is an initial difficulty: the author must recognise that symbols drawn from art have a more restricted and restrictive power of suggestion than traditional classical, Biblical and folk archetypes, and so must be used sparingly and consistently if they are to be apt and not dominate or distort the focus of the thematic effects they are to elucidate. In *A Room With A View* for example, Forster demonstrates the effect of Renaissance art, its aspirations, serenity and humanity on Lucy Honeychurch, and so communicates her gradual perception that there are more valuable social and personal attitudes in life than are permitted in English middle-class society. One remembers too, in Forster's *Where Angels Fear To Tread*, the nervous 'shock' that stimulates Philip Herriton's awakening to the knowledge that a love that is passionate, imaginative and selfless is the divine spark in man, when he is momentarily arrested by a view of Caroline with Gino and his baby that has all the serenity of a painting of the Holy Family. In both these cases, the symbolism is simple enough; but it is an adequate foil to the falsely civilised values the novels elsewhere satirise, and successfully conveys a fulfilment of Forster's injunction 'to connect'. Neither case is open to the charge of Aestheticism, for in both the initial aesthetic experience is not total and exclusive; it stimulates moral awareness of a deficiency in character and prescribes a remedy. Art, for Forster, is less a refuge than the stimulus for a healthy concern for the quality of human nature. Italy, to use Forster's phrase, 'quickens' Lucy and Philip to tolerance.

Moore attempts something similar to define the sins of Aestheticism and one would expect the method to be ideally suited to the subject. However, he lacks the necessary discretion and sureness of touch. Take, for example, Evelyn's reconciliation with her father some years after she eloped and abandoned him; she is now a famous opera-singer. As she begs him to forgive her, she cannot resist drawing a parallel between their relationship and that of Brunnhilde and Wotan and the moment becomes for her not a genuine act of reconciliation but a self-conscious performance.[26] The reader is being invited to make a moral criticism of Evelyn here in a fairly direct manner but Moore mars the episode by himself pursuing the analogy between the 'living' characters of his fiction and their Wagnerian archetypes to an extreme, labouring every possible effect, when what is wanted to give the incident vitality is an appreciation of its possibilities for ironic comedy. The effect of this insight into Evelyn's capacity for self-delusion is further dissipated in that it is only one of many such moments: Watteau's *Bal Champêtre*; *The Rubáiyát of Omar Khayyám*; Balzac's novels; *Tristan and Isolde*; *Parsifal*; Celtic mythology are each in turn analysed by Moore – one is tempted to write 'ransacked' – in relation to Evelyn's psyche, until the symbolism runs amok to the reader's confusion in a litter of purple passages. When the same subjects recur elsewhere as themes for the arty conversations mentioned earlier, consistency and significance are lost; too many kinds and degrees of 'symbolic significance' only obscure the author's moral intention. On the one hand Moore is using such material to provide him with symbols whereby he can creatively define his characters' consciousness, while elsewhere in the same novels he criticises his characters for their obsession with these fashionable ideas and tastes because in his view they are life-denying. Certainly the reader must be made to perceive Evelyn's moral and intellectual confusion, but not by the confusing of his own values. The one solution to this predicament is for the symbols to become autonomous; but then it is essential that they have a complexity of reference, an elasticity and freedom of which the particular intellectual kind used by Moore is just not capable; it is, as I wrote earlier, too restrictive. Wagner's Brunnhilde and Isolde cannot respond to Moore's every purpose; as symbols they cannot be manipulated extensively, as James, for example, can manipulate his central image of the golden bowl, and Moore himself in a later novel that of Lake Carra.

Drawing these various points together, we can begin to see why Moore felt that, though failures, these novels were a valuable development in his career. All these new elaborations of technique have one common aim, that of finding a valid means of defining psychological and sensory activity, the life of the soul. Some kind of poetic or symbolic equivalent was essential; but what these novels taught Moore in contrast with *Esther Waters* was that a detached study of too exotic a personality was an over-ambitious aim for one of his creative powers; that action and situation could be as valid as contemplation as a means of defining essential personality; that the simpler, the more vital and consistent the symbolism, the more credible his related psychological analysis would be; and that other existing works of art – paintings and operas – could not furnish him with the kind of organic symbolism that he required for depicting the life of the subconscious, for they invited an intellectualised, mannered style at odds with his real purpose.

The return to Ireland was to stimulate his imagination afresh; the outcome is to be the subject of my final chapters. But even in *Sister Teresa*, which was conceived in London though written for the most part in Dublin, one may observe positive indications that a technical evolution was in progress. As one reviewer of that novel remarked: Moore 'has acquired a mellowness and a curious, wistful, chant-like quality which are very persuasive'.[27]

(6) Four Novellas

(i)

A Mere Accident is a traditional study: the tragic conflict that ensues when adult commonsense attempts to curb the wayward idealism of youth. The action focusses on three characters, John Norton, his mother and his future wife, Kitty Hare, and becomes tragic in that each is obsessed with an idea or an ideal which blinds him to the true nature of the others. John is suffering a prolonged adolescence and has developed the pet Victorian art-study, ecclesiology, into a 'delicate' principle of life that imitates medieval ascetic ritual. One's ideal, he argues, must be abstract: pure intellect contemplated amidst either an artificial luxury or austerity, such as only the Catholic Church affords. He plans to enter the Jesuit order because its discipline offers him an escape from his instinctive self which he fears is bestial. In his view a religion like the Catholic faith that embraces both art and ritual and that sanctions self-repression is the one real safeguard for purity of thought. To his mother this is nonsense; making a study of Christian Latin authors and furnishing one's rooms with uncomfortable chairs inspired by Durer engravings can only incite one's 'county' neighbours to mockery. John should be assuming his duty to his family and position; he should marry and get an heir. His way of life is a painful embarrassment to her. Neither can view the other charitably: John finds 'county' values, the hunting and house parties, tedious and restricting and cannot see that, for all her limitations, his mother is acting out of a desire to do what she considers the best for him. She in her frustrations cannot appreciate that her helpful hints about how he might 'improve' himself are a constant reproach to him and arouse his anger because they suggest that she sees his ideals as merely childish.

Though the struggle continues between mother and son, John is attracted to Kitty Hare, his mother's young companion; but it is the ideas she can represent in his imagination that appeal to him rather than the woman herself. Her beauty fulfils certain of John's literary and artistic criteria and she symbolizes for him his ideal of health and immaculate purity, a 'personal life' of 'sanctuary-like intensity'.[1] Kitty must remain enshrined and inviolate; John finds her soiled and weak even in responding to his love; till now John has believed that joy lies in admitting and repressing one's sensual instincts, and the strength of his affection for Kitty fluctuates, making her perplexed and self-conscious. In a melodramatic conclusion to the novel Kitty is raped by a tramp who attempts to rob her when she is returning one evening from a walk with John. The nightmares that haunt her afterwards always show Norton as the cold, righteous accuser casting her forth from bliss; never is he charitably forgiving. Subconsciously she has come to recognise the inhuman cruelty of his intellectual ideals, and in revulsion from his inexorable sense of principle she takes her own life. Her loss arouses no intense personal grief in Norton, only an elegy for the mutability of all things other than the life of the mind.

A Mere Accident is very uneven in quality, as this summary shows. What promises initially to be a fruitful conflict between Norton and his mother is not fully developed. Moore's inspiration here came from his knowledge of his friend Edward Martyn's emotional wrangles with his mother who, like Mrs Norton, refused to allow her finely developed intellect to influence her judgement over personal matters where the dictates of convention had to be taken into account.[2] Martyn, like Norton, was a figure of contrasts; a man with a strongly practical business sense yet, incongruously, a man devoted to the point of obsession with his intellectual and aesthetic pursuits. The potential for tragedy or at least pathos in this conflict within the family is never adequately developed, however, since Mrs Norton disappears from the narrative as John becomes involved with Kitty.

This sense of rich possibilities left unfulfilled is what mars the novel overall. The incongruities in Norton's character mentioned earlier, namely the practicality and the studiousness, the aesthetic sensuality and the physical prudery and asceticism, are amplified with considerable detail, both psychological (he has a morbid terror of death coupled with a disgust for living) and physical (imitating

Balzac here, Moore describes John as having large, powerful grasping hands but idealising, frenzied eyes). But they remain *stated* incongruities; Moore never takes us, either through the narrative or his commentary on it, to a region of John's psyche where the root cause of these tensions is explained. The progress of the tale offers us no satisfying enlightenment.

Kitty's rape is an infelicitous indulgence in sensational writing, particularly since Moore begins to intimate that she perceives the dangers to her that are latent within John's aestheticism through the way his feelings towards her waver so strangely. Her sudden realisation of his true nature would have made a more fitting climax to the novel. Bearing in mind Moore's success in charting the decline of Kate Ede's affection for Dick Lennox, we know such a resolution to the narrative was well within his analytical powers.

The most serious limitation concerns the inconsistencies of tone, of which the rape-sequence is a strident example. For much of the novel Moore adopts a detached, objective stance towards his material and particularly towards John, and his commentary echoes Zola's clinical language, referring to his purpose as a 'psychical investigation' and to the narrative as 'an experimental demonstration of the working of the brain into which we are looking'.[3] Moore abandons his detachment on several occasions, notably at the opening of the novel where he lavishly expatiates on the England which is Sussex, in mocking rhetorical terms which one can only suppose are intended as a satire on Mrs Norton's 'county' values. The shift to a flat objective stance in then introducing Mrs Norton to the reader is both jarring and confusing.

It might have been better if Moore had preserved throughout this mocking humorous attitude towards his subject. There is much about Norton, his tastes and his prejudices, that is both grotesque and pretentious, as when he pontificates against Sussex because it 'is utterly opposed to the monastic spirit. . . . In that southern county all is soft and lascivious'[4] or, to take another example, when he asserts his prudery: 'I don't think I could live with a woman; there is something very degrading, something very gross in such relations'.[5] Much that John does and represents in the novel would merit comic treatment since comedy thrives on such incongruities of temperament as he is prone to. Indeed Moore's most successful portrait of the type of Edward Martyn is in his comic autobiography *Hail and Farewell* where the prevailing humorous tone meticulously calls into play both the reader's critical insight and his sympathetic understanding. The portrayal of Martyn in *Hail and Farewell* is affectionately done and therefore psychologically convincing; that of John Norton in *A Mere Accident*, by contrast, is merely schematic, and it suffers because one is never sure either of Moore's attitude towards him or of the attitude that Moore expects the reader to adopt. As it is, one often roars with laughter at John's preposterousness yet is left uncomfortable in case this is not the response expected.

Moore might have preserved Norton's over-earnestness and presented it seriously to the reader had he abandoned the objective approach entirely and allowed John to present himself to the reader through a wholly subjective novel. This would have permitted the reader to register the absurdities of John's mental outlook while at the same time experiencing the emotional and intellectual anguish that afflicts him. By taking the reader right into Norton's process of thinking Moore would have made him perceive the logic, as Norton himself sees it, behind his incongruous behaviour. The reader would then have found him an acceptable tragic figure through apprehending the waste of intellectual effort that goes into his attempts to create order out of his own neurotically distorted perceptions of the world about him. There are times in the novel when Moore seems to be trying to do this by recording John's inner musing about his ideals and about Kitty, but these sections are somewhat spoilt by an insistent, over-rhetorical style: 'Could he abandon this? No, a thousand times no; but there was a melting sweetness in the other cup [that is marriage with Kitty as opposed to spending his life in a monastery]. The anticipation filled his veins with fever.'[6] The debased stage-rhetoric and the jaded poetic idiom of this make Norton's anguish seem merely factitious, thereby seriously reducing his stature. At this time Moore has not yet developed a prose style adequate for conveying the movement of a character's consciousness, instead he resorts to the monologue or stage-soliloquy. To compare passages such as this with the lyrical style of *Sister Teresa* and *The Lake* or the passages of personal reverie in *Hail and Farewell* is to realise how determinedly Moore worked to evolve a genuinely poetic prose to convey the delicate workings of the psyche and how versatile that style is in its command of a wide range of moods, tones and mental experiences. Discrimination and self-criticism are not qualities that are usually attributed to Moore but without them his development towards those late works could not have been so assured.

Neither a humorous detached treatment of Norton's predicament, then, nor a seriously conducted dramatic evocation of it from a subjective viewpoint lay within Moore's scope. Both approaches demanded a profounder understanding of the type than he yet possessed; it was to take a further twenty years of intimate acquaintance with Edward Martyn before Moore could render so idiosyncratic a breed of aesthete in fiction with a completeness of observation and with a technical mastery that did not denigrate the original.[7]

(ii)

Perhaps Moore was wise to abstain from following up the comic possibilities of his subject in *A Mere Accident*, if his one comic novel of this period, *Spring Days*, is anything to judge by. It is a trivial, repetitive piece and certainly his worst work of fiction. It fails because Moore with obvious strain tries to juggle with three narrative and thematic subjects without either quite fusing them into an imaginative whole or selecting one as of major interest while subordinating the other two to the level of subplots. The arbitrary, indeterminate effect produced by the structure is worsened by Moore's indecision about the kind of tone he should aim for throughout: he never truly relaxes and allows the full humorous potential of his situations and characters to flourish; his control is too cautious and exacting so that his funniest conceptions are not allowed to run riot. As a comic novel *Spring Days* is just not funny or witty enough. The method chosen for this work was a new departure for Moore and in reading it one is all too conscious of his anxiety to succeed, rather than his relishing the ludicrous foibles of the human condition.

Moore's narrative concerns the efforts of the three Miss Brookes to escape their stuffy middle-class family with its rigid routines and class-consciousness. Their rivalries, duplicity and sexual desperation are presented with some zest but compared with similar scenes in *A Drama in Muslin* the effect is slight since Moore shows little compassion for the girls' predicament. The man-hunting of the Irish debutantes in that novel had its farcical moments but Moore's sustained awareness of the social and financial necessity which was compelling them to this gross behaviour allowed him to preserve a rich balance between comedy and pathos. He offers no such insights into the condition of the Miss Brookes and the comedy is, as Henry James would term it, merely *louche*. Though the eldest sister is driven to marry the pompous, elderly, self-satisfied Mr Berkins through the combined pressures exerted on her by father, aunts and sisters, the consequences for her of this step are not explored; she disappears from the novel and does not return either as a victim of a way of life where money is the only mediator of existence or, like Charlotte Lucas in *Pride and Prejudice*, to take the reader by surprise with her new-found power and assurance. Moore does not work his plot to achieve such moments of illumination. Similarly, though another of the sisters, Maggie, loses her senses when she discovers that Escott, her fiancé, is courting a second woman, Moore simply ridicules her as preposterous and makes no attempt to elicit the reader's sympathy.

Moore's treatment of the adult world against which the sisters are rebelling is no more successful, when he sets out to expose the myth of bourgeois self-sufficiency. Both Mr Brooke and Mr Berkins are types of the self-made man whose values in life are based exclusively on vulgar considerations of cost:

'Talked too much about my money? – who would talk about it, I should like to know, if I didn't? I made it all myself.'[8]

To them, marriage is a matter of doweries and settlements, and infatuation and desire are either childish or indecent. They and the girls' two aunts are the stock butts of anti-materialist satire; their dialogue is comic at first, but becomes repetitively stereotyped. Moore does not creatively develop the humour of their idiosyncrasies, they do not take wing as Miss Bates or Sarah Gamp do where the exuberance of the character transcends the limitations of the type.[9] Moore does approach this virtuoso style of caricature with the girls' brother, Willy Brooke, a man who for all his painstakingly accurate and conscientious business transactions is forever becoming involved with firms that go into debt or liquidation and who, though he appears an old-maidish bachelor with his settled habits and slow daily routines, in fact secretly keeps a common-law wife and family in a discreet lodging house in Brighton. Willy leads the kind of double life which is the starting-point for many a good comedy (and indeed he deserves a novel to himself), yet Moore does not make real use of him thematically in *Spring Days*. It was presumably Moore's intention with Willy to show up the cruelty of a world that allows the brother this clandestine means of escape from his father's tyranny but offers no such outlet for the sisters. On one level, the novel aims to expose the moral confusion that underlies much contemporary behaviour that passes for propriety; but in contrast with this, Moore so obviously enjoys writing about Willy (the one character that he treats with any warmth and creative sparkle) that he undermines his thematic and moral purpose. Far from being a means to evoke pathos for his sisters and their plight, Willy is in fact a welcome relief from their tantrums and affectations.

Maggie Brooke's fiancé, the easy-going, convivial Frank Escott, provides the novel with its third narrative strand. Being the heir to an Irish estate he can rise above the petty financial considerations that dog the Brooke family in their pursuit of emotional fulfilment. Escott chooses to trust his instincts but finds himself drawn simultaneously to Maggie and to a jolly barmaid, Lizzie. His moral confusion steadily clears with time as Lizzie's earthy naturalness encourages in him a dignified, responsible attitude towards her, while with Maggie he indulges in ever more sensational games of passion, eventually even trying to persuade her to join him in a Wagnerian love-death. Maggie's unwillingness to drown herself merely to satisfy Frank's desire to be another Tristan affords some dialogue rich in bathos:

> 'I would tell how I became convinced that I am the one appointed by God to lead you to Him.'
> 'I thought you didn't believe in God.'[10]

Burlesque is a suitable vehicle here for exposing the lovers' pretensions to a consuming passion they do not feel; and the dialogue achieves some witty deflations. However the passage is marred by Moore's intrusively pompous commentary. Where at most deftly ironic asides are all that is required of the author so that situation and dialogue can carry the full impact of the satire, Moore gives the reader mock-lectures on algolagnia and sexual incompatibility.

Here as elsewhere Moore reveals he has no sensitivity to the special demands of pace in the comic novel; indeed throughout as a narrator his style is too heavy-going.

Given so many major characters and such a wide variety of styles of comedy, it is not surprising that the various themes never quite integrate and complement each other to the point where they create an autonomous comic world. *Spring Days* remains stubbornly episodic. It might have been possible to manipulate so much activity in the novel and it still have found a positive, unifying factor in the narrator's own humorous vision but that would have required Moore to be more assured, witty and interesting in the role of puppet-master than he is, more in control of his material and more intimate in his relationship with the reader.

(iii)

Mike Fletcher is Moore's attempt to treat the myth of Don Juan in contemporary terms. Mike, a personable young Irishman, has dedicated his life to a pursuit of sensual gratification; he is gifted with great charm of manner and with a Celtic fluency in complimentary and persuasive speech. Women, Moore informs us, quickly succumbed to him, yet when they were as quickly abandoned by Fletcher they could never totally obliterate him from their memories or cease to be sympathetic and loyal. The weakness here is that Moore *tells* the reader all this; he does not present Fletcher to us dramatically in a way that makes him beguilingly and dangerously attractive, disarming our moral judgement, as Wilde does with Lord Henry and Dorian Gray and James with Gabriel Nash. Mike's animal magnetism and his eloquence have to be taken on trust (indeed in the one seduction scene we are shown he is very firmly put in his place by his intended victim: "Love! You profane the word; loose me, I am going").[11] Moore's imaginative coldness towards his hero derives from a basic uncertainty about what he intends to do with the subject. Mike has, we are told, all that boisterous vitality, that adventurer's delight in the challenge of life that the eighteenth-century novelist and novel-reader relished but which nineteenth-century moral fervour has sought to quell and castigate as sinful.[12] This would suggest that Moore's aim is to liberate his readers from emasculated forms of living and loving. But the novel as it unfolds brings hero and reader not a revelation of forgotten paths of joyousness but a growing despair that finally compels Fletcher to commit suicide. Mike ridicules his friend John Norton (of *A Mere Accident*) for submitting to the dictates of the Catholic church, and Frank Escott (of *Spring Days*) for marrying and becoming the family man; they have capitulated in his view to the social pressures of the age. Yet though they have struggled and been forced to compromise with themselves they have eventually achieved some contentment, whereas he experiences only greater tedium in living. The novel starts as a challenge to orthodox attitudes but ends by enforcing them with some severity.

Moore's cautious distrust of Fletcher's sensualism is a manifestation of a profound dilemma in Moore's creative life and thinking at this time: he wished to promote a creed of shamelessness, a recovery of pagan delight in instinctual living free of puritan scrupulousness, but could find as yet no way of imaginatively expressing that personal freedom except in terms of contemporary fashionable Aesthetic poses which as he explored them in his fiction proved to be all too limiting in their turn. The problem was how to reconcile this shamelessness with his powerful, humanitarian conscience, and Fletcher's way of life as he developed it signally failed to do this. Anyone wishing to treat the Don Juan myth must first decide what psychological explanation he will give for the hero's relentless sexual buccaneering. Moore offers us in Fletcher a Don Juan who is a failed Romantic artist frustrated in his quest for knowledge of the Ideal: 'I have always hoped to love; it is love that I seek';[13] and every new love is 'a voyage of discovery'[14] but every attempt is an inevitable failure: 'I have possessed nothing but the flesh and I have always sought beyond the flesh'.[15] Weary with the limitations of life as opposed to the imagination ('the real is mean and trivial, the ideal is full of evocation'),[16] Fletcher has embraced the pessimism of Schopenhauer. Living and loving come to be merely animal functions, monotonous in their routine; his writing celebrates with glittering cleverness whatever is unnatural – the Sphynx, the faun and the pierrot – in Gautier-like cadenced prose, and the masterwork he envisages is a poem in praise of pessimism in which the last man, a type of Adam in a world of paradisal beauty, murders his mate rather than prolong the human species and thus leaves a virgin world. The poem represents, Fletcher argues, the triumph of reason over mere natural instinctive will. He delights in shocking his friends out of their complacency but can offer them no compensation for what his intellect ravages. Nothing for him has permanent value except the law of natural change; he worships transience because it sustains his one sanction for conduct which is not his conscience but his curiosity. His life is a monstrous assertion of his own ego. Fletcher's obnoxiousness is nowhere more evident than in his treatment of Lady Helen (the wife of Lewis Seymour from *A Modern Lover*) who in a highly distraught state encourages him to talk to her of his philosophy; insensitive to her frame of mind, Fletcher expatiates on suicide; later he discovers that after leaving him she drove to a hotel, hired a room and took her own life. He sees her corpse but shows neither feeling nor scruple over the incident; he merely discusses its suitability as the subject of a prose-poem.

In time, life takes a suitably ironic revenge on Fletcher's lust for the transient. All his old friends drift away and Mike finds himself the centre of a circle of pathetic middle-aged bachelors, all lonely failures, spiritually and emotionally paralysed, all struggling to pretend they are still the bright young blades full of promise that they were at twenty. (These sad nonentities show Moore at his descriptive best in Chapter VIII; one is only sorry that Moore did not build on the effect and render through situation and dialogue a more climactic realisation by Fletcher that he too is a grotesque parody of his former self, just the lecherous roué of stage melodrama and farce.) Though he acquires a vast fortune by the death of one of his former mistresses, Mike cannot escape from the increasing sense of his own worthlessness; all he can claim in life is that he 'wheedled a few women who wanted to be wheedled'.[17] Such knowledge kills whatever energy he might have had to effect a regeneration; true to his life's philosophy, though aware of its absurdity, he shoots himself. Fletcher's pessimism is tragic because it offers nullity as the ideal; it denies even the regenerative possibility of Byron or Baudelaire's conscious pursuit of damnation. As Eliot writes of the latter: '. . . it is better, in a paradoxical way, to do evil than to do nothing; at least we exist'.[18] As with William Golding's heroes and with Moore's own Evelyn Innes, the deliberate sinners, the conscious challengers of divine omnipotence, are still potentially vehicles for divine grace and charity. But Fletcher sets his own ego and its desires at the cohering centre of the universe and finds that life quickly ceases to be potent, mysterious, challenging and evocative.

Moore offers here a valid and accurate insight into the mind of the Aesthete and as an analysis of the psychology behind much of the writing in the late Eighties and the Nineties the novel has an undoubted value, though there is none of the exciting stimulus that Wilde's combative paradoxes bring to his treatment of similar discussions of Aesthetic interest. It was profitable for Moore's own writing in that Mike Fletcher was a good preparation for his more subtle study of the type, Sir Owen Asher. Frank Escott's successful marriage to the barmaid, Lizzie (begun in *Spring Days*) that cost him his title and inheritance, affords a suitable positive contrast to Fletcher's self-sufficiency; the problem arising from Lizzie's social position ensures that the marriage is not sentimentalised, although it would merit more development from this standpoint.[19] Moore would seem to be offering through Frank's career a tentatively explored counter-statement to Mike's philosophy, show-ing a form of passion which involves Frank in serious choices in life but which sustains him when the consequences of those choices bring him social ignominy. Certainly Frank is a more authoritative figure than his farcical younger self in *Spring Days* and is used by Moore to voice some salient criticism of Fletcher's decadence, caddishness and affectations.[20]

The principal weakness of the novel is its lack of narrative drive, its monotony of incident, pace and character. (Mike after all only learns about himself what the reader has known for a long time.) It has no real development, being too obviously the exposition of a given thesis to arouse a complex response in the reader towards the central character. More tension and bite might have been achieved if the presentation of the material had been orientated to a wholly subjective viewpoint but Fletcher's brand of world-weariness is so alien to Moore's own staunchly resilient temperament that he would have found it difficult to sustain the heightened degree of sympathetic involvement and creative self-discipline necessary for such a treatment. In the final pages Fletcher's realisation of the desert that he has created in his consciousness fails to elicit sympathy since, as with John Norton's soul-searching at the close of *A Mere Accident*, Moore resorts for this inner musing to a hackneyed rhetoric totally lacking in verisimilitude: 'Wisdom! dost thou turn in the end and devour thyself?'[21] Moore's growing coldness towards his central character makes for an increasing flatness in the writing; *Mike Fletcher* at the last is a chilly, depressing fable for the times.

(iv)

Vain Fortune tells of the tragedy that comes of a failure of vision, both artistic and moral. Hubert Price, an aspiring dramatist, suffers a seizure of his imaginative faculties, and finds he cannot shape his ideas into original works of art; he supposes that he will break free of the morose indolence that besets him only through another's sympathetic understanding of his plight. An unexpected inheritance from a deceased uncle brings him into the company of that uncle's ward, Emily, who has been disinherited, and her companion-chaperone, Julia. The vicious triangular relationship that follows exposes Price's inadequate perception of psychological motive and responsibility, despite his pride in defining these matters in his pseudo-Ibsenite dramas. The *impasse* is finely conceived. Price is conscious of a duty to protect the ward whose income he jeopardised, yet is attracted to Julia for her power to console him as an artist. Julia is in love with Price, yet, having been financially dependent in the past on Emily, feels morally in her debt. Emily, deprived throughout her life both of security and of all she loved, is now a prey to self-pity; she childishly idealizes Price as a kind of Sir Galahad and jealously resents his affection for Julia. Each of them senses an altruistic duty to abandon the relationship out of honour to a second member of the triangle, but masochistically accepts the misery of maintaining it to satisfy a sexual attraction to the third. Price and Julia are married; Emily commits suicide; and ironically, Price begins to doubt whether Julia's love will be the creative and sustaining force in his life that he had expected; his new-found material security and Emily's sacrifice cannot alter the basic failure of his own personality.

In a rueful prefatory note to the revised edition of the novel in 1895, Moore admits to his dissatisfaction with *Vain Fortune*; it is, he states, 'probably not my best book but it certainly is far from being my worst'.[22] It is uneven in quality: in its later stages it offers a fine study in types of selfishness that in the subtlety of its psychological discrimination and its remorselessly sustained tensions is comparable with the claustrophobic family wrangles explored in *A Mummer's Wife* and *A Drama in Muslin*. The early chapters of the novel describing Price's theatrical activities and his decline among the down-and-outs of London lack punch and seem rather literary in inspiration. The choice of a theatre-hack as hero, a man of middle-class tastes and scruples whose willpower is sapped by the increasingly shabby lodging-house society he has to frequent, inevitably invites comparison with Gissing whose *New Grub Street* had appeared the previous year. Like Gissing, Moore can evoke the inner misery of such an existence with considerable power: the oppressiveness of a life of fervent longing for literary success where the longing is not matched with the rigour necessary to realise the ambition and where adverse criticism quite crushes the morale under abject self-pity. But Moore's portrait of the type lacks the density of Gissing's, because he is unable to realise imaginatively the niceties of the social predicament of the failed intellectual as he clings desperately to the remnants of his genteel existence to avoid 'contamination' by the lower classes and absurdly welcomes the bitter loneliness that is the outcome of this snobbery. In Gissing, the sterility of such a man is total.

Moore offers a parallel with Price's career at various stages in the actress, Rose Massey, who has the 'irresponsible passion'[23] which is genius. One is tempted to wonder whether Rose is modelled, deliberately or unconsciously, on James's study of the actress Miriam Rooth in *The Tragic Muse* of 1890, a woman confident of her vocation and ferocious in her self-discipline and in her pursuit of success. Moore expects the reader to take Rose very much on trust as simply a structural device; he does not try to realise as James does either the psychological and social miseries that accompany such a single-minded devotion to the theatre or any of the consummate artistry that is the mark of her genius. This failure to make Rose Massey a truly organic part of the novel has repercussions regarding Moore's treatment of the theatrical back-ground to much of the plot. The detailed factual account of methods of rehearsing and mounting plays in this period is of undoubted value to the theatre-historian and so too is the witty satire both on contemporary orthodox tastes in drama and on typical theatre reviewing in newspapers and journals but its lavish treatment (amplified in the revised version) seems like wanton padding as it is not closely integrated (as the account of life with the touring company in *A Mummer's Wife* is) with the personal tragedy which is the focus of the reader's attention. A fuller treatment of the psychological contrast between Price and Rose Massey might have enabled Moore to shape this background material more relevantly to his purpose.

And so Price's fortunes are suddenly transformed by an uncle's legacy, as crude a device as it always is in the Victorian novel, but more noticeable than ever here since it accompanies a complete transformation in the style and method of the novel itself from a rather low-keyed performance from Moore to one of incisive, dramatic force, as his imagination comes to grips with what he really wants to write about and no longer struggles with an irksome but necessary exposition. The excellences of this latter half of *Vain Fortune* are numerous; the fine overall conception of the battle of wills and the fluctuations between lust and responsibility of the three contestants; the meticulous balance and complexity of Moore's treatment of three characters and their particular dilemmas; the controlled but gathering atmosphere of tragic inevitability that accompanies the struggle from its casual beginnings to its violent climax; the carefully realised sense of place in the mansion, its gardens and estate so that the reader experiences Price's particular agony as his pleasure in the house and its comfort, which offers such a sharp contrast with his previous way of life, is steadily destroyed by the growing bewilderment and enervating frustration that he suffers in coping with Emily.

Emily herself is a new creation for Moore: the girl who has led such a closeted youth that she carries her childishness into adulthood, seeking to gain her way by either petting or petulance; her every speech hits a tone of assertive, monopolising banter, demanding instant attention like a peevish child. As her neurotic jealously of Julia grows, her only form of conversation becomes a string of unjustified paranoid rebukes which undermine whatever feeling of liking Julia and Price have for her. She knows the moral grounds which prevent them leaving her and yet she goads them beyond endurance to do so, luxuriating in her physical and mental weakness because she knows it is her way of tyrannising over them. When eventually they do have the courage to abandon her she takes her life, calculatedly certain that it will be an eternal reproach that will harrass them with remorse. Till this point in the narrative

Moore preserves a studied objectivity towards Emily but he mars the account of her suicide initially by presenting it melodramatically through her hysterical talk with her pet dog and to herself. Her first attempt with an overdose of laudanum fails and though nauseous and haunted with waking nightmares, Emily is compelled, to avoid detection, to struggle across her bedroom to retrieve her suicide-note. The grotesque plausibility of this and the sheer power of will in Emily that it demonstrates arouse a complexity of emotion in the reader that redeems the earlier lapses into melodrama. Her second, successful attempt is recounted in a quiet, unemotional prose that avoids sensation and sentimentality yet works disturbingly on the reader's imagination because of its very restraint:

> When she approached the brink, the swans moved slowly away . . . hastening her steps, she threw herself forward. She fell into shallow water and regained her feet and for a moment it seemed uncertain if she would wade to the bank or fling herself into a deeper place. Suddenly she sank, the water rising to her shoulders. She was lifted off her feet. A faint struggle, a faint cry, and then nothing – nothing but the whiteness of the swans moving through the sultry night slowly towards the island.[24]

Though a maddening and in many ways evil woman, Emily is also a victim of circumstance and her death is the death of a suffering human being, however malicious her intentions may have been in taking her life; and the factual austerity of the prose allows a complex but charitable balancing of responses to her plight.

This balance is carried over into the final chapter which records Julia and Price's reception of the news of Emily's death. They have returned from the theatre where they have seen Rose Massey triumph as Lady Macbeth and Price is already prone to misgivings about his own art and envy of Rose's resolution and mastery. Emily's suicide provokes a complex of reactions both petty and generous; chagrin, self-reproach, relief, vexation. Each is conscious that the death they wished for has created a barrier between them that their marriage, entered into in a spirit of desperation, cannot surmount. The night passes in fragmented, inconclusive discussion, analysing the past and planning for the future. Eventually at dawn Julia falls asleep and Price sits contemplating her in the cold, distorting light; the strangeness of the scene etches itself into his memory, fixing the moment for all time as an epiphany to trouble his consciousness endlessly with knowledge of his own failure as a man, a husband and an artist. That insight surfaces in his mind with lucid precision despite the confused welter of ambivalent emotions, moral evasions and tortured perceptions that has formed the atmosphere of the preceding scene with his wife. Moore attempts no irony and reaches after no explanations; confidently he allows the full weight of the novel to create a context for this scene so that every response, each brief snatch of conversation, carries a wealth of implication from what has gone before. The narrative method is restrained and simple, the emotional allusiveness is profound, and the pathos that results is deeply moving, as we watch Price confront the truth of his moral being:

> The fire was sinking; dawn divided the window-curtains. He looked at his wife. She seemed to him very beautiful as she slept, her face turned a little on one side, and again he asked himself if he loved her. Then, going to the window, he drew the curtains softly, so as not to awaken her; and as he stood watching a thin discoloured day breaking over the roofs, it again seemed to him that Emily's suicide was the better part. . . . He felt a terrible emptiness within him which he could not fill. He looked at his wife and quailed a little at the thought that had suddenly come upon him. She was something like himself – that was why he had married her. We are attracted by what is like ourselves. Emily's passion might have stirred him. Now he would have to settle down to live with Julia, and their similar natures would grow more and more like one another. Then, turning on his thoughts, he dismissed them. They were the morbid feverish fancies of an exceptional, of a terrible night. He opened the window quietly so as not to awaken his wife. And in the melancholy greyness of the dawn he looked down into the street and wondered what the end would be. . . .
>
> He would hang on for another few years, no doubt; during that time he must try to make his wife happy. His duty was now to be a good husband, at all events, there was that.
>
> His wife lay asleep in the arm-chair, and fearing she might catch cold, he came into the room closing the window very gently behind him.[25]

One is not surprised to find that James Joyce considered *Vain Fortune* 'fine, original work'[26] in view of the way Moore presents this moment of revelation; indeed he admired it so much that he accommodated and imaginatively reworked Moore's material, as Richard Ellmann has shown, into his story 'The Dead' in *Dubliners*.[27] Amusingly, Moore found this tale so perfect in its composition that he wished he himself had written it.[28] It is unfortunate that Ellmann dismisses Moore's novel as 'overpraised' by Joyce[29]; admittedly, as we have seen, the early chapters give no promise of the novel's magnificent close, but there is no denying the power of that resolution. Moore's epiphany differs in kind, of course, from Joyce's; Price's insight into his mediocrity is moral and artistic, his only hope for the future is a bleak one – a life of studied kindliness and pretended devotion towards Julia whom he now knows he does not love. Gabriel Conroy in 'The Dead' suffers as painfully as Price, but what he learns is his deficiency in *passion* in his relationship with his wife, in his failure to commit himself wholeheartedly to the Gaelic revival and the cause of Ireland, and in his lack of charity towards friends and acquaintance. Gabriel's wit and humour so much in evidence throughout the early scenes in the story are a device to keep himself aloof from imaginative and emotional engagement with life. Joyce having registered the pain of this awareness brings Gabriel a degree of peace denied to Price; as the snow falls, Gabriel has a lyrical vision of death, and sympathy for his fellow-mortals begins belatedly to well forth from his being.

The seminal importance of *Vain Fortune* for Anglo-Irish literature does not, I think, stop with Joyce. Given Samuel Beckett's known interest in Moore's work, stimulated initially no doubt by Joyce himself, it is tempting to see *Eh Joe* as another imaginative redeployment of the same source. Once again an emotional failure, Joe's abandonment of his fiancée, has revealed to Joe his moral inadequacies; for him, there is no peace as for Gabriel, nor is there even Price's more austere consolation in performing his duty by his wife; Joe is left only with the harrowing fact of his own disgust with himself. His remorse is endless, obsessional. Where Beckett's play comes closest to Moore's novel is in the account of the girl's suicide;[30] her first feverish attempts at death, like Emily's, are botched; the details, sordid and verging on the comic, are in both treatments disturbingly immediate in their frank admission of human fallibility. In both instances a real tragic stature is invested in the dying girls through their willed determination, their absoluteness for death, which carries them onward in the face of initial defeat and allows them to surmount the sensational and comic potential of their situations. Neither Price nor Joe can make a necessary leap of the imagination and sympathetically experience the plight of the dead one as Gabriel does finally with Michael Furey, thereby finding an inner calm denied to them. Joe tries to stifle all memory of his fiancée's act; and Price responds to Emily's death with peevish self-concern. For them the epiphany is abortive and brings no promise of redemption.

(7) Wagner and the Novel

It is not making exaggerated claims for Moore's achievement with the ending of *Vain Fortune* to borrow Joyce's term and describe the incident as an epiphany. Moore was not like Joyce a scrupulous theorist adept in Thomist language nor was he keen as Joyce was to analyse and justify continually his fictional methods; Moore worked more intuitively, discovering his methods through the imitation of techniques that pleased him in his reading or through chance accidents during the process of composition. What Moore was struggling to depict in these transitional works was the 'underlife', 'that vague, undefinable yet intensely real life that lies beneath our consciousness, that life which knows, wills and perceives without help from us', where he believed 'resides the true humanity', 'the wonder and mystery' of a particular personality.[1] From this under-life the artist derived his inspiration and there he should look for his subject for it is there that any man's soul quickens in its own unique manner to the rhythms of nature. It is this under-life which controls a man's mode of perception. What Moore was questing for in these years was a new way of painting in words 'intimate pictures of the soul'.[2] It necessitated finding a way in which incidents in a character's daily life in time could be invested with representative status (what Joyce calls *quidditas*) by being shaped into resonant symbols which for the sensitive reader, and sometimes for the character himself, would bring some apprehension of that character's total being. The details of his active life in other words would steadily be converted into images that would depict by implication the play of forces within his consciousness, that inner destiny which constitutes selfhood.

Moore's initial mistake was in assuming, after Pater and Huysmans, that this quickening of the soul is best revealed when a man is experiencing intense aesthetic or intellectual excitement; but

133

such transcendent moments, as Moore discovered, are not always representative of the total self, for a man's emotional and moral being can at such moments be suspended. By contrast, the epiphany that concludes *Vain Fortune* reveals to us the truth about Price morally, emotionally, imaginatively and socially since it is his failure in his responsibilities towards the two women in his life which brings about the crisis.

Interestingly, *Vain Fortune* is not the first novel in which Moore created a complex epiphany of this kind, though the earlier example in *Mike Fletcher* is less well prepared for and less climactic than this. After Lady Helen Trevor's suicide, Fletcher, Escott, the novelist Harding and several of their friends are invited to view and identify the body by the proprietor of the hotel in which the death has occurred. The men stand in the doorway of the room and Moore gives a factual but precisely detailed description of its appearance – the crude colours of the cheap carpet, the changing shadows cast by the fire upon the ceiling, the flowers slowly withering that Lady Helen had worn at Mike's party earlier that evening, a stray beam of sunlight through the closed blinds that highlights a flounce of petticoat. The specific detailing has its purpose, for Moore is concerned to show how the minds of the men numbed with shock hypersensitively register these visual responses in an effort to come to terms with their grief. Moore concludes: 'So the room fixed itself for ever on their minds'.[3] What we watch here is the room becoming an image, an emblem through which memory may recall the event so that the mind may gradually accommodate itself over the years to the tragic implications of the scene; Lady Helen's death is becoming part of the fabric of the men's consciousness. But Moore does not stop there. Most of us respond to tragic shock in ways that retrospectively may surprise us for being trivial or self-centred. Our normal social and intellectual defences are on such occasions often inoperative and a less scrupulous self can be disturbingly in evidence. Moore ends his chapter by recording tersely the first thoughts that begin to surface in his characters' minds as they leave the deathbed:

Harding mused on the ghastly ingenuity, withal so strangely reasonable. Thompson felt he would give his very life to make a sketch. Mike wondered what her lover was like. [He has reason to believe that Lady Helen has been abandoned by her lover

and that this is the motive for her suicide.] Frank was overwhelmed in sentimental sorrow. John's soul was full of strife and
suffering. He had sacrificed his poems, and had yet ventured in
revels which had led to such results! [4]

There is considerable psychological insight in the way Moore brings
his characters through the flux of emotions here to reveal their
quintessential selves to the reader with such exactitude. This
epiphanic moment reveals more about these men in three pages
than whole chapters of aesthetic debate between them elsewhere
in the novel.

The terms and phrases I quoted earlier showing how Moore's
thoughts about rendering the under-life in fiction were approaching
Joyce's concept of epiphany without being so carefully formulated
were all drawn from an article he contributed to *Cosmopolis* in
1896, about the time that he was embarking on *Evelyn Innes*.[5]
'Since the Elizabethans' is largely devoted to a comparison between
Thackeray and Tolstoy, in which Moore justifies his claim that
the Russian is the superior novelist by drawing attention to his
finer capacity to depict 'inwardness' in his characters. He illustrates
what he means by extensively analysing a particular scene in *Anna
Karenina*, were he feels Tolstoy arrests historical time and renders
in detail the effect of the passing of a sequence of emotions in
Levin's being; in terms of historical time the experience is momen-
tary but it brings a depth of self-awareness to Levin the repercussions of which will continue to influence him throughout his
future life. The moment is Levin's realisation of his need to marry
Kitty: he has been mowing with the serfs and, watching the sky,
is reflecting on the vanity of things, when he is suddenly filled with
an overwhelming sense of peace; inexplicably the thought enters
his mind that he must marry one of the peasant women working
beside him and by that means secure his present contentment for
good, but chance at that moment brings Kitty past him in her
coach and the sight of her face changes his sentimental resolution,
flooding him with knowledge of the depth of his love for the girl.
Levin's sudden enlightenment as to his emotional need gives him
access to a complete maturity of personality.

The essay is one of Moore's finest; the comparison it effects is
just and well substantiated and it is conducted without any of the
quirky lapses of expression that can mar the tone of Moore's
critical writing at times with touches of slick journalese which in-

evitably make one question the seriousness of his judgements. Nowhere else in his work does Moore express such whole-hearted admiration for Tolstoy's novels and one can but suppose that his enthusiasm here derived from his recognition that Tolstoy had perfected a method remarkably like that which he himself had conceived as his goal but towards which he was still hesitantly groping; reading and writing about Tolstoy brought Moore new powers of discrimination. The commentary on *Anna Karenina* is tantamount to a statement of Moore's own intentions; over the ensuing years Moore came to abandon the Huysmanesque way of evoking consciousness, preferring poetically rendered epiphanic incidents. Indeed the slow growth to maturity of his heroine Evelyn Innes in his next two novels is conveyed by the author's steady transition from the one method to the other and Evelyn's early limitations, moral and emotional, seem directly related by Moore to the limitations of the method with which he is presenting her. With *The Lake* Moore achieved his goal: here all the wonder and mystery of the under-life of his character, Gogarty, is communicated to the reader through his modes of perceiving the natural world about him, modes which change under the controlling impact of Gogarty's shifting emotional and moral responses to his friend Nora Glynn. With the characterization of Gogarty, Moore attained that illusion of completeness which he so much admired in Turgenev. Significantly, in looking back on his success with this novel and commenting on his creative development towards it, Moore came closest to using Joyce's term 'epiphany' to define his aim; he was writing about consciousness and the novel to his friend, Edouard Dujardin:

> For many years now I have been engaged on realistic works, always trying to create characters, and today it seems to me that it is not sufficient merely to find appropriate words for them. It is necessary that from time to time they should rise beyond themselves and utter unexpected things, and it is by such *illuminations* that characters are really created. At all events, it is my method.[6] (My italics.)

It is fitting to mention Dujardin in connection with Moore's finally achieving completeness of characterization in *The Lake*, for it was chiefly through Dujardin's encouragement expressed in conversation, correspondence and through the medium of his own experimental creative work that Moore began to study the work of Wagner, to the extent that, with Balzac, he became a truly formative influence on Moore's development: 'My life,' Moore wrote, 'would have been poor without them.'[7] It was his deepening understanding of the literary possibilities of Wagner's ideas and method which saved Moore from the imaginative poverty into which he had sunk, making what Edwin Muir has described as but 'bad translations of aestheticism'.[8] Dujardin of course was not the only Wagnerite amongst Moore's circle of friends in the late Eighties and Nineties; there were such notable enthusiasts as Lady Cunard, Edward Martyn, Miss Annie Horniman, Catulle Mendès and Arthur Symons,[9] but none of these were as avid as Dujardin for exploring ways of compelling language in poetry and the novel to yield effects analogous with Wagner's use of leitmotival musical phrases for psychological penetration and emotional intensity in his music dramas. In *Conversations in Ebury Street*, Moore remarks of his friend: 'To none have I given so ardent an ear as I have to Édouard Dujardin. . . . I have harvested most profitably' from his work.[10] Dujardin is one of those interesting figures – Arthur Symons is another – who helped to create the particular intellectual environment of their time, generated endless stimulating ideas for projects which their friends brought to fruition but which, somehow, they never had quite the necessary creative energy to produce themselves: generous, enthusiastic, inventive, yet lacking the determined application necessary to write the masterpiece that would establish a new language for the contemporary sensibility and a new school of writing.

Moore's interest in Wagner was of long standing: his early years in Paris in the Seventies coincided with the great Wagner boom amongst the intelligentsia that followed the publication of Baudelaire's *Richard Wagner et Tannhäuser*; he made at least three visits to Bayreuth[11]; his novels and his letters to Lady Cunard and to Dujardin abound in references to the operas; and he contributed articles on the composer to *The Musician*.[12] Dujardin's seminal role lay first in offering detailed thematic interpretations of the operas for Moore, thereby defining Wagner's recurring preoccupations with the conflicts of sensuality with intellect, of passion with religion, of Pagan with Christian ideals, of the life-force with renunciation, which Moore was to make the central subjects of his own late novels. Secondly he fostered in Moore a desire to evolve a Wagnerian style and method of prose fiction. Over the many years of their friendship, Dujardin's involvement with the changing aspects of literary Wagnerism in France is reflected in Moore's various experiments with style and structure in his novels. When they first became acquainted Dujardin was the editor of both *La Revue Indépendante* and *La Revue Wagnérienne*; the former serialised a translation of the *Confessions of a Young Man* and the latter carried what Moore considered the only really sympathetic appreciation he received of *A Mere Accident*. This is understandable as the *Revue Wagnérienne* had for some time been considered the leading organ for disseminating the views of the Symbolist movement, since the publication in its pages of a series of articles on the significance of Wagner's ideas for literature by another of Dujardin's friends, Téodor de Wyzewa. The Symbolist philosophy of art is not far removed from Huysmans', so the review of Moore's novel by de Wyzewa is predictably sensitive.

The attraction of Wagner for the Symbolists lay in his belief that ideas or thoughts are but images of the perceptions of the senses, symbols which make these perceptions apparent to one's understanding and which facilitate the recollecting of emotion in a state of tranquillity. In *Opera and Drama* for example, he argues:

> Thought and memory are therefore the same; thought being, in fact, the return to memory of that picture, which as the impression of the object upon our sensation, was formed by the sensation itself.[13]

Art, he continued, must perform a service like memory, recalling the images of experience; the true artist is he who can give himself 'without reserve to the impressions which move his emotional being to sympathy';[14] and the source of that sympathy in his view lay in nature and a proper concern for one's fellow men. Developing Schopenhauer's theory of the dream-organ which is capable of exciting the brain to function by extrasensory force, Wagner advocated a similar function for operatic music: it was to be a visionary force carrying its audience to a world of emotions materialised as dramatic metaphors.

What the Symbolists hoped to do was to invest language with the symbolic potency with which Wagner had succeeded in investing music; Edmund Wilson in the process of defining Symbolism has pointed out how the poets in their practice and de Wyzewa in his theories were the victims of a basic misapprehension:

> . . . it is the poet's task to find, to invent, the special language which will alone be capable of expressing his personality and feelings. Such a language must make use of symbols. . . . The Symbolists themselves, full of the idea of producing with poetry effects like those of music, tended to think of these images as possessing an abstract value like musical notes and chords. But the words of our speech are not musical notation, and what the symbols of Symbolism really were, were metaphors detached from their subjects. . . . And Symbolism may be defined as an attempt by carefully studied means – a complicated association of ideas represented by a medley of metaphors – to communicate unique personal feelings.[15]

The function of literature, according to de Wyzewa, was the creation of the life of the mind, 'une vie plus vivante',[16] where ideas are born from repeated and classified sensations. (This is precisely Huysmans' aim too in *A Rebours*.) The sensations that Wagner depicts and which his characters analyse in themselves always have a definable source, either in natural phenomena or in the dramatic interaction of the characters with each other; in other words to borrow Wilson's terms above, the metaphors have a specified subject. The Symbolists, while drawing on Wagner's method, committed themselves to Schopenhauer's rather different belief that 'the world is my representation'.[17] Mallarmé, for example, with the collapse of his social and religious ideals, underwent a crisis of emotional and mental anarchy and decided that the only way to salvation lay in deliberately accepting the dark night of the soul, 'le rien qui est la vérité'.[18] The stable world came to exist therefore only in so far as he personally perceived it: 'peindre non la chose mais l'effet qu'elle produit'.[19] This is but one step away from Wilde's extreme definition of truth in art as entirely and absolutely a matter of style. With their relation to a definable subject severed, metaphors and symbols however musically patterned to please the ear may be little more than empty rhetoric and hyperbole. Wagner criticised contemporary Romantic opera as existing simply to exhibit the bravura technique of the performers; it was, he argued, capricious, 'a mere product of culture and not sprung from life itself'.[20] The same criticism can be made of many Symbolist works; mannerism triumphs and life escapes.

Moore's attitude to the Symbolists becomes increasingly non-committal; in his criticism he always deals with them carefully and sympathetically, limiting his articles to autobiographical reminiscences of his meetings with them rather than attempting any form of analysis. In his late revision of his first novel, which was retitled *Lewis Seymour and Some Women* (1917), Mallarmé actually appears as one of the characters and in circumstances that imply a kind of criticism. The revised version stresses more forcefully than *A Modern Lover* the second-rate quality of Seymour as man and artist. In a new central episode, Mrs Bentham and Seymour seek in Paris a dangerous escape from reality: she, from a moral condemnation of her relations with Lewis and from her fears of growing old; he, from his failure as a creative artist ever to express in his art what he truly feels and imagines and from his inability to evolve an original personal style. Moore presents the dream-world they attempt to create by a mass of analogous literary and artistic images; in imagination they want to live in an artificial world, the world conjured up by the paintings of Boucher, Fragonard, Watteau and by the Petit Trianon. At Fontainebleau they encounter Mallarmé, a man of the nineteenth century, living in a world of wish-fulfilment 'amongst the off-scourings of the eighteenth'[21] and pleading that all that is best and beautiful in man and nature should remain elusive and a dream, like that experienced by his own *Faune*. There must be no healthy sense of perspective, no irony: illusion must be consummate. At the close of the novel Seymour's shallowness, his lack of personality and character stand revealed and condemned, despite his material success: true art, Moore argues, is difficulty overcome and great art that where difficulty is surmounted with apparent ease. It is a constant theme in his criticism that art is a manifestation of the creator's personality: 'there is no art so indiscreet as painting and the story of the painter's mind may be read in every picture'.[22] Inevitably therefore that art must suffer where, as with Seymour, and by implication with Mallarmé and the artists of the rococo, 'life was but make-believe'.[23]

So Moore's first effort at being a literary Wagnerite by imitating Huysmans' Symbolist novels showed him that that form offered little scope for development. *Esther Waters* was a return in some ways to his earlier social thematic preoccupations but the technique was innovatory: his aim as we have seen was to present the sensibility of a working-class woman who had no 'mind-life' as such (indeed her few attempts to reason out and articulate her predicament are pathetically confused and inadequate) and who was motivated entirely by her instincts. The pattern of narrative events became the reader's guide to an appreciation of Esther's complex psyche. Interestingly this relates very closely to a comment made by Moore in 1888 in the *Confessions* about Wagner's influence on the novel:

> Wagner made the discovery . . . that an opera had much better be melody from end to end. The realistic school following on Wagner's footsteps discovered that a novel had much better be all narrative – an uninterrupted flow of narrative. Description is narrative, analysis of character is narrative, dialogue is narrative; the form is ceaselessly changing, but the melody of narration is never interrupted.[24]

Esther Waters is by this criterion a Wagnerian novel and by another criterion too, in that Esther's moral and emotional being is organic, her inner life is, as it were, placed in a historical dimension. All the great decisions that confront her have definite roots in her past actions and choice and will have consequences too for her future which is embodied in her child and its welfare. Esther has a memory and it comes actively into play in her consciousness whenever her resilience is put to the test and she must choose a new way of life. Norton's or Fletcher's mind-life lacks by contrast this historical or temporal dimension, because that mind-life is cultivated as an escape from the pressures of moral choice and responsibility; their minds are not organic but closed. Wagner's conception of thought as both a symbol of and an index to one's emotions was distorted by the Symbolists to a belief that experience was moulded by one's subjective reaction to it, that the symbol *was* the reality and that artistic creation was the one positive compensation for the anarchy and frustration of the world; evil and consequently morality were in their view illusions and so memory and conscience played no part in shaping consciousness. Pursued to its logical extreme, Symbolism completely inverted Wagner's original premise.

In his music-dramas Wagner had used the words of his libretto as analogous to thought-symbols and his musical phrases as more nearly allied to the emotional sources from which those thoughts derive; hence in the great ruminative monologues or passages of sustained narration, such as Waltraute's account to Brunnhilde of the misery of Wotan and the gods in Valhalla since her exile, the words defining present action or moods are conveyed by musical phrases reminiscent of past emotions and situations in which, whether consciously or not, the immediate action and its sensations had their birth. Through the uniting of music and poetry Wagner was striving to present a given action with its full complement of significance for both the thoughts and the emotions of his characters: memory and its associations colour and affect life in the present moment and must be recorded if the recreation of experience is to be full and composite. The active, the mental and the emotional are interdependent and inseparable. Monologues, soliloquies and narrations in the great operas are not excrescences or emotional padding; they are, as both Symons and Moore perceived, moments when the characters are compelled by changing circumstances to reinterpret their past experience and in so doing apprehend some truth about themselves and their condition.

The 'epiphany' with which Moore concludes *Vain Fortune* has something of the power and density of implication of one of Wagner's monologues, as memory, moral conscience and frustrated desire coalesce in Hubert Price's imagination to create out of his view of his sleeping wife a symbol of his delusions of emotional security in the past and of the imprisoning frustrations that are to be his future. It might be argued that this kind of 'epiphany' is coming very close to Symbolism and the words of Axel that one sees the external world through the medium of one's soul; in practice as we have seen the Symbolist evocation of the soul tended to be through fixed and restricting images whereas the epiphany here is more dynamic, a sudden intense manifestation of what is a continum of feeling, awareness and self-discovery. The problem that faced Moore now was how to depict growth and change in the soul of a character by relating a sequence of such epiphanic moments to a progressing narrative structure.

His next experiment, a logical one, was to build the narrative in *Evelyn Innes* out of thinly disguised parallels with situations, relationships and characters in Wagner's operas. The various conflicts that trouble Evelyn Innes' psyche are deliberately modelled by Moore on the tragic predicaments that face Wagner's heroines. Working within such a framework of analogies was, of course, what D'Annunzio had recently been attempting in two of his novels, *The Flame of Life* and *The Triumph of Death*. As one of his contemporary English critics wrote:

> Music, the most personal and the most emotional of all the arts, possesses for D'Annunzio a haunting power. It plays a part in each of his novels in turn. It is by music that lovers converse; it is through music that the depth of their passion is revealed to the reader. . . . Ippolita and Giorgio Aurispa spend long hours over the scene of 'Tristan and Isolde' and afford the novelist an excuse for a dozen brilliant pages of analysis of the most marvellous drama of sex-emotion ever interpreted by music.[25]

(This would serve equally well as an interpretation of Moore's aim in *Evelyn Innes*.) 'Musical' too was in that same critic's view the most apposite term for D'Annunzio's style, for 'there is in his writing . . . an exquisite fluidity which carries the reader forward in a rhythmical progression'.[26] This critic was a Mrs Virginia Crawford, who according to Hone was introduced to Moore by W. T. Stead in the course of 1895;[27] she remained a life-long friend and assisted Moore with the composition of *Evelyn Innes* and its sequel and with Moore's later novel about convent life, *Héloïse and Abélard*. What precisely the help was that she offered Moore with *Evelyn Innes* is not known but it is significant that Moore began to refer enthusiastically to D'Annunzio's novels in his letters to Dujardin and Lady Cunard in 1897 as his own work was in its final stages of composition.[28] Mrs Crawford's *Studies in Foreign Literature*, which includes a chapter on D'Annunzio from which these quotations have been drawn, appeared the year following the publication of *Evelyn Innes*.

In *The Triumph of Death* the hero, Aurispa, senses within himself the capacity for a unique sensory response through romantic love but cannot achieve it in his passionate relations with his lover, Ippolita. Finally in brooding over his memory of a performance of *Tristan and Isolde* he recalls Tristan's cry 'To desire and desire unto death but not to die! ' and realises that Wagner's opera exactly expresses his own sensual aspiration. Aurispa seizes Ippolita while walking with her on the clifftops and plunges with her to death in the sea. The more closely Aurispa models himself on Wagner's hero, the more ominously predictable grows the tragic outcome of his neurosis. The analogies are simple, consistent and so are gradually invested with a force like fate.

Mrs Crawford, like Henry James, considered it a limitation in D'Annunzio's work that he was preoccupied with a singularly one-sided view of life rooted in the sexual: 'he is', she argues, 'less immoral than devoid of all sense of morality'.[29] James even goes as far as questioning whether there is not something essentially bogus, even tasteless, in investing with mythical grandeur characters and a situation like Aurispa's passionate murder of his lover which are morally vulgar.

> Here at all events we put our finger, I think, on the very point at which his esthetic [sic] plenitude meets the misadventure that discredits it. We see just where it 'joins on' with vulgarity. That sexual passion from which he extracts such admirable detached pictures insists on remaining for him *only* the act of a moment, beginning and ending in itself and disowning any representative character. From the moment it depends on itself alone for its beauty it endangers extremely its distinction, so precarious at the best. For what it represents, precisely, is it poetically interesting; it finds its extension and consummation only in the rest of life. Shut out from the rest of life, shut out from all fruition and assimilation, it has no more dignity than – to use a homely image – the boots and shoes that we see, in the corridors of promiscuous hotels, standing, often in double pairs, at the doors of rooms. Detached and unassociated these clusters of objects present, however obtruded, no importance. What the participants do with their agitation, in short, or even what it does with them, *that* is the stuff of poetry, and it is never really interesting save when something finely contributive in themselves makes it so. It is this absence of anything finely contributive in themselves, on the part of the various couples here concerned, that is the open door to the trivial.[30]

Such a criticism could not be levelled against Moore's novel, for Evelyn Innes has an implacable and scrupulous conscience and is terrified when she discovers that the cultivation of her art as a singer is deeply related to her need for erotic fulfilment. Where Moore's work does approach D'Annunzio's closely is in the depicting of the 'irreparable void in a life dedicated solely to pleasure',[31] which Mrs Crawford sees as D'Annunzio's great psychological strength. The oppressive inevitability created in a novel by relating the narrative to a pattern of Wagnerian analogies delighted the Italian writer's *penchant* for melodrama. Moore, however, came to find the technique as restricting as Huysmanesque symbolism and condemned both his own and D'Annunzio's novels as dealing in 'worthless externalities'.[32] The satisfying Wagnerian novel would require a profounder degree of influence; it must strive for a different kind of musicality. '*Evelyn Innes* is externally musical', Moore wrote in later life, '. . . but the writing of *The Lake* would not be as it is if I had not listened to *Lohengrin* many times.'[33]

The sequel to *Evelyn Innes*, *Sister Teresa*, brought Moore one stage closer to his goal, for having confined his heroine to the seclusion of a convent cell, where there was nothing for her to contemplate but her new vocation and her past life with all its frustrations, he had created a situation where the revealing of Evelyn's mysterious under-life and inner being was of necessity his only possible subject. Her daily life was now rooted in the cycle of rituals of the convent; her world had shrunk to the chapel, the nuns' house and garden, but the myriad specific details of that circumscribed existence took on the intimacy and familiarity which signify meaningfulness to the consciousness that observes and delights in them. Moore now had a justifiable source out of which to evolve leitmotival phrases that would define the changing moods of Evelyn's psyche. Here at last he had found a subject and a situation that would permit him to write a patterned, rhythmical poetic prose that would not defy verisimilitude. Moreover Evelyn's deep and urgent self-communing was obviously closely allied to the dramatic reveries of Wagner's heroes and heroines. Her quest for serenity with its fluctuating hopes and setbacks offered Moore too a narrative line with subtle emotional climaxes where the epiphanies marking the stages of her progress towards her goal would assume specific religious connotations.

In the event *Sister Teresa* was not the perfect achievement one might have assumed it would be, for the composing of the novel coincided with, indeed may in some measure have aggravated, a series of crises in Moore's life which made both for an undercurrent of anxiety in the tone of much of the writing and for an indeterminate conclusion to the heroine's quest.[34] Once again Mrs Crawford assisted Moore with the novel (she was herself to enter a convent in 1903) and she patently had high hopes for their achievement for when in 1899 she published her essay on Huysmans and wrote appreciatively of his studies of monastic life she noticeably took care to prepare the ground for Moore's new novel:

Monasticism, the life of the cloister, where alone the contemplative life can flourish, hovers unceasingly before his [Huysmans'] vision as the ultimate goal. Both his latest books are penetrated by the sense of its beauty, of its extraordinary fascination. He brings it before the reader in a way that no great novelist has done before, that no English novelist has ever attempted.[35]

Here, patently, we can read Mrs Crawford's ambitions for Moore; but he completed his novel away from her influence in Dublin, where perhaps he was beginning to realise how fervently she was begging the question, for the contemplative life can flourish outside the convent; reverie does not depend on one's withdrawal from society. Ireland was teaching Moore how to relax while renewing and strengthening the flow of his inspiration. His perfect Wagnerian novel was yet to be written.

(8) *Evelyn Innes* and *Sister Teresa*

The desire of the flesh is more necessary to the life of the world than the aspirations of the soul, yet the aspirations of the soul are more human. The root is more necessary to the plant than its flower, but it is by the flower and not by the root that we know it.[1]

Evelyn Innes is a novel of quest, a quest for a centre, for a code of values in which the demands of the flesh and of the spirit will fall into a true and natural relation. Evelyn's acute awareness of sin acts as a tether that draws her away from public success on the stage to the convent. Her seducer, Asher, argues that 'she was the kind of woman who, if she once let herself go, would play the devil'.[2] She defies the rules of her Roman Catholic faith and, like Fletcher and Kate Ede, follows the dictates of her capricious desires and comes indeed to experience hell; but the moral conscience that her faith has instilled is so deep-rooted that it gives her in time the power of will to resist her desires when they lead only to frustration and misery. Talent, intelligence and passion have a place in Evelyn's life but she discovers that they are not the goal of her quest. She begins by abandoning her familial responsibilities and accepts Asher's persuasion that the sacrifice of one's whole self for such ends is a sin against life. Her initial move is in error but through the course of the novels Evelyn learns in what precise sense Asher's advice is sound. She does, as he says, have a paramount duty to herself but the precise nature of that duty when Evelyn discovers it is beyond his conception or understanding.

Asher makes it the condition of his paying for Evelyn's tuition as an opera-singer that she leave her widowed father and become his mistress in Paris. Her choice is a nicely balanced question of varying degrees of selfishness: her ambition and love for Asher in conflict with her duty to a father who depends solely on her as his contact with and shelter from the everyday world; Evelyn has spent her life till now preventing any intrusion into Mr Innes' privacy which he devotes exclusively to the study of medieval liturgical music. Evelyn chooses Asher. As so regularly in his work, Moore evokes well the web of emotionally charged duties that complicates personal ethical decisions.

Owen Asher is a dedicated narcissist: he has devoted his life to 'self-culture' and financially can afford to materialize his illusions and sustain a pose he acts consciously to perfection. Like Mike Fletcher, he has wittily argued God out of his personal universe and cherishes love and art as the only oases in the desert of life. Asher's philosophy is that of the poet Omar Khayyám, whom he is so fond of quoting: life is but as a rose to be plucked and relished for a brief moment. All his particular social set live on the surface of life, 'in the animal sensation rather than the moral idea'; by sophistry they confuse their terms of moral and artistic reference in order to justify a life in which dilettantism and 'good' living (in the palatal sense) are sexual stimulants. Passion and art alone influence Asher's moral conduct: that Evelyn should let her operatic talent lie fallow is immoral in his code, but not so his urge to seduce her; while her scruples seem to him a lack of taste. Creating temptations and succumbing to them is his one occupation. When he seduces Evelyn with whispered erotic fantasies it is characteristic of Asher that the bliss he offers her is in no way depicted in physical and sensual terms but is intimated through light innuendoes with which he entertains her while they are studying the paintings by Watteau in Dulwich art gallery. Here is exquisite tact and taste but how effete the love is which he proffers.

The image of the cultured rose comes, in time, to have a more ominous significance: Evelyn is to be an embodiment of his ideals; she is to have no life other than as a realisation of Asher's Aestheticism. He purchases her since he wishes to mould a work of art out of the living substance of her flesh and mind. As he has no critical detachment, no ideals higher than what is self-sufficient, Evelyn is to be an image of his own egoism, the Echo that flatters his Narcissus. He indoctrinates her with his agnostic opinions to break her self-control; even his love-making is to be a testimony of his taste. He loves her clothes, her singing, everything that is consummate artistry in her, but not the vital woman and her heart. The reality is less dear to him because more inexplicable than the Evelyn he has created in his mind. No man has the divine right to create another in his image; Asher's need to do so with Evelyn marks the complete lack of the frank but sympathetic understanding that should be the basis of any intimate relationship. He is merely using her. Like Oscar Wilde in his treatment of the relationships between Lord Henry Wootton and his protégé, Dorian Gray, and between Dorian and his actress-lover, Sibyl Vane, Moore is reworking and adapting the myth of Pygmalion here to give narrative form to his exploration of the psychology of the Aesthete. Having formerly played the type in his own person but rejected it as limiting his identity, Moore can lucidly expose the subtle sophistries that sustain the posture.

To achieve success on the stage Evelyn must conquer her moral scruples; but, for a Catholic, that is to sacrifice eternity for the satisfaction of a moment in time. The life of the world and the flesh is permitted by her Church only to the woman who seeks to fulfil herself in marriage and motherhood; Asher and her career dictate that the full force of her creative instincts be channelled into interpretative art. Art is Evelyn's one means of exposing the potent sexuality that through Asher she has discovered in herself; her energies are to be devoted entirely to a studied demonstration of the all-consuming power of instinct; this is the personal mark of her interpretation of Wagner's heroines, especially of Isolde. The danger is that art will come to be her only means of satisfying her instincts, a danger that Asher's attitude deliberately provokes. He lives constantly for 'the memory of life' carefully selected and aesthetically arranged and heightened; he rarely embraces direct experience.

Even his love-making with Evelyn is savoured as much for the pleasant memories it will afford him in old age as for the immediate ecstasy. Self-consciousness always prevails; and in this Asher is a debased artist in that he is trying to fabricate and control his own moments of epiphany and so they are never true epiphanies, sudden revelations, remarkable because unexpected, disturbing and enlightening because unprepared for. Asher works to create epiphanies that confirm his self-hood and self-indulgently orders life so that it affords no lasting challenge to his ego. He encourages Evelyn to approach her roles in the same fashion: acting for her is not to be an imaginative withdrawal of herself in response to the author's conception of the part, an act of meticulous deperson-alization. She is not to interpret, rather she is to identify totally with the character she is portraying by imposing aspects of herself upon the role. She is to sift her memory for experiences analogous with the situations she is playing and is to 'live' moments of her life again through recall during the performances. This is not artistry, but self-display; and it carries with it a terrible penalty, for art comes to be Evelyn's only means of gratifying her instincts. Having reduced her faculty of imagination to the level of self-indulgence she no longer has any control over it. The strongly emotive and sensual qualities of Wagner's music amplify her memories with an intensity of passion that physical life cannot stimulate; and life begins to appear weak and 'lifeless' by com-parison. Art becomes not an 'art' at all but a 'medium through which [Evelyn] was able to relive past phases of her life or to exhibit her present life in a more intense and concentrated form'.[3] Asher, in seeking to destroy her conscience in order to recreate her personality has destroyed in the process her instinct for life itself, and this brings about a total dissolution of her personality: as 'acting' is to Evelyn perfectly 'natural', so she can be again the pious virgin she once was by performing as Elizabeth in *Tann-häuser*, while off-stage a growing sexual dissatisfaction with Owen who cannot compete with the ecstasies she experiences in playing Isolde forces her to take another lover, Ulick Dean, and indulge in frenetic promiscuity. She has reduced experience to sensations which acquire meaning for her only in the context of Wagner's music and so has lost the power to discriminate morally, imagina-tively, perceptually.

When Evelyn returns home to Dulwich and sues for her father's forgiveness she does so in the precise words of Brunnhilde's plea to Wotan; the familiar music sounds in her imagination and she loses all power to distinguish; the act becomes a self-indulgent 'playing' at penitence as the imaginary cadences seem to lift her out of her fleshly self and to purge it of the corruption of her daily existence. Music is perversely now her escape from an aware-ness of sin:

> She was conscious of the purification of self. . . . But she did not know if the transformation which was taking place in her was an abiding or a passing thing. She knew she was expressing

all that was most deep in her nature and yet she had acted all that she now believed to be reality on the stage many times. It seemed as true then as it did now – more true; for she was less self-conscious in the fictitious than in the real scene.

She knelt at her father's or at Wotan's feet – she could not distinguish: all limitations had been razed. . . . She knelt like the Magdalen. The position had always been natural to her, and habit had made it inveterate. . . . She could only think of her own grief . . . she was so lost in it that she expected him to answer her in Wotan's own music; she even smiled in her grief at her expectation.[4]

The moment fails to act as quite the climax to the first novel that Moore seems to have intended, because Evelyn's own doubts about her sincerity do not enlighten her as to her true predicament. Given the frankness of Moore's analysis of Evelyn's mind, his handling of the conclusion to the situation rings false, as Mr Innes wholeheartedly and uncritically responds to his daughter.

It was he who had been acting. He had pretended an anger which he did not feel. . . . She was shrined in his heart, the dream of his whole life.[5]

That the old man's affection for his daughter should triumph over the moral stance he feels he should adopt in the situation is credible enough, but in view of the obvious self-consciousness of Evelyn's 'performance' the reader expects either that the full flow of his feeling will be arrested by some apprehensive doubts or that Evelyn, hovering on the verge of renewed self-knowledge, will be horrified by the power of her dissembling to convince others of her sincerity. Subsequently to escape from the painfulness of this appraisal of herself by basking in her father's effusive love would be a logical step for her to take next; but Moore does not chart the later stages of this psychological development as confidently or as distinctly as the initial ones and the reader is left confused. This is a crisis in Evelyn's life; potentially it is a turning-point, marking the start of her dogged return to sanity, but the significance of the moment is blurred in the telling; a controlled sense of irony is wanting to place either Evelyn's blindness or her father's here in their true perspective.

Evelyn now begins a long review of her past life. Her increasing dissatisfaction with Asher as a lover had made her critical of his principles. Her atheism, which she adopts under his guidance, is not like his a deliberate intellectual achievement, but an acquired culture, sustained as an act of deference and trust. Criticising him begins to crack the shell of his ideology and the kernel of her innate moral sense is slowly revealed again to her. To condemn his existence is equally to repudiate her own self.

> To sin is the common lot of humanity; but she had done more than commit sins, she had committed *the* sin, she had striven to tear out of her heart that sense of right and wrong which God had planted there.[6]

Total surrender to desire, she realises now, lays waste the very will to live: Isolde's fate has a maturer, tragic significance than Evelyn's interpretation took into account.

She had done wrong in flaunting Owen and art in defiance of God. She twice sought to challenge God's presence in Church but she had instinctively bowed in submission before the Host. The evil had turned on itself and left her a weary prey to her own consciousness. Without Owen's influence she can no longer maintain in art the illusion of escaping her sense of guilt; but her recognition of it is a step in the path to Grace. 'Her mistake from the beginning', she decides, 'was in trying to acquire a code of morals which did not coincide with her feelings.'[7] She goes to Confession and tells Monsignor Mostyn: 'What we feel matters much more than what we know.'[8] And she renounces as arid the intellectualising about art's superiority to life which occupied so much of her time with Asher and Ulick Dean. What she 'feels' now is that she can free herself from the taint of Owen and Ulick's decadence, not by cherishing her conscience as a means to control her passion, but only by a total renunciation of this world. But this is to flee from one extreme, Aestheticism, to another which is a kind of perversion of the Victorian adage that cleanliness is next to godliness. Such a quest for perfection can be as limited to the physical as Owen's Aestheticism is, and just as fiercely egotistical. It is not simply, as Evelyn now thinks, 'by denial of the sexual instinct that we become religious.'[9] The convent may, for the immature mind, be just a recoil from the united effort of all the faculties that must accompany any deliberate remoulding of the personality to accord with the dictates of one's conscience. The veil may be yet another illusion if it offers only a defence for purity and is not founded in conviction.

The fine psychological insight behind Evelyn's reasons for entering the convent is somewhat marred by the prolonged account of her indecision whether to retire from the stage and return to her father, to marry or to leave Asher, or whether to sing out of charity to help free the convent from debt. The detail is excessive and many of the situations add little to the narrative except an unnecessary amplification.

A further weakness in the latter half of the novel is the very shadowy characterization of Ulick Dean, who is much less successfully achieved than Asher.[10] The two men are not forcefully enough distinguished and provoke no dilemma of choice for Evelyn (as Fred Parsons and William Latch do for Esther); instead the conflict is between what Asher and Dean represent intellectually and the dictates of Evelyn's faith. Moore says that Ulick Dean is a compound of his newly-acquired friends Yeats and AE and this may account for some of the inadequacies of his presentation. In the moral pattern of the novel Ulick takes a position which the reader is expected to criticise, yet he utters ideas to which in life Moore was currently responding enthusiastically. His interest then in Ulick is frankly exploratory and his attitude is consequently indecisive; there is not the detachment and the resulting clarity of definition which he brings to his portrait of Asher. Dean has a Shelleyan absorbtion in the things of the mind, 'never speaking for effect, stripping himself of every adventitious pleasure in the service of his idea';[11] and he seems to represent religious Aestheticism.

We can best compare Evelyn's two lovers in their attitudes to Wagner's *Parsifal*. Wagner sought through the sensuous quality of music and poetic legend to re-kindle a perception of the value of Christian ideals of penitence, sacrifice, purity and communion. The response he wished to evoke was not to be limited to the given symbols but was to be creative, exploratory, educative and fulfilling; they were to be organic like the art-symbols in Forster's novels. Asher responds merely to the musical and dramatic qualities and admits, as does Evelyn, that he is confused as to the significance of *Parsifal*; Dean reverses Wagner's intentions and sees in all the operas a vindication of his belief that spiritual truths exist exclusively in art. He tempts Evelyn with aesthetic piety, a worse perversion than Asher's frank atheism. (Moreover his theories on Celtic revivalism, transcendental mystery and exultation are responsible for much of the tedium at the close of *Evelyn Innes*.) Moore was to offer a more perceptive and typical analysis of aesthetic piety in Evelyn herself in *Sister Teresa*.

Evelyn enters the convent to gain moral strength which she equates with her 'quest for happiness', yet is still uncertain of her faith. The prioress, trusting in Evelyn's willingness to submit to the authority of the Church, attempts to mould her to the contemplative life of the Order, in the mistaken belief that the dutiful fulfilment of her vows will inspire conviction. As in her earlier relationship with Asher, Evelyn is surrendering control over her own life to another. The prioress misunderstands Evelyn's equating of morality with happiness; it would be absurd to suppose that dejection inevitably implies immoral conduct. Revulsion from her frantic sexuality has led Evelyn to accept Ulick's belief that 'by living . . . and by suffering for our ideas, . . . we raise ourselves above our animal nature.'[12] She imagines that religious contemplation will become a means to a spiritual perfection pleasing for its freedom from actual and physical circumstances. But this is to cultivate the inner conscience at the expense of one's daily life, and that is essentially to fall into the sin of pride through seeking a perfection analogous to the divine. A nun does not renounce her physical self, but controls and cherishes its imperfections and desires as a witness of her humility; she offers her weakness and faults as her sacrifice. Penitence demands an awareness of sin, if absolution is to be valued fully.

The penitential exercises so 'humiliating' to the other nuns are for Evelyn the 'etiquette of the convent'; she delights at first in their simplicity but they come rapidly to irritate her by failing to satisfy her fierce desire for spiritual intensity. Yet humility is the bed-rock of St Teresa's teaching: ecstasy is to be the unexpected reward not the coveted goal of contemplation. Prayer and self-confession are to be the contemplative ideal, tapping the core of one's self to acknowledge the unworthiness of one's desiring flesh in contrast with the pure motive of Christ's suffering. From the depths of this humility springs a nun's patience, accepting this life in its proper perspective and honouring the divine gift of rapture when it comes as a pearl of inestimable value.

Evelyn, however, refuses to catechise her personality and come to terms with its deficiencies. Such 'active thought', she argues, 'interferes with the ecstasy of contemplation', which she interprets as purging, but which is really to be another escape from her conscience into dangerous illusion.

> The inward satisfaction one gets by living for an idea is infinitely greater than one gets by the pursuit of artistic or other pleasure. It is delicious to feel that one is not prompted by selfish motives.[13]

The adjective 'delicious' exactly reveals Evelyn's true sensual motive: the very wish to receive satisfaction rather than to give in devotion is the epitome of selfishness. Rapture, even of the saintliest order, has a limited duration, and is valid, according to St Teresa, only when it derives from and returns to a state of quintessential patience.

> Anyone who tries to pass on and raise his spirit to taste of pleasures that are denied him will, in my opinion, lose in a double sense. For these pleasures are supernatural, and when his understanding is asleep, his soul is left desolate and very dry. Moreover, as the whole edifice is founded on humility, the nearer we draw to God the more this virtue must be developed, and if it is not, all is lost. It seems a sort of pride in us too that makes us wish to rise higher when God is already doing more for us than we deserve by drawing us, in our condition, near to Him.[14]

Evelyn requires total self-effacement, frequent and of long duration; when her rapture passes she has nothing but contempt for ordinary prayer as mechanical, as so much sterile mummery. Even the ecstasy she attains is self-conscious, an acted, imitated art, stimulated as much by her dress as her scruples. Like Asher compelling memory into aesthetic patterns, Evelyn tries to force and control her experiences of transcendence. Her faith is but a type of sensuality and her ecstasy merely cerebration. That Evelyn finds so much misery in meditation is because her personal intention is dishonest.

> Like imperfect sleep which, instead of giving more strength to the head, doth but leave it the more exhausted, the result of mere operations of the imagination is but to weaken the soul. Instead

of nourishment and energy she reaps only lassitude and disgust: whereas a genuine heavenly vision yields to her a harvest of ineffable spiritual riches, and an admirable renewal of bodily strength.[15]

Having failed to analyse adequately the cause of her former confusion of art with fact, Evelyn cannot now control the profane and sacrilegious memories of Asher and Dean that intrude upon her contemplation of her duty as the symbolic bride of Christ; like Pope's Eloisa, her reverie is self-indulgent and her rapture gratified desire. She flees in terror from her conscience to the deceptive shelter of the illusions she calls her faith, only to find in them nightmare visions of her former sins. She cannot humble herself and so attain divine forgiveness; rather she will reject God because He will not countenance her self-pity. She refuses the Host and suffers a mental collapse, for, as she acknowledges: 'I have never known myself; it is so difficult.'[16] Others have wrongly sought to control her will for most of her life, forcing her to seek her own self in illusions, which have inevitably made her unfaithful both to her mentors and her innate but undeveloped conscience. Moore's method of demonstrating Evelyn's power of self-deception strongly resembles Flaubert's treatment of Emma Bovary, in pitting lyric feeling – here sterile and falsely pious – against the hard reality of conscience.

That final admission to a failure in perception and integrity, 'I have never known myself', saves Evelyn at the very moment she abandons herself utterly to the hellish chaos of her own mind. As the Prioress says: 'God will not abandon one who desires Him so ardently' however perverse that desire may be. Grace lies beyond the hope that is a comforting play of illusions; with her convalescence comes Evelyn's slow regeneration:

> No one can lay before another the life that passes in her soul. . . . Words are ineffectual to explain it. With words you can tell the exterior facts of life, but you cannot tell the intense yet involuntary life of the soul – that intricate and unceasing life. . . .[17]

Moore faced the difficulty of communicating Evelyn's uncertain movement towards equanimity by reserving for a certain kind of response in her a markedly simple but lyrical tone and cadence that anticipates the style of his final novels. Gradually these moments gain in momentum as Evelyn perceives and learns to cherish that 'involuntary life' within, until the pattern that is her real self finally evolves.

After her father's death, which in part induces Evelyn's psychological crisis, the Prioress wisely puts her to work in the convent garden. Activity wearies her physically and occupies her mind in relief from sorrow. The work becomes more than mere toil as, with the encouragement of her close friend, Sister Mary-John, she becomes interested in the constant activity of nature even in the soil itself that she digs. At first, her awareness is purely sensory: colours, activity, sounds, the healthy atmosphere. But the experience is direct, not the imitation that is art. She readily agrees with the Sister's remark that 'God created the earth before He created man. . . . Our love of the earth is deeper than our love of art';[18] she responds deeply to the calm inevitability of the cyclic pattern that controls all this activity, to a tranquillity seemingly reverential that begins to inspire her if only in pointing a contrast with her own mental turmoil. Attending to the garden soothes her more lastingly than the prayers of her faith; but this, in time, adds only to the bitterness of her despair at the convent's prison-like sterility. When memories of the past throng her fantasies and nightmares she longs for a new kind of bliss, for Brunnhilde's 'rapture when she awakens to the beauty of the world'.[19] She fears she must sacrifice her immortality, like Brunnhilde, to be at one with this great creating nature – 'death follows all delight'.[20] Once for her 'the whole world was a shadow and my belief was the one real thing in it. But that belief has passed from me'.[21]

As she convalesces after her breakdown, she watches the slow change of autumn, as 'the garden seemed to struggle against death', while she herself 'yields . . . to the sweet pressure of returning life'.[22] But with strength comes renewed agony of mind, although at least she now understands how close her former delusions brought her to madness. She has life and must quest onwards. Throughout all her bitterness, almost subconsciously, she studies the garden about her, finding in its barren winter melancholy images for her own sorrow. Spring slowly returns and as the cycle begins again the vitality of the natural world stirs as if from sleep in response to the renewed warmth of the sun. The pattern of this struggle, submission to healthful sleep and returning vigour – so close a parallel to her own health – works on her subconscious mind until in a moment of illumination she perceives through its significance the mystical Christian truth – that he who loses his life shall find it; that the simple but enjoyed fact of daily life can itself be an act of faith. Patiently and confidently to submit to the universal pattern, as Esther found, brings its own reward, when merely to live becomes in its particular compensations a rapturous communion with the divine.

> The sunset seemed to steal into her heart, and to become a source of secret joy to her. She wondered what was the influence of the sun; it made the woods grow green and the flowers blossom, it drew all things into itself . . . and she stood . . . watching the light, breathless and delighted. She saw the beautiful earth quiescent like a nun watching before the sacrament. The plants lifted their leaves to the light. Everything knew it, even the stones in the centre of the earth . . . her soul dilated and knew its light; the shell broke which till now had darkened it from her; her flesh and spirit seemed to become one with it; her immortal spirit seemed to ascend into the immortal light. . . .
>
> The great secret was revealed: she understood the mysterious yearning which impels us in turn to reject and to accept life; and she had learnt these things merely by watching the flowers raising their leaves to the light.
>
> She sat down in the grass and watched a sunflower till it seemed a sentient being whose silent adoration of its distant shepherd in the heavens was turning it into the likeness of the glory it longed to reach. She closed her eyes to imagine it better and the sunflower in her thoughts grew and expanded and went upwards to the brimming love which gave it life; and the imagined ecstasy of the meeting thrilled her heart, and she remembered that yesterday the elevation of the Host had left her unmoved. Why was it that the mere sight of a flower evoked a vanished sweetness which no ritual could awaken in her? And in another moment of revelation she knew that to seek the Real Presence on the altar alone is a denial of the Divine Being elsewhere, and she felt the door would be closed to her until in every mood and in every place she could recognise the sacrament as an eternal act in nature.[23]

Evelyn finds herself at last truly at one with Nature, no longer needing the convent as a shelter from the temptations of life, nor art as a gratifying stimulus for her imagination. A force has gener-

ated in her subconscious that has gradually quelled the introspec-
tion which weakened in her the energy to live. The striving for
Huysmanesque effect that formerly defined Evelyn's consciousness
has been resolved into a truly poetic prose. Here is lyricism, but the
feeling no longer is illusory.

The psychology underlying Moore's account of the epiphany is
accurate. William James lists many case-histories for whom the
countryside became endowed with a potent mystical force, or who
were visited with this type of pantheistic conversion, photism, in
which, as with St Paul on the road to Damascus, the world suddenly
emanated the blinding glory of the Lord. James defines the
character of 'affective experience' as 'the loss of all the worry . . .
the *willingness to be*, even though the outer conditions should
remain the same'; 'the mysteries of life become lucid'; and ' "An
appearance of newness beautifies every object" the precise opposite
of that other sort of newness, that dreadful unreality and strangeness in the appearance of the world, which is experienced by
melancholy patients.'[24]

After the magnificent climax of this epiphany the conclusion of
the novel gives a disappointing shock. One reviewer called it
bathos.[25] Evelyn plans to escape from the convent; she stands at
the door watching the spring, but feeling 'that something had
broken in her . . . she closed the door'[26] and returned to worship
the Virgin. The nature of her *éclaircissement* here is left ambigu-
ously vague. It contradicts the earlier epiphany, and yet nothing
has led us to suppose that this is the kind of quest-novel to which
the answer is itself nullifying; that, as in Kafka, there can be no
answer. From the rest of his work we know that the epiphany was
for Moore a positive force and not another of Evelyn's self-
delusions. She had found what Moore felt to be the true sanction
of conduct, the conscience that is rooted in the very instinct for
life. In the final chapter Evelyn is visited by a former actress-
colleague to whom she offers a seeming explanation:

> 'The important thing to do is to live,and we do not begin to
> know life, taste life, until we put it aside. . . . Life is the will of
> God, and to enter into the will of God we must forget ourselves,
> we must try to live outside ourselves in the general life.'[27]

In the secluded convent, Evelyn had submitted to the nun's death-
in-life and had discovered through their very absence the valuable

qualities that life itself can offer. From this standpoint her decision to remain in the convent is nothing less than a rejecton of
her new-found purpose and identity. One cannot accept that the
freedom she finally chooses to sacrifice was simply an illusion; for
if it were, we should expect her to feel elation and a quickening
of moral sense, but she speaks of herself only as 'a broken spirit'
and 'Louise was not certain if she were speaking in bitterness or in
jest'.[28] Are we therefore to interpret the ending as a final tragic
failure of will; that once again Evelyn could not personally accept
the challenge to bear the burden of her consciousness? If so, then
Moore's purpose needs ampler exposition, for it would still seem
to contradict what the epiphany had shown. The ambiguity is not
deliberate and ironic, as when in *Esther Waters* the personal moral
triumph is placed in a realistically judged social context. Here,
the ambiguity is ill-defined and suggests a failure both of vision
and of construction.

The totally revised ending of the later version of the novel in
which Evelyn quits the convent and engages in social work by
founding a home for crippled children indicates Moore's dissatisfaction with the original.[29] Was the uncertainty the result of
attempting to repeat the successful minor cadence that ends
Esther Waters? This is one possibility; but there are autobiographical factors which arguably offer a more cogent explanation
for Moore's failure to resolve the narrative. For Evelyn to have
left the convent would have amounted to a rejection of the Roman
Catholic position. To accept the conscience as the gauge of one's
responsibility and the visible world as exemplary of God's bene-
ficence and not as a vanity to be spurned in preference for eternal
treasures hereafter is to challenge the power of the Confessional to
act as a mediator between God and man.[30]

It would not be absurd to see Moore at this time as facing something of a religious as well as an intellectual crisis. His novels were
mostly critical and moral analyses of types of religious experience;
his most successful studies had led him to express a view alien to
the orthodox faith of his birth; and his friendships with AE, Lady
Cunard and Dujardin stimulated his enquiries and deepened his
tolerance. His dissatisfaction with Irish Catholicism was augmented by the numerous battles that were waged in defence of the
literary and dramatic activities of the Irish Renaissance; but he
seemed reluctant for several years actively to pursue the course

towards which his thoughts and his art were tending. It may be that he feared the rebuke which Mostyn levels against Asher, that 'when a Catholic loses his faith it is because he desires to lead a loose life.'[31] That reluctance is expressed in the conclusion to *Sister Teresa*: as one reviewer wrote, the gordian knot is cut but not untied.[32] This explains one further weakness of construction in the novel: despite the finely written scenes between Evelyn and the Prioress, Moore does not treat the life of the convent with detachment or generosity; the narrator's response is too closely allied to Evelyn's. She is a valid study of what St Teresa would define as a false vocation but no adequate case is presented for the virtues of the contemplative life by way of contrast in the novel and far too much attention is given to the trivialities of the nuns' lives, the petty squabbles, the supposed lesbian tendencies and the fears of demonic possession.[33] Evelyn's response to the nuns is too egocentric to evoke for them the kind of sympathetic understanding in the reader, that, for example, Esther's response does for Fred Parsons. Her ungenerous attitude to most of the other nuns again makes Evelyn's return to the convent inexplicable.

Sister Teresa was published in 1901. By 1903 a new assurance is discernible in Moore: 'Life has no other goal but life,' he wrote to Dujardin, 'and art has no other end but to make life possible, to help us to live.'[34] Three months later he made a public avowal of his Protestantism.[35] *The Lake* and *The Brook Kerith* were to fulfil the promises of Evelyn's epiphany – the attaining of a sense of responsibility in harmony with a joy in the vitality of Creation that makes every lived moment an act of faith and endows that moment with an intensity free of aesthetic illusions:

> Not the intense moment
> Isolated, with no before and after,
> But a lifetime burning in every moment.[36]

PART THREE:
STYLES FOR CONSCIOUSNESS

(9) *The Lake* — The Wagnerian Novel Perfected

(i)

At the end of the century in a restless, often bitter mood, Moore began to effect a number of partings that appear in retrospect to have been a response to some urgent impulse to sever old ties and form new friendships in the hope of renewing his jaded inspiration. The cycle started with a final and irrevocable break with Zola whose attitude to Moore had been steadily cooling since the publication of the *Confessions of a Young Man*. In 1894 Moore wrote a lengthy study of Zola for the *English Illustrated Magazine*.[1] It is a brilliant but cruel account of a visit to the patriarch of Medan; the house, the writer, his study, his working methods are elaborately described; everything has in Moore's view a monumental vulgarity, evidence of Zola's soulless and tasteless materialism. The novels demonstrate great industry but lack refinement of thought, sentiment and literary expression; Zola is voracious, he must grasp all life in his art but he is so greedy that in his haste he misses much: he rarely depicts 'souls'. The article is a clever pastiche of Zola's literary method judging him relentlessly in terms of his own art. Next Moore's painter friends, Steer, Tonks and Sickert began to bore him with their cosy Englishness; England infuriated and disgusted him by its jingoistic conduct in the Boer campaigns;[2] and in 1900 he quarrelled with his most intimate admirer, Lady Cunard, that earnest Wagnerite, energetic pursuer of new aestheticisms and dedicated sensualist.[3] Moore, the disappointed cosmopolitan, was shedding a past self; simultaneously he was rediscovering he was at heart one of the 'indomitable Irishry'. Yeats and Martyn's theatrical ventures[4] were a welcome intrusion on his struggles with the revised text of *Evelyn Innes*

165

and the composition of *Sister Teresa*. The incisiveness and discipline necessary for good dramatic writing were an invigorating challenge in marked contrast with the expansive meanderings of his current style of fiction. The talk amongst his Irish associates of the supremacy of Gaelic over Saxon culture and of their preference for a vigorous revolutionary commitment to Ireland rather than a disspiriting conformity to England in intellectual and artistic as well as political affairs chimed in perfectly with Moore's mood and the current needs of his imagination. Ireland, his first home, which had once seemed to him only a place for weed and ruin, had in his long absence changed utterly; now it alone offered him a future. Never one to dither in uncertainty, Moore completed the round of partings, personal and aesthetic, and moved house from London to Dublin to begin a new life in 1901.

Moore's involvement with the Irish theatre movement did not long survive his move to Ely Place; it virtually ended early in 1902 after the production of *Diarmuid and Grania*, which he wrote in collaboration with Yeats. Working together had encouraged a wariness and reserve rather than a deepening amity and some unseemly wrangling over their next joint venture (*Where There Is Nothing*, which Yeats finally took over as his own composition) ended their friendship; their subsequent relations veered between the deferential and the malicious. Martyn immersed himself in reviving Gaelic folk customs, polyphonic choral music and ecclesiological arts, whither Moore had no inclination to pursue him. As Douglas Hyde had taken care that Moore's activities with the Gaelic League should be at best peripheral, Moore found that for all his enthusiasm he was in the Irish Renaissance without exactly being of it. But he was far from dejected, for a renaissance of a different kind was taking place in his life under the influence of a new companion, Clara Christian, a painter, the 'Stella' of *Hail and Farewell*.[5] Moore probably met her sometime in 1897 or 1898 through the New English Art Club or through her teachers at the Slade, Moore's erstwhile friends, Steer and Tonks. When Moore settled in Dublin, she joined him there and bought a house at Tallaght. Clara Christian was witty, forthright in stating and defending her opinions and utterly devoted to her art. To judge from Moore's account of their relationship in his autobiography, she calmed his injured vanity at this time when he felt that his fellow-Irishmen had deeply insulted him; she treated him with consummate tact and, while being acutely responsive to his volatile moods, began sensitively to re-educate his sensibility, purging away his stale affectations and inculcating a freshness of response. Together they became great walkers, for Clara was ever in search of new motives and scenes to paint and listening to her comments on the landscape Moore discovered new themes for writing.

Clara opened Moore's eyes to the beauty of the Irish country-side and taught him how to appreciate its subtle seasonal changes and how to respond to that beauty simply and directly and so avoid intellectualising his reactions as he strove to define and express them. Other Irish influences strengthened this insight – AE (George Russell) with his mystical perception of landscape, his keen sense of the atmosphere of place generated by its historical and religious past; Kuno Meyer translating Gaelic nature poetry for Moore's delight and showing how a belief in an immanent deity had been an enduring aspect of Irish piety in both pagan and Catholic times; and later Synge evoking in his plays the imaginative com-pensations that accompany a life however harsh lived close to the soil and the simplicity, zest and unselfconscious poetry of speech that is the token of such an excited mental condition[6] – but it was at Clara Christian's instigation that these and other ideas, aims and influences both past and immediate suddenly began to fall into a new constructive relationship.

When Moore conceived an idea for a series of short stories on Irish peasant life that might be translated into Gaelic and used in teaching the language in schools, it was she who encouraged him to follow the project through with the Revd. Tom Finlay and the Gaelic League; she who saw that Turgenev's *Tales of a Sportsman* would be a fine model and one that might in the long term woo Moore away from Huysmans' perverse influence; she who insisted he should 'put the finishing hand' to the tales before they went off to the translator so they might be published also in English. (They became the collection entitled *The Untilled Field*.) She helped him find some of his subjects and most importantly of all with her 'fine ear for idiom drew my attention to the beauty of peasant speech in our walks through the Valley of the Liffey'[7] and thereby attuned his ear to the rich variety of speech rhythms on which his later style came to depend so strongly.

Ireland was wholly new to Clara Christian and her 'cordial un-moral response'[8] helped Moore to see his native land with new understanding free of bias. But her considerable influence did not rest there. In his youth in Paris Moore had known many of the Impressionists; for over a decade in his art criticism he had helped to foster their reputations in England;[9] Clara was a pupil of the first generation of English artists to respond to Impressionist principles and through her Moore came to appreciate what he had not seen till now: that the precepts behind such art could be applied creatively to prose fiction. As Moore observed Clara on their walks constantly measuring the landscape in her mind's eye, searching out what was particularly shapely and picturesque to her and delighting always as an Impressionist in those forms of natural beauty which were transient, he realised that her painting as a recording of her mode of perception was an expression of her temperament as he had come to know and admire it. Clara was a living example of how he might achieve his long-standing objective of finding a fictional method to render the 'under-life' of the soul: by recording a character's impressions of the world about him, his idiosyncratic mode of perception, he could define the quality of that character's innermost self in a lyrical prose that was poetic without being purple.

The two most satisfying innovations he had made in his recent phase of experiment with fictional styles were the final epiphany of *Vain Fortune* when Hubert Price confronts the extent of his own moral failure and that sequence of epiphanies that Evelyn experiences in the convent-garden in *Sister Teresa*, which wins her slowly back from despair. One of the principal themes of the autobiography that Moore was to write about his life in Ireland concerns his recovery of confidence in himself as an artist when he felt his inspiration had been played out. It was Clara Christian who showed him how this recovery might be effected and who unobtrusively watched over its progress. Through that personal recovery Moore perceived how he might relate these isolated episodes into a new structure for the novel. In *The Lake*, Moore's next novel, the protagonist has experienced, like Price, an overwhelming vision of his own moral failure; obsessively his mind tells over and over again to itself the story of the events leading to his epiphanic awareness, seeking through constant recall its full implications; when these are learnt the mind collapses but freed from shame and guilt it slowly recovers a sense of joy in living by responding with wonder to the beauty of the natural world. The epiphany that troubles the mind's repose by insistently activating memory and then the growing intensity in the character's perception of nature as repose is restored once again are here used as metaphors for a sustained process of psychic healing going on within consciousness. Moore had found a way of intimating the activity of the subconscious; he had found too a new structure to accommodate his developing moral insight and a new lyrical style with which to present it. All his late fiction employs this structure and method in some measure.

Something akin to Moore's verbal impressionism had been attempted earlier by his friend Dujardin in *Les Lauriers Sont Coupés* (1887-8). This records all the sensory perceptions of the character Daniel Prince as he moves during one day of his life around Paris trying to face up to his knowledge that his actress lover, Léa, wishes to leave him. It is an extended mood-piece capturing Prince's fluctuating bursts of hope and misery, written in a kind of verbal *pointillisme*: an unending cumulation of short phrases recording each of the stimuli that are registered by Prince's mind, all the 'myriad atoms' of experience that influence one's mood at a given point in time. Many years later, after Joyce had elaborated on this technique in *Ulysses*, Dujardin wrote an account of his intentions in his novel: he was trying to give voice to the interior monologue of the mind; his inspiration as with so much of his own and Moore's work was Wagner:

> A l'état pure, le motif Wagnérien est une phrase isolée, qui comporte toujours une signification émotionelle, mais qui n'est pas reliée logiquement à celles qui précèdent et à celles qui suivent, et c'est en cela que le monologue intérieur en procède. De même que le plus souvent une page de Wagner est une succession de motifs non développés dont chacun exprime un mouvement d'âme, le monologue intérieur est une succession de phrases courtes dont chacune exprime également un mouvement d'âme, avec cette ressemblance qu'elles ne sont pas liées les unes aux autres suivant un ordre rationnel, mais suivant un ordre purement émotionnel, en dehors de tout arrangement intellectualisé.[10]

While this has a certain truth about Wagner's style, it is not the whole truth. If one did not know Wagner's music, the impression one would get from Dujardin's description here is of a style that is like that of Dujardin's novel: haphazard and fragmented. Wagner's melodic line and often too the texture of counterpoint in the orchestration is built out of a series of short phrases each related to and developed from the basic group of leitmotifs for a particular opera. But put like this it all sounds fearfully schematic and repetitive; Dujardin does not take into account Wagner's virtuoso brilliance at improvisation, the ability (which he admired in Beethoven and carefully imitated) to intimate a musical phrase while developing and transforming it. One is conscious in performance not of reiterated phrases but of an onward-pressing organic growth of melody. The effect is not of sequence but of continuous movement. The minds portrayed by Wagner's musical characterizations are dynamic not static; the long arias of reflection and self-analysis culminate in new insights and decisions. While Dujardin's term, interior monologue, is apt as a definition of Wagner's intentions here – Wagner's great arias are essentially monologues for some inner voice of his characters' consciousness – it is not really an accurate description of his own work. The ordering of reflections, Dujardin states, is not rational but wholly emotional and that is true in Wagner's case; the point is that there is *an* order. The voice that speaks the interior monologue in Wagner speaks for the conscious life of the mind; it is, however, the mind's unconscious receptive activity that Dujardin is rendering in his novel, not the monologue of consciousness. Perception implies a degree of awareness. It is with modes of perception that Moore is concerned in *The Lake*, therefore he can accurately be described as using interior monologue. Moore's impressionism comes much closer than Dujardin's to rendering the Wagnerian experience in prose.

(ii)

With the exception of some letters that stimulate Father Gogarty's self-questioning, the whole drama of *The Lake* 'passes within the priest's soul; it is tied and untied by the flux and reflux of sentiments, inherent in and proper to his nature. . . . there is as much life in *The Lake* as there is in *Esther Waters* – a different kind of life'.[11] The principal action of the novel has occurred in the past: Gogarty, an Irish Catholic priest, publicly denounced one of his parishioners, Nora Glynn, because she was expecting an illegitimate baby, and this caused her to flee to England. The life and drama are reflective, meditative, psychological: the agony of a self-centred man becoming aware, through his dissatisfaction with his own life, of the spiritual aridity of his chosen creed.

In 1903 Moore had rejected orthodox Irish Catholicism partly on the grounds of clerical intervention in political and cultural affairs and partly because of the priests' emotional tyranny over their parishioners; he resented priestly interference in matters of the heart's affections that, by robbing them of privacy, deprived them of an intimate holiness and wonder which, he believed, could be a fruitful source of communion with the divine. Gogarty's career can be seen as a detached record of Moore's own experience and spiritual questing at this time; and one important issue that Moore takes care to establish in Gogarty's case must be emphasized if Moore's own future development is fully to be appreciated:

> . . . when religion is represented as hard and austere, it is the fault of those who administer religion, and not of religion itself.[12]

When Gogarty questions the validity of Catholic ritual and the power of the Confessional he undermines the intellectual and material foundations of his existence but does not destroy his inherent faith, that 'inner light' which the novel seeks to define as his 'conscience', that gives him in time the confidence to build anew:

> He seemed to himself a much more real person than he was a year ago, being now in full possession of his soul, and surely the possession of one's soul is a great reality. By the soul he meant a special way of feeling and seeing. But the soul is more than that – it is a light; and this inner light, faint at first, had not been blown out. If he had blown it out . . . he would not have experienced any qualms of conscience. . . . The question interested him, and he pondered it a long while, finding himself at last forced to conclude that there is no moral law except one's own conscience, and that the moral obligation of every man is to separate the personal conscience from the impersonal conscience. By the impersonal conscience he meant the opinions of others, traditional beliefs, and the rest. . . .[13]

The Lake and Moore's later novels are a statement of his personal convictions: faith is innate, creative, open and generous;

religion man-made, intellectual, restrictive and corruptible; sanity lies in a glad worship of the visible world.

Gogarty was attracted to Nora Glynn because the originality of her temperament and manner afforded such a striking contrast with his peasant parishioners: 'her independent mind informed every sentence. . . . she was happy and wore her soul in her face.'[14] She had an energy of mind and purpose akin to the vitality she taught him to admire in nature. Troubled and uncertain as to her fate since her disappearance from Garranard, he begins to ask himself what motivates this concern for her and more importantly to ponder what is the cause of her fearless joy, a quality of mind that he had never experienced before meeting her, and that conflicts so strongly with his own earnest piety.

To escape the nagging insistence with which his mind forces him to think about Nora, Gogarty recalls memories of his youth: how dismayed he was in his adolescence at the prospect of an arranged marriage to perpetuate the family business, and how he sought satisfaction in romantic day-dreams of re-working the local mills as an industrial magnate and later of retiring completely from society as a hermit. While affecting this state of piety he was caught out by his sister, Eliza, in a way that forced him to pretend a vocation for the priesthood as a proof of his integrity. Later at Maynooth he sustained this pretence by suppressing his full scholastic abilities and by indulging in various masochistic penances of a medieval barbarity under the naive illusion that such a disciplining of the self was a true act of faith and therefore to the glory of the church. His absurd earnestness reminds one of Maggie Tulliver, so determined 'that her part should be played with intensity . . . that she often lost the spirit of humility by being excessive in the outward act'.[15] Like that other would-be medieval saint, Gogarty found that the reward for his pains and 'delicate conscience' was merely to get his 'little half-fledged wings dabbled in the mud'. But Gogarty has allowed the mud to dry and harden about him like a shell, till his life has become all but dead to the spirit, imprisoned as it is within the round of his clerical duties. Confident of his own purity, he felt justified in taking upon himself, as God's instrument, the responsibility for wielding His righteous anger against Nora. These grandiose, Mosaic terms are Gogarty's own and expose the pride to which his 'humble' zeal has betrayed him. He spoke then in his function as priest, but his concern now for Nora's safety, his sense of guilt and need to atone show that his feelings as a man were not a part of his clerical reasoning. With Nora's departure he lost his one cultural equal in the parish and the resulting isolation and monotony of his life reveal to him in time the falsity of his vocation. He has become a prey to his own mind; he despairs at its relentless insistence on telling again and again the pattern of events that led to Nora's disappearance. Only in watching the spring transform the woods that border Lake Carra or in musing on the inner freedom that he knew in his childhood can he find peace.

A letter arrives from a Father O'Grady in London telling how he has helped Nora since the birth of her child and found her work teaching music. This opens a correspondence between the two priests which permits Moore, through his character O'Grady, to offer detailed, serious but benevolent criticism of Gogarty and his self-justifying reveries. O'Grady is an elderly man; years of work amongst the urban poor have made him relaxed, genial, compassionate, even worldly in comparison with Gogarty. Quickly and sensitively he reads between the lines of Gogarty's letters, assesses the precise nature of his turmoil and with great tact begins to enlighten the Irish priest about his condition. He sees that Gogarty's aggression towards Nora and his morbid, over-scrupulous concern with his own conscience about her are produced by a sexual interest in the girl which he cannot admit to himself. Technically these letters afford a useful change of tone and pace and thematically they initiate a process of growth towards self-awareness in Gogarty. O'Grady condemns Gogarty's treatment of Nora as inhuman and un-Christian and forces Gogarty to think about his own motives more deeply and thus to realise that a priest's true responsibilities are never merely parochial:

> He asked himself if he were wanting in natural compassion, and if all that he had of goodness in him were a debt he owed the Church. It was in patience rather than in pity maybe that he was lacking.[16]

Gogarty plans to secure Nora's return to the district by persuading his sister Eliza to employ her as a music-teacher in the local convent school but his efforts are frustrated when O'Grady informs him that Nora has taken employment as a governess and secretary in a Protestant household. Gogarty's renewed anxiety at this causes O'Grady to offer a detailed portrait of Nora: she knows no shame for her past but has taken her life confidently into her own hands, for 'she is one of those women who resent all control; . . . she is bent now on educating herself'.[17] To enquire into the nature and origins of religion as Nora seems intent on doing is not, O'Grady advises, to forfeit one's faith; indeed to try to restrain a woman of Nora's temperament would be fatal, as Gogarty's past experience should prove. But Gogarty equates Nora's new free-thinking with free-living and the possible loss of Nora's soul provokes in him a hysterical remorse of conscience. His impulse here is entirely one of sexual curiosity, which on a subconscious level his mind recognises as is evident from his long-winded special pleading in asking O'Grady for more and more information about Nora. His motives are transparent; he alone refuses to see them for what they are. O'Grady finally asks whether his concern is exclusively spiritual. Seeing the letters as a kind of confession, the elder priest grants Gogarty absolution for his public hounding of Nora. But absolution fails to free him from the shame and despair and this is proof of the depth of his feelings and of his need for some insight into a more deeply rooted conflict within his psyche before he can forgive himself and find freedom from his overwhelming sense of guilt.

Nora herself now writes to Gogarty about her new way of life. Her employer, Walter Poole, is a writer who is researching into the historical origins of Christianity; she tells of the excitement and challenge of working with a man like Poole, whom she accompanies to continental libraries and academic conferences. Her letters have a quiet assurance that reveals a genuine not histrionic zest for living; hers is a frankly sceptical mind but of a kind that is warm, open and enthusiastic not crabbed and mocking. Pondering on the joy that Nora's letters reveal, Gogarty realises that her attitude comes from a response to life that is wholly creative. There is an exuberance in her that he finds reflected about him in natural life in the landscape and which he recognises as a characteristic of medieval, but not of modern, faith. One of the islands in Lake Carra was the home of Marban the hermit, whose devotional poetry he has much admired since his youth for a serenity that he now realises is sadly lacking in contemporary religious ritual with its narrow insistence on dogma. An inevitable emotional storm which accompanies Gogarty's growing critical attitude to the

Churches leaves him sympathetically prepared to accept Nora's position; he is no longer anxious for the security of her soul.

> You have created a life for yourself. You have shown yourself to be a strong woman in more ways than one, and are entitled to judge whether your work and the ideas you live among are likely to prove prejudicial to your faith and morals. By a virtue of forgiveness which I admire and thank you for, you write telling me of the literary work you are engaged upon. If I had thought before writing the letter I am now apologizing for, I could not have failed to see that you write to me because you would relieve my loneliness as far as you are able. But I did not think: I yielded to my mood, and see now that my letters are disgracefully egotistical. . . . Loneliness begets sleeplessness, and sleeplessness begets a sort of madness. . . . But why am I writing about myself? I want to escape from myself, and your letters enable me to do so.[18]

The recurring pathetic touches of self-pity here testify to the real strain of the mental revision he has undertaken; his demands for Nora's understanding and consolation become increasingly urgent as his despair deepens: '. . . life is after all a very squalid thing – something that I would like to kick like an old hat down a road.'[19] His emotional exhaustion is reflected in the autumn landscape about him, where 'the season seemed to stand on the edge of a precipice, will-less, like a sleepwalker.'[20] Nora's refusal to offer the consolations he demands of her he excuses at first as prompted by revenge for his insults to her sexual pride; but that is absurdly ironic when one considers how his whole action has unconsciously been motivated by wounded vanity. He too is 'will-less, like a sleep-walker', torn between his subconscious impulses and his inadequate conscious self-justifications. More subtly than Asher with Evelyn Innes, Gogarty tries by asserting his clerical authority to mould Nora to his will, but her healthy independence frustrates this abuse of his calling. Her response is healthy because, though aware of her power to satisfy his uncontrollable desire, she resists the obvious temptation to assert that power to break or subjugate him out of spite. By sustaining a wholly passive detachment she charitably encourages his continuing self-exploration and development.

Gogarty is not alone in finding the intellectual and emotional isolation of the priesthood an agonising test of his duty to his faith and his parish. Moran, his curate, is a prey to drunken fantasies, which are his means of sublimating the need of the inner man to find some private release from the tensions occasioned by the necessity of leading a public life of relentlessly ideal standards. Moran's dreams are harmless enough, but for the obvious scandal of his being seen in a drunken stupor; Gogarty's are more dangerous in being centred on something much more vital and nearer reality. In pitying Moran's struggles to regain self-control Gogarty purges some of his own self-pity and so can ask, with a degree of detachment, 'if it were the end of man's life to trample upon self' constantly in this way.

> 'Nora,' he said, 'would answer that self is all we have, and to destroy it and put in its place conventions and prejudices is to put man's work above God's.'[21]

This marks a first breach in his rigorously maintained self-discipline and his desire now bursts forth in an anguished prayer that Nora's sin may fall on his shoulders and her soul be saved so that he might possess her in heaven as a reward for his earthly continence. His conscious mind recants from such indecent blasphemy, but he can no longer disguise from himself his real feelings for Nora. Courageously he writes to her confessing at last that his jealousy derived both from a perverted sexual curiosity about the men in her life and, more importantly, from envy of her spiritual freedom. He admits he has betrayed both his sensibility and his vocation. By recognising his hypocrisy towards her he also perceives the false values that till now have sustained his faith as a Catholic and this poses a new challenge to his integrity.

If he were publicly to abandon his parish, his act would be seen by his family and congregation as moral delinquency; yet to be obedient to a creed that for him had lost all significance would be to reduce his life to a ludicrous travesty. His thoughts tend by way of suicide to an inevitable mental breakdown. Mind and body need repose for recovery. Just as winter's seeming desolation is really a time of recuperation and strengthening of organic resources, so Gogarty's discontent passes through the period of his convalescence to full self-knowledge:

> After a severe illness one is alone with one's self, the whole of one's life sings in one's head like a song, and listening to it,

I learned that it was jealousy that prompted me to speak against you, and not any real care for the morality of my parish. I discovered, too, that my moral ideas were not my own. They were borrowed from others, and badly assimilated. . . . But while dozing through long convalescent hours many things hitherto obscure to me became clear, and it seems now to me to be clearly wrong to withhold our sympathy from any side of life. It seems to me that it is only by our sympathy we can do any good at all. God gave us our human nature; we may misuse and degrade our nature, but we must never forget that it came originally from God.[22]

From what was at first merely an aesthetic appreciation of natural beauty, Gogarty has, like many of Forster's characters in similar circumstances, developed a full response to life. He now has the courage and moral conviction to build his life again and in a fresh, direct style he communicates his decision to Nora. Through her reply, Moore can vindicate Gogarty's new strength and integrity:

Has it not often seemed strange to you that we go through life without ever being able to reveal the soul that is in us? Is it because we are ashamed, or is it that we do not know ourselves? It is certainly a hard task to learn the truth about ourselves, and I appreciate the courage your last letter shows; you have faced the truth. . . . We live enveloped in self-deception as in a film; now and again the film breaks like a cloud and the light shines through. We veil our eyes, for we do not like the light. It is really very difficult to tell the truth. . . .[23]

All too easily, man can deceive himself with the belief that the religious and social conventions that make up that film are mechanistic forces. They become determining factors, according to Moore, only if man chooses that they should be so: man has the moral right to mould his life, emotions and aptitudes to a condition that accords with his individual desires and need; but to make such a sense of his duty to himself a lived experience requires courage. It is this appreciation of life as a personal adventure that Nora has offered to Gogarty:

You dared to stretch out both hands to life and grasp it; you accepted the spontaneous natural living wisdom of your instincts, when I was rolled up like a dormouse in the dead wisdom of codes and formulas, dogmas and opinions.[24]

To the Church Nora constitutes a temptation because of her cult of personality; but Nora is not Eve and there is here no Fall, rather she shows Gogarty that the whole concept of Eden as a paradise lost through woman's weakness and sensuality is a priestly connivance to bolster the Church's power over the individual. Gogarty likens an existence under such doctrines to 'an old, decrepit house . . . all the doors and windows nailed up. . . . In the dusty twilight, creatures wilt and pray'. Nora came, like Primavera, 'and the shutters fell and I found myself looking upon the splendid sun shining on hills and fields, wooded prospects with rivers winding through the great green expanses'.[25] The Church castigates woman through fear, he argues, for 'woman is life'.[26] Nora ceases in time to be merely a sexual female to Gogarty; his joy in her becomes with his maturer response relaxed and all-embracing and his sense of the richness of her individuality stimulates in him an appreciation of what Lawrence would describe as 'the quick of self'. It is with no degree of blasphemy that Moore describes Nora's cumulative effect on Gogarty in the image with which St Teresa defines Grace as a fountain nourishing the garden of the soul; Nora has transformed what initially in Gogarty was blind lust into a wholehearted generosity:

> A fountain springs out of earth into air; it sings a tune that cannot be caught and written down in notes; the rising and falling water is full of iridescent colour, and to the wilting roses the fountain must seem not a natural thing, but a spirit, and I too think of her as a spirit.[27]

This appraisal of Nora's character would seem a suitable point at which to pause and comment on Malcolm Brown's criticism that *The Lake* is a typical product of the Aesthetic decadence.[28] The basic theme of the lapsed Catholic is so, certainly; but Nora is no *femme fatale* and Gogarty is no Tannhäuser submitting to the forbidden and evil rites of the Venusberg. Moore's whole attitude is healthier, anticipating Forster and Lawrence. One has only to compare *The Lake* with Zola's *La Faute de l'Abbé Mouret*[29] to perceive the force of this distinction, for Moore's narrative is closely modelled on Zola's and so is his trio of central characters, yet the finished work is radically different in its intentions, attitudes and method. The Abbé Mouret is obliged to choose the lesser of two evils: on the one hand a spiritual prison if he commits himself to the life-denying dogmas of the Catholic church and to celibacy as a priest and on the other the equally entrapping world of his lover Albine which is symbolised by her tropical garden, a degenerate Eden where rank vegetation and putrescent fruit are conducive to a forbidden eroticism. Zola creates in the novel a world where all pleasure is inevitably synonymous with lust and self-abandon. Brother Archiangias, an older priest, who strives to secure Mouret's soul for the Church, seems at first to be a caricature of a typical Catholic view-point. Once he has Mouret in his power he forces from him a terrible confession:

> Yes: I renounce life. I maintain that the death of the race would be preferable to the unceasing impurity which propagates it. Sin besmirches everything. It lurks in the chamber of the newly-married, in the cradle of the newly-born – nay! even in the flowers dropping in the sun and the trees putting forth their buds.[30]

The confession is depressing in its ferocity because Zola offers us in the world of his novel no alternative to this black zealous hatred of existence and disgust with man's sexuality and one begins to resent the lack of a more generous perspective. There is no denying a sickness in Gogarty's soul which makes him prone to self-loathing at times; in a crisis Gogarty may speak for example of his 'morbidly excited imagination' in comparing the bare autumn trees in 'farfetched and unhealthy' Huysmanesque terms to consumptive invalids;[31] but his ability to recognise the fact critically is a positive step towards sanity and change. Nora is worldly but she means more to Gogarty than carnal experience. There is an authentically realised joy in living at the heart of Moore's novel.

There is one difficulty, however, that must be faced here and that is the existence of two versions of *The Lake*, the first markedly inferior to the second. (Malcolm Brown may be basing his judgement simply on a reading of the 1905 text.) The basic difference lies in the characterization of Nora. Faced with the stylistic problem of creating a free-thinking heroine, Moore unfortunately endowed Rose Leicester (the heroine of the 1905 version) with all the Aesthetic gossip about music, painting and Wagner that made parts of *Evelyn Innes* so factitiously turgid, as well as a rather tasteless line in witticisms about sinful school-mistresses. Freedom in Rose is simply lack of reticence; her style of expression is aggressively shrill and it seems incongruous, even comic, that Gogarty's restoration should be effected by such a vulgar hussy. It is essential to Moore's structuring of the novel that the reader respect Rose but as he presents her she alienates rather than attracts one's sympathy.

In the revision Moore wisely extends O'Grady's role and function: he is given four letters in the 1921 version as against two in the 1905 edition; his presence and authority in the novel are much amplified by Moore's adjusting the narrative to allow him a personal visit to Gogarty in Ireland. Much of Nora's character is now conveyed to the reader through O'Grady's quiet and incisive comments. Nora herself is more passive than Rose and her intelligence and determination make her judgements of Gogarty the more acceptable. We respect her shrewdness of perception and her tact. Her undemonstrative strength makes it easier for Moore to effect the transitions from the real Nora to the symbolic and comprehensive Life-figure, the Primavera, that she becomes in time in Gogarty's imagination. Both Nora and Gogarty observe the natural world with sympathy and sensitivity, both are cultured and so Moore can develop psychological and mythical imagery in his rendering of their responses without any sense of strain or affectation. The 'naturalness' of the description is genuinely lyrical and healthy.

Gogarthy decides he must leave the parish but, to avoid a scandal, he will swim across the lake; his abandoned clothes will give searchers the impression that he has been accidentally drowned. He cannot remain a priest without sacrificing his potential:

> . . . we cannot sacrifice ourselves all our life long, unless we begin to take pleasure in the immolation of self, and then it is no longer sacrifice.[32]

The shedding of the masochistic fantasies that have beset him since his youth is complete. Gogarty's last hours in Garranard are occupied with some bizarre incidents of parish-life: Philip Rean, the child of a mixed marriage, receives a double baptism as a

Catholic and a Protestant because of a violent conflict between his two grandmothers; the bishop of the diocese has scruples about roofing Kilronan Abbey so that Moran's parishioners can communicate in comfort because local folklore tells of a centuries-old curse that death on the high road will meet whoever repairs the Abbey ruins; and Pat Kearney comes to barter with Gogarty over the price of a marriage-ceremony. The comedy is perhaps unfair to Catholicism but Gogarty's humour and Moore's is compassionate in this demonstration of the pathetic parody of itself that a dogmatic religion can become in a rural and predominantly illiterate community: intolerant, superstitious and grasping. The record of cultured exiles from an Ireland resistant to change testifies to the validity of Moore's analysis: Gogarty's exile is, however voluntary, not an expulsion from a second Eden. Like Stephen Dedalus, he goes off in quest of life – 'to live, to err, to fall, to triumph. . . . On and on and on and on', but whereas Stephen's assurance is precarious Gogarty's resilience comes of having learnt 'what the heart is and what it feels'.[33]

There are two aspects of the conclusion that require more detailed attention. The first is the unexpected intrusion of the curate Moran that prevents Gogarty's escape on the night he originally planned to leave. The curate speaks of some mystical compulsion that has forced him to come and save Gogarty from himself, to wrestle with him till he regains control. There is an obvious parallel with Moran's earlier predicament when Gogarty walked for hours with his curate while he strove to exhaust himself and so stifle his cravings for whisky. When Moran has left, Gogarty at first interprets his visit as an act of providence saving him from the windstorm that settles over the lake that night in which he would certainly have been drowned; then later he dismisses the matter: 'God doesn't bother himself about such trifles as my staying or going'.[34]

It could be argued here that Moran is acting as a foil to test the strength of Gogarty's new-found convictions and whether he will have the will-power to make a second attempt at swimming the lake, having been frustrated when he had first nerved himself to the effort. But the effect of the incident is ambiguous and, by contrast with the carefully sustained detail of Gogarty's psychological awakening that we have been examining, it is pointlessly melodramatic. By making Gogarty talk of a watchful, organizing providence, Moore has introduced a concept at variance with the overall pattern of the novel. If this episode is to be interpreted as a visiting of divine grace, (a miracle no less, since Gogarty is saved from certain death) why, we may ask, is the situation subsequently belittled by Gogarty himself? Though his adherence to the Catholic Church has been shaken, Gogarty has never denied the need in his life for faith and reverence. As if Moore himself was troubled by the inconsistency of all this and saw the necessity of reasoning it out clearly, he now has Gogarty write to Nora telling her of his delay in leaving Ireland and discussing at length the strange coincidence of Moran's visit and the storm that same evening on the lake. Gogarty now asserts that 'these were part of God's providence sent to warn him against leaving his parish'.[35] This is a completely new interpretation of the event with providence seen not as a benevolent but as a threatening power, yet Moore offers no explanation for this sudden shift in Gogarty's thinking. Gogarty now recalls various experiences from the past few months which seemed as he contemplated them to have the signficance of omens. One such memory is of a curlew:

> I can still see it in the air, its beautifully shapen body and wings, its long beak, and its trailing legs; it staggered a little in its flight when the shot was fired, but it had strength enough to reach Castle Island: it then toppled over, falling dead on the shore. . . . At first I believed that this bird was sent to warn me from going, but it was that bird that put the idea into my head how I might escape from the parish without giving scandal.[36]

Faced with a problem he cannot solve, Gogarty throws up his hands: 'Life is so strange that one doesn't know what to think. Of what use are signs and omens if the interpretation is always obscure?'[37] Sensing that perhaps Moore might not be sure either of the precise nature of the events he is handling is unsettling for the reader. Moore certainly admitted to Lady Cunard that he found 'the greatest difficulty in writing the end' of the novel; *The Lake*, he told her, was a troublesome as *Sister Teresa*.[38] And yet this sudden failure to be completely in control of his material and of the reader's response is not as detrimental to the overall movement of *The Lake* as it is with *Sister Teresa*. This is because, for all his scruples and questions, Gogarty does finally follow through the course of action he has planned for himself and in so doing does vindicate Moore's belief in the sovereign power of man's instinctive responses as the finest sanctions for his conduct, which is his principal theme and motive for composing the novel. That being so, why, we may ask, does he allow Gogarty to waver and distrust his intuitive insights? Why is Gogarty compelled to seek for rational explanations when the subjecting of experience to such intellectual analysis distorts, blurs or trivialises its complex nuances of meaning?

The answer is that it is in keeping with Gogarty's personality as we have come to know it. When we first encounter him he is a man whose intellectual maturity has been acquired at the expense of his emotional integrity. The acquisition of that integrity, that wholeness of being, is the goal of his psychological quest. But as Moore knew well from his own experience and that of countless other educated Irishmen, the old self is long in dying, however potent the forces for rebirth. Brought up within the authority of the Catholic Church, Gogarty has needed the security of succinct explanations of experience and as his new self has emerged he has turned repeatedly to O'Grady and Nora as spiritual guides of superior understanding for their approval of his new insights. Faced with the most decisive stage in his growth towards wholeness, with the need once and for all to commit himself to a way of life that accords with his new beliefs, it is psychologically right that his old self should assert its voice most powerfully and insidiously, unsettling his will and provoking nervous tensions. It is an act of remarkable courage for Gogarty to prepare himself emotionally and psychologically a second time to escape. That he refuses to debate the rightness of his action any longer is in fact proof that he now trusts wholly in his instincts and accepts total responsibility for his future life. Moore's conception of the conflict of thought and impulse has an accurate verisimilitude here; the weakness lies in the actual presentation of that conflict and its aftermath. Understandably enough Gogarty gives up the search for explanations perplexed and exhausted but Moore does not make as much as he should of Gogarty's subsequent calm determination to pursue his resolve. Psychologically the moment is climactic and decisive but Moore's actual rendering of it is surprisingly down-beat, even half-hearted. For once Moore's dramatic sense failed him and he does not realise anything like the full potential of the episode. It may be that Moore hoped at this point that he could rise to a specific philosophical statement of his beliefs and found that he could not adequately do so, so that the tired quality of the writing reflects his disappointment. One can appreciate why he should wish to do this though it is not a necessity that he should; we do not expect it of any novelist providing he can communicate the validity of his convictions as a felt and judged experience through the terms of his art as Moore himself does superbly through his special use of narrative in *Esther Waters* and as he does elsewhere in *The Lake* through lyrical symbolism. Indeed it is because the conception of the novel as a whole is so strong (and that is true psychologically even of this episode) and because its method and style are so finely and scrupulously sustained elsewhere that, though irritatingly it occurs at such an inauspicious point, this lapse is not seriously detrimental. One is impelled to take the desired intention for the accomplished fact.

There is a second failure of judgement of a like kind in the final chapter. As Gogarty waits by the lakeside for the moon to rise so that he can begin the first stage of his journey he ponders on the consequences of his exile: 'He was following what? Life? Yes; but what is life?'[39] His exit is not a grandiose Romantic gesture of defiance; Gogarty has no illusions about the struggle that his future life in America will bring, but it will be a struggle for, and not against, his better, instinctive self. He tests the possible interpretations of the word 'instinctive' against his own experience and intentions. A life devoted exclusively to adventure, he realises, would be as monotonous in its pursuit of change and excitement as the Aesthete's jaded appreciation of 'a flower that yields up its perfume only after long cultivation' or 'a wine that gains its fragrance only after it has been lying in the same cellar for many years',[40] for such pleasures, unconnected to any central purpose in life, offer ever-diminishing returns. To seek merely for adventure would be as withering spiritually as to go on acquiescing in a social and religious tradition that his whole personality has proved stagnant.

> He liked better to think that his quest was the personal life – that intimate exaltation that comes to him who has striven to be himself, and nothing but himself. The life he was going to might lead him even to a new faith.[41]

The nature of that faith is implied in Gogarty's final words: 'In America, I shall be living a life in agreement with God's instincts. My quest is life.'[42]

But after this precise analysis there is a rather serious failure of vision; it marks interestingly one of the few places where the first version of 1905 is superior to the second. 'Instinct' has come to mean in the course of the novel an understanding comprehensive of sympathy and conscience, which act as curbs to prevent individuality reverting to egoism. While it is obviously inclusive of sexual love, it has a wider application. The first version places any physical reconciliation with Rose Leicester as 'beyond the light of commonsense', but in the revision Gogarty enjoys a brief mystical union with Nora, 'through the exaltation of some sense latent or non-existent in him in his waking moods'.[43] It could be argued that the episode symbolizes the final integrating of Gogarty's personality, his achieving the goal of his quest. But the ghostly visitation follows directly after the observation that 'his heart cried out that his love must bring her back to him eventually'.[44] Moore is at pains to define Gogarty's passion here as Platonic, totally unselfish and without jealousy but as the vision fades Gogarty asserts his conviction that 'she who was today an adventure, would become in the end the home of his affections'.[45] This is the more surprising since earlier in the chapter he had stoically resigned himself to the fact that in going to America 'he would never see her again – at least, it was not probable that he would. He was not following her, but an idea, an abstraction, an opinion'.[46] If his future struggle is to be sustained by such a delusion then the reason for his exile, if not open to question, becomes somewhat limited in its significance and Gogarty is for the reader an object of pathos rather than of joy.

This narrowing of perspective is matched by stylistic imprecision; a false, breathless quality is introduced in the prose which invites a women's-magazine type of sentimentality:

> A little surprise rose to the surface of his rapture . . . it would be as vain to lament that her eyebrows were fair as to lament or reprove her conduct.[47]

It is precisely this tendency in Gogarty to sentimental fantasies that Nora has chastened.

Once again as with the episode of Moran's unexpected intervention and its consequences this lapse does not jeopardise the novel as drastically as might be expected, and mercifully it is short and the content virtually redundant. *The Lake*, like many fictional studies of the nature of consciousness, is a novel in which the inner meaning remains for the reader a powerfully apprehended, rather than a comprehended, fact. It communicates to the reader's imagination an understanding of the quality of the characters' lives and personalities through lyrical statement and through their individual styles of expression in letters, in conversation and in Gogarty's case quintessentially in his private communion with himself. The written style carries much of the weight of the novel's significance and meaning; on it alone Moore had to expend most of his imaginative energy and invention. The control, the discipline demanded by this technique of presentation is formidable. Lapses are regrettable but, given Moore's volatile temperament, it is remarkable that there are so few and that he could submit to the rigours of craftsmanship with such sustained persistence. The lyrical, the apprehended pattern of the novel is already complete in Gogarty's decision to swim across the lake; the theme has by this stage become more important for the reader than surface detail and so the sentimental soul-trysting with Nora, though tiresome, is ultimately irrelevant.

It has here been suggested how important the style is in *The Lake* and how fine for the most part Moore's writing is as a result. The novel seeks to portray Gogarty's innermost private self by depicting the nature and quality of his sensory and sensual perceptions as they are affected by his changing feelings towards Nora Glynn. In this the novel is neither landscape painting in words, nor a virtuoso performance in the art of pathetic fallacy. Gogarty's wandering beside the lake is a private voyage into his own consciousness but Lake Carra and its district is more than the landscape of his mind; it has a vital life of its own, related to a dynamic cycle of change, of growth, fruition, decay, and rebirth. Nora before their quarrel had taught Gogarty to recognise these 'mysteries that common things disclose'.[48] In her absence the woods become for him an obvious satisfying correlative, stimulating at first memories of her. Later he perceives that Nora's idiosyncratic energy is at one with the natural cycle; she is fearless of change, content only in seeking out the best that life can offer. This invites the inevitable comparison between Nora's sanity and his jaded lassitude that initiates Gogarty's progress to maturity. Unlike the limited artistic symbols of Moore's earlier novels, the lake is flexible and complex, sugges-

tive at once of the permanent and the transient, of a still geo-
graphical point in a constantly changing cycle. Its varying moods
under different atmospheric effects and its greater seasonal change
afford Gogarty the means to articulate with precision and immediacy his fluctuating emotional conflicts: '. . . my loneliness
helped me to perceive the loneliness of the wood and the absence of
birds made me feel it'.[49] His pursuit of the analogy defines this
particular psychological state; but even in his mind the analogy
never becomes a static symbol: the stagnant pent-up claustro-
phobia of autumn and winter passes into the energetic release of
vigour in spring. Awareness of the inevitability of this change
allows him mentally to encompass the need for emotional conflict
in himself as a prelude to growth. By accepting all his fluctuating
moods he gains the strength to scrutinise them carefully and perceive the pattern behind their ebb and flow, the truth within their
seeming inconsistencies. That controlling force which is his instinctive being, he comes to realise, is the only real permanence in self.
By recognising this enduring and unifying principle which imposes
pattern on change, Gogarty can pass from enervating unrest at his
predicament in Ireland to a creative awareness of his potential.
A healthy, sensory response to natural beauty slowly stimulates a
moral response to the facts of his own existence: moral, because
it permits him at last to be truly generous to others and especially
Nora, in whom he has learnt to welcome the excitement of change
as a means to a really intimate friendship with her that transcends
physical separation. No longer does he seek to impose meanings
on her life and actions and define her personality through restricting and insulting images of her as innocent companion and soul-
mate, fallen woman, repentant Magdalene or *femme fatale*.

Moore's writing is controlled in such a way that the play of
associations is only in Gogarty's mind, it is not pathetic fallacy;
thus his perception of the permanent sources of vitality coincides
with a progress beyond mere association to an awareness of the
'quick of self' that is both the source of all instinctive and imaginative creativity and the point of union between man and nature. It
is only in apprehending this fundamental reality that the mind's
superstructure of imagery and association becomes viable and
free of illusion and fantasy.[50] Substantiating this by quotation is
difficult, as the lyrical pattern is cumulative in effect, but let us
consider some representative passages.

He was fortunate enough to catch sight of an otter asleep on a rock, and towards evening he came upon a wild-duck's nest in the sedge; many of the ducklings had broken their shells; these struggled after the duck; but there were two prisoners, two that could not escape from their shells, and, seeing their lives would be lost if he did not come to their aid, he picked the shells away and took them to the water's edge, for he had heard Catherine say that one could almost see little ducks growing when they had had a drop of water. The old duck swam about uttering a whistling sound, her cry that her ducklings were to join her. And thinking of the lives he had saved, he felt a sudden regret that he had not come upon the nest earlier, when Christy brought him Father O'Grady's letter.[51]

O'Grady's letter is the first that brings news of Nora in London, and in retrospect the picking open of the shells and the drop of lake-water that stimulates growth have an obvious symbolic connotation. But the incident conveys most about Gogarty emotionally: his observation has developed into an actively sympathetic interest in nature, which is breaking down the intense self-consciousness and the emotional stagnation that are the cause of his misery. The accuracy of the observations of the ducks' behaviour is a token of Gogarty's complete absorption in the event. What impresses too is the ease with which the various apparently random processes of the mind are rendered and shown to have a pattern of relevance: for much of the novel Gogarty resents his housekeeper, Catherine, as he finds her peasant shrewdness and curiosity about his life intrusive (indeed much of his wandering by the lake is motivated by his desire to escape her inquisitive and, as he thinks, judging eye). Yet in his mind's play of associations we see here and elsewhere that he respects Catherine's authority on animal and folk lore, her natural wisdom. Catherine has an intuitive intelligence and acquires some stature as the novel progresses for her honesty and devotion as a servant which make us perceive why Gogarty in his struggles with his conscience over Nora should fear her.

To take another example, consider this passage where Gogarty recalls denouncing Nora in his sermon; he cannot explain that action; he feels in retrospect that he was possessed by a being not his own. The memory breaks off as Gogarty is exhausted with the persistence of his remorse. The consciousness is for the time being numbed into silence and a different activity of the mind takes over, bringing some solace:

> All night he had lain awake; he must have been a little mad that night, for he could only think of the loss of a soul to God, and of God's love of chastity. All night long he had repeated with variations that it were better that all which our eyes see – this earth and the stars that are in being – should perish utterly, be crushed into dust, rather than a mortal sin should be committed; in an extraordinary lucidity of mind he continued to ponder on God's anger and his own responsibility towards God, and feeling all the while that there are times when we lose control of our minds, when we are a little mad. He foresaw his danger, but he could not do else than rise from his bed and begin to prepare his sermon, for he had to preach, and he could only preach on chastity. . . . His brain was on fire that morning, and words rose to his lips – he knew not whence nor how they came, and he had no idea now of what he had said. He only knew that she left the church during his sermon. . . . And from that day to this no news of her nor any way of getting news of her.
>
> His thoughts went to the hawthorn-trees, for he could not think of her any more for the moment, and it relieved his mind to examine the green pips that were beginning to appear among the leaves. 'The hawthorns will be in flower in another week,' he said; and he began to wonder at the beautiful order of the spring. The pear and the cherry were the first; these were followed by the apple, and after the apple came the lilac, the chestnut, and the laburnum. The forest trees too had their order. The ash was still leafless, but it was shedding its catkins, and in another fifteen days its light foliage would be dancing in the breeze. The oak was last of all. . . .
>
> His eyes dwelt on the lake, refined and wistful, with reflections of islands and reeds, mysteriously still. Rose-coloured clouds descended, revealing many new and beautiful mountain forms, every pass and every crest distinguishable. It was the hour when the cormorants come home to roost, and he saw three black specks flying low about the glittering surface; rising from the water, they alighted with a flutter of wings on the corner wall of what remained of Castle Hag, 'and they will sleep there till morning,' he said, as he toiled up a little path, twisting through ferns and thorn-bushes.[52]

The style exactly captures the movements of Gogarty's mind: the obsessive reiterations evoke his growing desperation and horror as he remembers in detail his former cruelty; after the anguished statement that Nora is now lost to him he forces his mind to concentrate on his surroundings to gain some respite and he intellectualises about order in nature; that activates memories based on his past observations of seasonal change; the generalised gives way to the particular; then remembered details excite a growing appreciation of immediate beauty in the countryside about him till the mind finds a kind of rest. As Gogarty discovers and fosters his capacity for sympathy, so his perception of the colour, sound and continuous movement of the woods and the lake by day and night becomes the more subtle and detailed and his insight into his own psyche the more exact: ' "There is a lake in every man's heart," he said, "and he listens to its monotonous whisper year by year, more and more attentive till at last he ungirds." '[53]

The most troublesome factor for a novelist involved principally in depicting the nature of consciousness is how to relate the inner life of the character being observed to his daily physical existence in time. In terms of the whole novel of course the quality of Gogarty's consciousness has a direct bearing on his vocation as a priest with its duties and responsibilities. As such he is a fitting subject for a novel of this kind since to be true to his calling he must lead an exemplary public and private life. But there remains the continuous local problem for the author of effecting easy transitions in the writing between the two levels of experience. All too easily the balance can be broken and the tone or mood dissipated by an unintended bathos when either the physical act appears trite or the play of the mind seems pretentious. Mrs Ramsay's efforts to create and sustain an emotional security amongst her family and friends in Virginia Woolf's *To The Lighthouse* which contrasts so courageously and yet so absurdly with the routine of her household chores and her supervision of the dinner table never wholly rises clear of this hazard. In the third section of that novel, where Virginia Woolf attempts to redefine feminine sensitivity in terms of the artist Lily Briscoe's percepton of colour and form as she works away at her canvas, she is on much safer ground: mood and meaning here are created and sustained in an uninterrupted flow of finely cadenced poetic prose. Moore was right to focus on Gogarty's perceptions in a similar fashion as the means of effecting smooth transitions between the temporal and psychological conditions of his character. Unity of tone is rarely lost and one is left with a sense of the real completeness of one's knowledge of the character thus communicated. One has only to compare Moore's writing with Dujardin's in *Les Lauriers Sont Coupés* to perceive the immense technical advances that Moore achieved. Dujardin also gives us his character's perceptions in detail but far from using this to achieve an intense rapport between reader and character as Moore does, Dujardin alienates the reader from his hero as the style seems to pin him down as a specimen for detached observation:

> La rue est sombre; il n'est pourtant que sept heures et demie; je vais rentrer chez moi; je serai aisément dès neuf heures aux Nouveautés. L'avenue est moins sombre que d'abord elle ne le semblait; le ciel est clair; sur les trottoirs un limpidité, la lumière des becs de gaz, des triples becs de gaz; peu de monde dehors; là-bas l'Opéra, le foyer tout enflammé de l'Opéra; je marche le côté droit de l'avenue, vers l'Opéra. J'oubliais mes gants; bah, je serai tout-à-l'heure à la maison; et maintenant on ne voit personne. Bientôt je serai à la maison; dans . . . d'ici l'Opéra, cinq minutes; la rue Auber, cinq minutes; autant, le boulevard Haussmann; encore cinq minutes; cela fait dix, quinze, vingt minutes; je m'habillerai; je pourrai partir à huit heures et demie, huit heures trente-cinq. Le temps est sec; agréable est marcher après dîner, à ce moment du soir, jamais beaucoup de gens dans l'avenue.[54]

Dujardin locates Prince for the reader at a precise time of day in a precise setting yet we cannot say we ever really come to *know* him in the novel. The staccato style is wearing, moreover the quality of Prince's mind-life as rendered here is so mundane as to be trivial. Dujardin's mistake here is in recording every one (or so it seems) of Prince's sensations as if they were perceptions; it is little more than traditional authorial description given in a terse nagging prose reminiscent of the stage-directions for a play. The point is that though the mind subconsciously registers a wealth of sensory stimuli only a selected few actually impinge on one's conscious thoughts and it is that process of selection that creates the precise idiosyncratic tenor of an individual mind, its unique mode of perception. There is little in the passage here that marks Prince off from any other man walking along the pavement that same evening, other than certain trite physical details. Prince unlike

Gogarty is not a dramatically realised character. For all Dujardin's concern with perception, there is a want of deep imaginative engagement with his character's precise subjective self. Though Moore owed a debt of inspiration to Dujardin, he was not uncritical of his model: what was needed, he realised, was a disciplined impressionism and a subtly varying, fluid and compelling style. The reader must be made aware, as the spectator is in viewing certain styles of painting, that a selection of sense-data has been made for a private subjective purpose. The nature of that purpose, that inner controlling force which determines the essence of a character at a given point in time, will reveal itself only gradually and by implication through the total pattern of the novel. The ability to relate the moment-by-moment actualising of the character's experience to the total purpose of the novel becomes a far more pressing concern for the author than in the traditional form of the novel; a scrupulous discipline is demanded as style becomes intimately bound up with meaning, which is why, as we have seen, a lapse in tone or expression can seriously disturb the verisimilitude.

It is obvious that to support this greater weight of significance the imaginative recreation of Lake Carra should not strike the reader as mere description. Both accurate observation of detail and a feeling for transient atmospheric effects are called for; and Moore was wise to choose the countryside of his home as his setting. (Exactly the same technique is used to describe most movingly the author's last visit to Moore Hall, which is the subject of the final chapters of 'Vale': the experience is so intensely concrete and immediate that the intimacy of the memory never lapses into the sentimental.) Throughout *The Lake*, Moore's writing achieves a cogent sense of place without the lifelessness of too precise a geography. Gogarty's drive to Tinnick, for example, has a sense of joyfully renewed acquaintance with a landscape that arouses delight because of its very familiarity:

> Then, shading his eyes with his hand, he peered through the sun-haze, following the shapes of the fields. The corn was six inches high, and the potatoes were coming into blossom. True, there had been a scarcity of water, but they had had a good summer, thanks be to God, and he thought he had never seen the country looking so beautiful. And he loved this country, this poor Western plain with shapely mountains enclosing the horizon. Ponies were feeding between the whins, and they raised their

shaggy heads to watch the car passing. In the distance cattle were grazing, whisking the flies away. How beautiful was every- thing – the white clouds hanging in the blue sky, and the trees! There were some trees, but not many – only a few pines. He caught glimpses of the lake through the stems. . . .[55]

The incident is enlivened by being presented through Gogarty's response; colloquial rhythms are continually breaking through to give an immediacy and tension to the writing that is quite absent from set-piece descriptions or from Dujardin's evocations of Prince's walks round Paris, where because of the insistent style, everything seems remarkable and nothing appears really special or familiar. In Gogarty, however, we see a man who has known and rarely quitted a particular world in over thirty years suddenly finding that world transformed as the direct result of a force long suppressed now awakening in his psyche. The lands, the churches, the ruins, the villages about the lake and the numerous islands in its waters have their history, pagan, medieval and modern, their legends and their folklore; all play their part in moulding Gogarty's sensibility. As in life, the feeling for place has many levels of signi- ficance. And over it all is cast the growing pathos, apparent ulti- mately even to Gogarty himself that he is seeing it all with such acute intensity because he is seeing it for the last time. If he cherishes it profoundly now it is because he wishes to etch the experience deep in his memory.

Subtly Moore's prose links together multiple levels of response and weaves them into the fabric of Gogarty's consciousness. With considerable invention, Moore transforms all the material of the novel into this psychological dimension, yet such is the rhythmic versatility of his prose that there is no danger of a monotony of mood. The unity of *The Lake* in design and execution, in its analysis and meticulous realisation of processes of the mind, is masterly. Without Dujardin's example Moore's novel might not have been written; but with *The Lake* Moore transformed what in the Frenchman's work is a crude sketch for a new style of fiction into a perfected work of art.

(10) *The Brook Kerith* and the Late
Historical Novels

(i)

A decade elapsed between the publication of *The Lake* and
Moore's next novel, *The Brook Kerith* – a period in which he was
preoccupied with compiling, devising and writing his long, brilliantly witty autobiography, *Hail and Farewell*. For this work he
evolved an intricate structure and a new style. The book is at
once a record of the efforts of the Dublin intelligentsia at the turn
of the century to effect a renaissance in Ireland with the founding
of the Gaelic League, the Abbey Theatre and the Irish Agricultural
Organisation Society and also an account of Moore's own role in
all the revolutionary activity. Public life is everywhere matched
with private experience; as Moore assesses the achievements of his
friends and associates – Yeats, AE, Synge, Lady Gregory, Edward
Martyn and Sir Horace Plunkett – so he sets in motion a process of
self-discovery and appraisal. Their ambitions for the political
liberation of Ireland encourage Moore to explore his past life to
discover the cause of his own sense of complete spiritual freedom,
his energy and shamelessness. The narrative of events both public
and personal has an objective historical validity but it is also a
complex process of memory; the method of telling cumulatively
reveals the personality of the teller so that the substance of *Hail
and Farewell* is both social fact and a dramatization of Moore's
own mind.[1] The prose moves effortlessly between precise observation and reminiscence, impression and intimate reverie, showing
how the active, the intellectual, the pensive and the emotional
selves are interdependent and inseparable and how the past finds an
enduring and creative vitality in the life of Moore's consciousness.
The style is relaxed and lucid; the simplicity of expression allows

Moore to endow the narrative line with a wealth of allusions and implications. With his autobiography Moore finally achieved a style of narrative that paralleled Wagner's complex use of melody, which had been Moore's ambition since the late Eighteen-Eighties and which he had in varying degrees realised in *Esther Waters* and *The Lake*. If one substitutes 'narrative' for 'melody' in this account of Wagner's practice by Arthur Symons one comes closest to appreciating what Moore strove to accomplish:

> Wagner's aim at expressing the soul of things is still further helped by his system of continuous, unresolved melody. . . . it partakes of the nature of thought, but it is more than thought; it is the whole expression of the sub-conscious life, saying more of himself than any person of the drama has ever found in his own soul.[2]

Hail and Farewell is a triumph of style.

Moore now set about applying this technique to fiction, always admitting his debt to Wagner:

> I went to Bayreuth again and again to hear Wagner, and to Munich to hear Wagner and Mozart, and for some years was seldom absent from the symphony concerts . . . thinking how a story might be woven from start to finish out of one set of ideas, each chapter rising out of the preceding chapter in suspended cadence, always, never a full close; and as an example of the kind of book that comes out of such ideas as these, I will name *The Brook Kerith*, for the story begins like a brook; the old woman telling stories to her grandchild may be compared to the 'Fanfare of the Rhine' and the book widens out as it flows, a smooth current, not very rapid, but flowing always, turning sometimes east, sometimes west, winding, disappearing at last mysteriously like a river.[3]

Hail and Farewell is a synthesis of history, biography and autobiography and in his late novels Moore similarly attempts a subtle fusion of the objective and subjective forms of narrative. Most fiction concerned to depict consciousness reduces plot to an absolute minimum and is intent on allowing a formed and therefore static personality to reveal itself; Moore by contrast in his last novels as in *The Lake* is preoccupied with growth in consciousness either towards maturity or to total intellectual or emotional stagnation. As with *Hail and Farewell* there has therefore to be a double movement: a linear progression recording a particular character's life in time is presented in such a manner that events are less important for what they are in themselves than for what they reveal of the conscious and unconscious activity of the character's mind. The autobiography had shown Moore how the skilful combining of the many ways of presenting a story – the juxtaposing of observation with involuntary memory; the comfortable reminiscing that passes into serious debate or into a nagging obsessional concern with a particular detail; the impressions that suddenly cohere into judgements – can make narrative cumulatively a portrayal of consciousness. Much obviously depends on a flexible prose style.

A good *oral* storyteller will always dramatize his characters and enact his tale through their distinctive voices and Moore attempts to reproduce this effect on the page: as narrator he identifies himself in his imagination with a particular character's responses, selects a prose rhythm suited to that character to evoke both his speaking voice and the inner 'voice' of his conscious mind, and then arranges and conducts the narrative in a way that suggests a subjective viewpoint though the method allows him the freedom when the occasion demands it to act as omniscient author too. (In *The Brook Kerith*, for example, it permits him to shift the focus of interest from Joseph of Arimathea to Jesus, then to Paul and finally to Jesus again with considerable ease.) Moore's success in this derives from his preserving an overall colloquial rhythm (he used to compose at this stage of his career by oral dictation) and from the subtle variety and ambiguity of the tenses of his chosen verbs which provoke a lively and creative confusion in the reader's mind of subjective and omniscient perspectives. Thus Moore can move easily to develop either perspective in detail as the need arises. The advantage of this compared with many techniques for depicting consciousness which seem over-studied and composed is its effect of supple spontaneity; a design is patently there exercising control but it is not insisted upon. Let us examine a typical passage in the later style:

> But to reach Chécy before nightfall they would have to hasten, and the innkeeper told them that the road through the forest looped so that the village of Lorris might be taken into the circuit; but there was no need for him to follow this winding, he would find a by-path across certain low hills which he could not

miss. Abélard did not feel sure that the by-path might not be missed, but to hear the road explained out again would be merely a waste of time, and so they hastened towards the forest in a sort of half-knowledge of the way, allowing the horses to trot a little, thinking that they might draw rein when they passed through the fringe of birch trees that encircled with their pallor the great district of pines that showed in black masses over against Etampes. Now we are well within the forest, Abélard said . . . and he asked Héloise to peep over the undergrowth that lined the rutted path down which they were riding, so that she might see the pines. . . . Like the spears, Héloise said, of crusaders going into battle; and how penetrating is the smell of resin.[4]

Or again, consider the shepherd, Jesus, meditating on the hills above the Jordan:

His thoughts began again, flowing like a wind, as mysteriously, arising he knew not whence, nor how, his mind holding him as fast as if he were in chains, and he heard from within that he had passed through two stages – the first was in Jerusalem, when he preached against the priests and their sacrifices. God does not desire the blood of sheep, but our love, and all ritual comes between us and God. . . God is in the heart, he had said, and he had spoken as truly as a man may speak of the journey that lies before him on the morning of the first day. In the desert he had looked for God in the flowers that the sun called forth and in the clouds that the wind shepherded, and he had learnt to prize the earth and live content among his sheep, all things being the gift of God and his holy will. . . . He had striven against the memory of his sin, he had desired only one thing, to acknowledge his sin, and to repent. But it seemed to him that anger and shame and sorrow, and desire of repentance, had dropped out of his heart. It seemed to him as he turned and pursued his way that some new thought was striving to speak through him. Rites and observances, all that comes under the name of religion, estranges us from God, he repeated. God is not here, nor there, but everywhere: in the flower, and in the star, and in the earth underfoot. He has often been at my elbow, God or this vast Providence that upholds the work; but shall we gather the universal will into an image and call it God? – for by doing this do we not drift back to the starting-point of all our misery?[5]

The transitions here from reported to direct speech, from dialogue to description, from thought to response, from perception to contemplation are easily effected. Always the verbs convey a sense of growth and activity; they rarely lapse into the conventional historic present or simple past tense of traditional omniscient narrative. Professor Jeffares rightly describes the liveliness of this later style as the result of 'its picture of the ceaseless shifting of the human mind on earth'.[6] Moore invites the reader in his imagination to live through a character's experience and response but he would also have the reader pause, consider and assess. This is especially the case with *The Brook Kerith*, which is a study of how men intellectually shape God to their liking in their own image and of the effects this has on their total selves.

(ii)

The idea of writing a life of Christ had long hovered on the horizon of Moore's imagination. It first found expression as early as 1889 in *Mike Fletcher*, where Fletcher himself talks of composing a trilogy of plays on the subject. 'His idea was the disintegration of the legend which had united under a godhead certain socialistic aspirations then prevalent in Judaea.'[7] Fletcher's aim, typical of the fin-de-siècle, is calculated to shock. The interest of the passage lies in the decision to structure the material as a trilogy; each play is to concentrate on a different biblical figure: John the Baptist, Jesus and Peter. The tripartite structure is the one thing which survives from this embryonic conception into *The Brook Kerith*, where with far greater seriousness of intention Moore uses the biblical events to effect three contrasting studies of different religious temperaments in Joseph of Arimathea, Jesus and St Paul.

The second notable discussion by Moore of the life of Christ occurs in a review he contributed to *The Musician* in 1897[8] of an English translation of a posthumously printed work of Wagner's: *Jesus of Nazareth*, which comprises a detailed scenario for a five-act opera examining Jesus's ministry, betrayal and trial before Pilate; a lengthy section of philosophical jottings which are presumably Wagner's first thoughts towards the libretto for Jesus's long arias either of preaching or private meditation; and lastly an assemblage of quotations from the Lutheran Bible which may have been intended for inclusion in the libretto or as substantiating evidence for Wagner's interpretation of Jesus's life and teaching. The opera was never completed, largely, one would suppose, because of the insuperable difficulty of cogently fusing the philosophical themes that Wagner outlines in his second section with the narrative events of his scenario. Plot and thematic purpose in no way coalesce. When Wagner came eventually to treat the events of the Last Supper, Good Friday and Easter in an opera he moved right away from the actual gospel story and explored them as psychological states in the legendary figures of Parsifal, Gurnemanz and Kundry. Interestingly in his review Moore comments only on the scenario as demonstrating Wagner's superb dramatic instinct; he quotes in full the plan for Act II which is set beside the Lake of Genesareth and analyses with considerable imaginative insight Wagner's conception of Pilate.[9] Moore's Jesus in *The Brook Kerith*, especially in the early stages of the novel, bears a marked resemblance to the 'love-athirst soul' that Wagner envisages Christ as being both in this sketch and in *A Communication to My Friends*;[10] but what is particularly of note is that, despite Moore's admiration as expressed in the review for Wagner's sense of theatre, Moore himself carefully avoids the public drama of Christ's life, often with considerable ingenuity, in his novel, to focus consistently on the relationship between his characters' beliefs and their specific identities. As with *Parsifal* so with *The Brook Kerith*, the action is largely private and psychological; the drama, as in *The Lake*, passes within the soul.

Throughout the Nineties, Dujardin's interests turned increasingly away from Wagner and Symbolism towards biblical exegesis (Walter Poole, Nora Glynn's employer in *The Lake*, is modelled on Dujardin in this respect); and as always Moore followed his friend's new pursuit with some excitement. The results of Dujardin's research were published in 1906 in *La Source du Fleuve Chrétien*, which argues that many of the problematic inconsistencies and paradoxes of the gospel accounts of Jesus's crucifixion arise from the evangelists' attempt to conflate an ancient fertility ritual involving a 'hanged god' (a rite common throughout near-Eastern religions in remote times) with a historical judicial execution performed by the Romans. The rite survived in Dujardin's view as an underground cult and the central actor-priest who assumed the divine role on this occasion was probably Simon of Cyrene. The book was in time immensely influential on Moore for its description of the political and religious climate of Palestine under Roman rule, but the one idea that took root initially in his imagination was not Dujardin's main thesis that the crucifixion of the gospels was really a sacred drama but a minor related historical fact that death by crucifixion as a Roman judicial punishment took never less than three days. Rather than try to resolve the inconsistencies of the gospel story by seeing the crucifixion along with Dujardin as a three-hour sacrificial ritual, Moore chose to exploit the inconsistencies Dujardin points out in the New Testament of a judicial execution lasting less than a day. There was a danger here. Moore at this time was engaged on the composition of 'Salve' for *Hail and Farewell*, which explores in detail his motives for declaring himself a Protestant. The anti-clerical feeling of this volume of the autobiography is particularly strong and threatens at times to overwhelm the comic mode Moore adopts in the trilogy.[11] Feeling he had a good story and motivated no doubt by this same anti-clerical fervour, Moore rushed into print a scenario for a three-act play, *The Apostle*, on the very eve of leaving Ireland. It was a silly and impetuous gesture. The play exists merely for its sensational ending: Jesus, revived rather than resurrected after the short duration of his crucifixion, encounters St Paul in Jericho some twenty-five years later; Paul is at first rendered speechless at this challenge to his belief in the resurrection and then in a headstrong rage kills Jesus so that 'Christianity [may be] saved by his dying'.[12]

The Apostle is an unfortunate lapse of taste in Moore, worthless but for what it reveals by contrast of the delicate discrimination of his handling of the biblical material in his later novel. Except for the final burst of crude action, the play is largely an arid exploration of ideas about godhead; again noticeably there are three differing attitudes: Mathias, a Platonist, who survives as such into the novel but becomes there a minor figure; Jesus, a kind of nature mystic; and Paul, a dogged fanatic, who reiterates the tales of the resurrection and of his own conversion 'even to satiety . . . like one that hardly believeth in the story himself'.[13] Here in a compressed schematic form is the germ of the novel; but it shows little promise of the richness and complexity of the finished work with its study of the varied manifestations of the religious impulse in the human mind. As Moore became involved with his subject so it imposed a decorum on his imagination and demanded a judicious commitment of his total sensibility. Gradually he discovered that his subject was not merely historical but one with an enduring timeless relevance, which allowed him to bring a density of implication to the work by drawing some unforced critical parallels between the attitudes of his various biblical characters and certain contemporary religious views – unforced, because *The Brook Kerith* has no pretensions to satire (the shaping vision is everywhere compassionate and Moore's anti-clerical feeling is now either exhausted or firmly under control), nor is it a rigidly devised thesis-novel. The focus of interest throughout is on the interactions in the human mind between philosophy and perception; idea is constantly explored in relation to being. *The Apostle* is to be regretted, though its existence does serve to highlight in a comparison with *The Brook Kerith* the strengths of Moore's responsible artistry. This novel was in some measure gestated for over twenty-seven years as if an instinct prevented Moore from tackling it fully until his technical skill was a true match for the subject.

(iii)

The novel begins with a leisurely prelude describing the childhood of Joseph of Arimathea. Moore is successful here, as later with Héloise's son, Astrolabe, in evoking the quality of an intelligent child's mind: the inquisitive wonder, the exuberance that tends to be selfish and thoughtless, and the comically precocious attempts to assume adult attitudes:

> . . . feeling his mood to be an odd one, [he] fell to thinking that his granny would laugh were she to see him, but unafraid or almost of her laughter he wandered on muttering softly to himself: Women have no sense of the Word of God. . . .[14]

Then there is the child's vanity so easily wounded when a parent is too tired or too busy to engage with his special point of view and the sulking that follows at this supposed injury to his sense of his unique individuality:

> And now, Joseph, my little prophet, 'tis bedtime and past it. Come. I didn't say I wanted to anoint kings, he answered, and

refused to go to bed, though manifestly he could hardly keep awake. I'll wait up for Father. Now what can the child want his father for at this hour? she muttered as she went about the room, not guessing that he was angry and resentful, that her words had wounded him deeply, and that he was asking himself in his corner, if she thought him too stupid to be a prophet. I'll tell thee no more stories, she said to him, but he answered that he did not want to hear her stories and betwixt feelings of anger and shame his head drooped. . . .[15]

Joseph's prattle frequently passes with a naive logic from immediate wants and pleasures to those profounder questions about existence that adults find it so embarrassingly difficult to answer.

But, Master, tell me, he added, is it true that God is going to destroy the world and very soon? Why dost thou ask, Joseph? Azariah replied, and Joseph answered: Because the world is so very beautiful. I never saw the world until today. My eyes are opened, and I shall be sorry if God destroys the world, for I should like to see more of it. But why should he make a beautiful world and then destroy it? Will not God relent when the time comes, if the day be as beautiful as it was this morning?[16]

Joseph innocently argues with his tutor about the nature of evil and intuitively perceives the resolution which it will cost Jesus a lifetime's experience to attain. However, he is ignorant of the significance of his reasoning: it is yet another childish question.

The opening chapters are full of beautifully observed details of family life, its frictions and its deep-rooted affections. Joseph is idolized by both his father, Dan, and his grandmother, but Moore carefully distinguishes between their ways of loving: Dan is stern, watchful but generous; Rachel is at once more expansive physically and intellectually more cunning in advising Joseph over the quickest ways to get what he wants. There is here an accurate precision of detail yet what is evoked is timeless in its truth to human behaviour. This is ordinary living yet such is Moore's narrative skill and accurate rendering that the very ordinariness captivates our interest completely: it becomes special as the reader is compelled to look at daily existence with a fresh perspective. That he should succeed in establishing this response in the reader is necessary to Moore's purpose if he is adequately to define later the nature of Jesus's mystical awareness.

The account of Joseph's development introduces other structural and thematic patterns in the novel. He is motivated entirely by the impulse of the moment; a creature, like all children, of unrestrained instinct:

> He'll roll among the grass and flowers like a young donkey, and then run hither and thither after insects and birds, desiring so many things that he'll know not what he desires, only that he desires.[17]

His innocence is naive, animal-like; it is totally at one with the natural state. Often in such moments of intense exuberance (increasingly so as he grows older) Joseph is visited with a sudden awe and an intuition of a 'presence' in nature beyond the reach of sight, hearing, touch or smell – 'A remote and mysterious life was certainly breathing about him'.[18] Sagely Azariah, his tutor, explains that such experiences often awaken religious emotions in man. The moments are epiphanies accompanied by a sudden and unexpected wonderment, seeming revelations, but they invariably leave Joseph dejected at his inability to understand their intimations: '. . . he regretted he was without a sense to apprehend this life'.[19]

> The lake had always seemed to him a sort of sign, symbol or hieroglyphic, in which he read a warning addressed especially, if not wholly, to himself. But the message the lake held out to him had always eluded him, and never more completely than now.[20]

His first momentous encounter with Jesus occurs one quiet evening by Lake Galilee; when Jesus departs, Joseph is left watching the stars and listening to the sound of the waves and a nightingale:

> Every breath of air brought a new and exquisite scent to him, and through the myrtle bushes he could hear the streams singing their way down to the lake; and when he came to the lake's edge he heard the warble that came into his ear when he was a little child, which it retained always. . . . But suddenly from among the myrtle bushes a song arose. It began with a little phrase of three notes, which the bird repeated, as if to impress the listener and prepare him for the runs and trills and joyous little cadenzas

that were to follow. A sudden shower of jewels it seemed like, and when the last drops had fallen the bird began another song, a continuation of the first, but more voluptuous and intense. . . . Again Joseph heard the warbling water, and it seemed to him that he could hear the stars throbbing. It was one of those moments when the soul of man seems to break, to yearn for that original unity out of which some sad fate has cast it . . . the stars and the stream, the odours afloat upon the stream, the bird's song and the words of Jesus: Whosoever admires the stars and flowers finds God in his heart, seemed to become all blended into one extraordinary harmony; and unable to resist the emotion of the moment any longer, Joseph threw himself upon the ground and prayed that the moment he was living in might not be taken from him, but that it might endure for ever. But while he prayed that moment was passing, and becoming suddenly aware that it had gone, he rose from his knees and returned home mentally weary and sad at heart. . . .[21]

Joseph is immensely perceptive of natural life – the movement of clouds, the line of the hills, the flight patterns of particular birds – and Moore deliberately presents much of the landscape-setting of the novel through Joseph's consciousness, but though Joseph *sees*, he cannot *feel* how beautiful it all is.[22] His epiphanies remain frustrating because they are in his consciousness simply moments isolated in time; their clarity fades in his memory; he cannot explore them through recall and find in them a way of making the joy they intimate to him a permanent condition of his being. He tries at first childishly to rationalise his despair: his failure to understand the silence of the woods as an adolescent, he decides, was because he felt guilty at the time for having escaped doing a school-task he had set himself. Later when such reasoning appears to him trivial and when hard work can no longer alleviate his melancholy, he journeys forth in quest of a teacher, a Messiah, who will enlighten him about how to discover in himself 'an intimate sense of God'.[23] This child is indeed ominously the father of the man. Dan and Rachel's possessive indulgence of Joseph's every whim encourages in him a 'capricious mind' which, though attractive in the child, is with time a moral weakness in the adult: 'he'll not know what he desires only that he desires', Azariah warns prophetically. Joseph cannot focus his mind to examine any experience or idea in depth; though he can reflect he cannot meditate, for he lacks the necessary inner repose.

The attraction of further novelty quickly extinguishes the ardour of each of Joseph's many conversions as he turns from Messiah to Messiah. He dramatizes his growing dissatisfaction with life as a form of demonic possession, but what he calls his fate is his willing subjection to the dictates of his impulses that makes his mind the sport of his feelings. The restless energy, the and-then-and-then-and-then quality of Moore's narrative in these chapters is an exact correlative for Joseph's mental temperament.

Depicting the waywardness of Joseph's mind through a sequence of conflicting religious inspirations in this way allows Moore quickly to sketch in the contemporary background of his novel: Palestine is under Roman rule and her political instability is aggravated by an age-old, decaying national religion riddled with warring sects, each jealously defensive of its temporal powers. Analogies with Victorian orthodoxy are apparent but not stressed. The frank, witty scepticism of a priesthood living on a preserved tradition while mocking its dupes is reminiscent of Browning's Blougram. The cant of the Sadducees echoes that of the High Anglican defence of established religion on moral grounds:

> It was necessary to observe the Sabbath and to preach its observances and to punish those who violated it, for on the Sabbath rested the entire superstructure of the Temple itself, and all belief might topple if the Sabbath was not maintained, and rigorously.[24]

Observance here has only a material value in that it helps to conserve the Sadducees' political and judicial stability. The Pharisees with evangelical fanaticism vaunt their hard-won and conscious sincerity and appear merely narrow-minded bigots. Clerical bickering over the letter as opposed to the spirit of the law has made the Jewish religion too self-conscious and rhetorical to satisfy Joseph's desire for a genuine faith.

Joseph turns from Jerusalem in revulsion to the community of Essene monks in the deserts of Jericho, but even there he faces dissension: on the one hand Hazael, the President of the Order, has a simple piety which informs his whole being: 'His goodness . . . is . . . natural. . . . His power is in himself for he is altogether without philosophy';[25] in marked contrast is Mathias, the Platonist, in whom religion has become limited to a cerebral philosophy based on abstract intellectual symbolism, which only his own verbal and interpretative felicity can make persuasive to others. Faith for Mathias is a moral ideology with God as a state of Ultimate Truth: '. . . our intellect being the highest gift we have received from God, it follows that we shall please him best by using it assiduously'.[26] To Joseph it seems as if he has deliberately restricted his vision because the total illumination would be too blinding. The simplification has robbed Mathias's doctrine of any essential significance; his religion is merely interpretative scholarship:

> He would return to the sage every day, but what if he were not able to remember, if it were all to end in words with nothing behind the words? The sage said that in a little while the discourses would not seem so elusive and evanescent. At present they seemed to Joseph like the mist on the edge of a stream, and he strove against the belief that a philosopher is like a man who sets out to walk after the clouds.[27]

Prophets, miracle-workers and hermits attract but fail to sustain Joseph's dilettante interest. His first encounter with Jesus is memorable because Jesus speaks to him immediately in terms of the inner calm that initially accompanied his epiphanic experiences: 'Whosoever admires the stars and the flowers finds God in his heart and sees Him in his neighbour's face'.[28] But as the heir to Dan's business and wealth and as a man tenderly responsible to his dying father, Joseph fails to live up to the standards Jesus demands of his followers and, to Joseph's great embarrassment, he is publicly turned away from Jesus's community. In recompense Joseph seeks to make a creed out of his very dissatisfaction and self-pity. He has frequently been bewildered by, or scornful of the inhumanity of what passes for religion, but he never has had the initiative to pursue these insights creatively. The assurance with which he began his quest for spiritual knowledge ebbs away through constant questioning into an acceptance finally of a negative philosophy of Heraclitean flux:

> All that is beyond doubt, he continued, is that things pass too quickly for us to have any certain knowledge of them, our only standard being our own flitting impressions; and as all men bring a different sensitiveness into the world, knowledge is a word without meaning, for there can be no knowledge.[29]

The resemblance between Joseph and Pater's Marius here is unmistakable: in both men a scrupulous observance of traditional
pieties cedes to a rejection of metaphysical certainty; both develop
a habit of 'tentative thinking and suspended judgement';[30] with
both this cautious reasoning of experience accompanies yet ener-
vates their quest in life for 'the focus where the greatest number
of vital forces unite'.[31] Moore's account necessarily simplifies, but
he presents through Joseph's character an accurate criticism of the
practical weakness of Pater's theories: Joseph constantly confuses
inner harmony and calm, the real goal of his quest, with sensuous
intensity; he judges all experience even the spiritual in terms of its
power to satisfy him emotionally. Inevitably nothing offers him
certainty on these conditions, so he comes to believe all values are
relative except for the one permanence that is death. It is fitting
that the only decisive action Joseph makes in the novel before his
recovery of Jesus's body from the cross is the carving of his tomb
in the hills beyond the Mount of Olives.

Because he is forever testing experience, Joseph is always a
recording spectator in life, and it is here that Moore's method of
presenting Joseph is so felicitous showing how his whole conception of existence, his ideology, is constitutional; how it is the product of his essential temperament and his mode of perception.
Joseph is the ideal focal consciousness and presenter of the novel
in its early stages: always he is the listener to other people's dis-
course; he speaks usually to question and so stimulate further
debate; statement occurs only in his introspective musing and
then is often tempered by the conditional tense. His judgements of
other characters depend entirely on empathy, which the most
inconsequential perceptions can easily disturb. His descriptions of
landscape and nature have a sensuous immediacy; the perceived
details are evocative and atmospheric but how very different in
quality the perceptions are from those of Jesus who scans the
landscape for signs that indicate suitable pasture for his flock,
hidden springs of water or caves deep enough to shelter him and
his sheep from preying animals at nightfall. The skies and the
movements of clouds and winds give Jesus knowledge of future
weather-conditions and the startled flight of a marsh-bird reveals
to him where Paul lies hidden and swooning. Joseph's perceptions
reveal a consciously poetic sensibility; Jesus's are charged with the
poetry of lived experience. Moore presents virtually the first half

of his narrative through Joseph's consciousness and the reader's interest is sustained by both the narrative content and what the manner of relating the material reveals about the narrator. In responding to the subtle implications of the prose style the reader shares Joseph's mode of perception and through it apprehends his character, his inner private self, and so discovers why he is incapable of growth. The style is the index of the man.

Making Joseph the first focus in the novel is a device that with great economy achieves several ends. The reader finds in him a credible portrait of a sensitive agnostic in whom there is an impulse to piety and mysticism but who lacks the mental and emotional stamina to realise these potentials actively; as such Joseph provides a good measure by which the reader can assess Christ's dynamic capacity for spiritual growth which makes his philosophy Moore's ideal. As it is with the philosophical and psychological meanings of his narrative that Moore wishes the reader to be engaged, there is every need to avoid sensational incidents or writing, though this is difficult given the dramatic events in Christ's life and the fact that Moore himself to serve his thematic purpose wishes radically to depart from the familiar Gospel story and suggest that Christ was not dead but in a severe coma when taken from the cross by Joseph and that the resurrection was a process of psychic healing. To have presented Christ's life from the standpoint of his own consciousness would doubtless have proved offensive to many readers and would have been an impossible imaginative feat to sustain; instead Moore wisely assumes the reader's familiarity with the details of Christ's baptism, ministry and crucifixion and concentrates on the effect of these events on Joseph's life and quest. The known facts of Jesus's life have to be rehearsed as a base for Moore's subsequent analysis; treated in this way they are covered rapidly but with a fresh emphasis in the new perspective that does not minimize their impact. Spectacular scenes in the Sanhedrin, Pilate's court and on Calvary are deliberately eschewed (the handling of the 'big' scene is not one of Moore's strengths as a novelist); but episodes like the crucifixion[32] are imagined and realised with a brilliant succinctness: Joseph, fully aware of the hatred of the Temple for Jesus and conscious of the danger of his mission, arrives to demand Christ's body and instantly engages in earnest conversation with the centurion to prevent himself looking at Jesus since if he were to do so he could not restrain an overwhelming

flow of horror, shock and pity which would frustrate his objective
and imperil his own life at the hands of the ever-watchful zealots.
The political pressures behind the crucifixion and its physical
horror are registered but all in terms of Joseph's need to preserve
a tight emotional control to achieve his humane intention. The
event fittingly impresses the reader as momentous but the account
is handled in a manner that does not disrupt the unity of theme,
method of presentation and tone. Only in retrospect is Jesus's
consciousness explored in relation to his ministry and persecution
through the meditations that accompany his psychological resurrection, at which point his mind has taken over from Joseph's as
the focus of the narrative. Moore's control both of his material in
relation to his theme and of the reader's response is confident, inventive and exact.

Jesus from his youth has been taught by Hazael's mysticism to
apprehend in Creation the presence of God as creative energy:

> . . . the law over the rock that crumbles into sand and the sand
> that is built up into rock again, was in that rock before Abraham
> was, and will abide in it and in the flower that grows under the
> rock till time everlasting.[33]

He has developed this apprehension into a statement of faith; to
cherish all things living as an expression of one's love of God is
the philosophy with which he attacks the meaningless blood-
sacrifices of the Temple: 'God hath no need of temples in Paradise
nor has he need of any temple except the human heart wherein he
dwells'.[34]

This is the substance of Jesus's preaching and the motive for his
healing; and on such doctrine of faith as love he seeks to establish
the Christian community in Galilee. To do this he invites his disciples to abandon their self-centred attitudes; but the altruism and
equality which he wishes to inculcate through his parables describing the new Kingdom of God are difficult to realise in practice, and
Jesus suffers the fate of many socialist teachers who nobly judge
human nature in general to be as high-principled as their own.
Once again there is conflict between the spirit and the letter of his
counsel. The moral significance that underlies the parables is
ignored by the disciples, who cannot resist the very human temptation to imagine themselves as the select aristocracy of the future
enlightenment: 'By what right are the saints of the Most High

coming here to ask for a share of this world, as if they hadn't a heaven to live in'.[35] Acting on a literal interpretation of his allegories, they squabble over matters of precedence and the distribution of power in the new kingdom, and, when invited by Jesus to meditate on God in creation, they indulge in visionary fantasies with a view to raising themselves in his opinion:

> As if dissatisfied with these answers, he looked into their faces, as if he would read their souls, and asked them to look up through the tree tops and tell him what they could see in a certain space of sky . . . John . . . said that he could see a chariot drawn by seven beasts, each having on its forehead seven horns; the jaws of these beasts, he averred, were like those of monkeys, and in their paws, he said, were fourteen golden candlesticks. Andrew, being misled by the colour of the cloud which was yellow, said that the seven beasts were like leopards. . . .[36]

Even Joseph's more sympathetic understanding of Jesus's aim is not free of intellectual snobbery:

> The conviction was always quick in him that he felt more deeply than these publicans and fishers, yet Jesus retained them and sent him away.[37]

The community is being wrecked on the shoals of materialism and self-interest even before its establishment: 'the hardness of heart and narrowness of soul that he encountered among his own people afflicted Jesus'.[38] For all his breadth of vision, he lacks imaginative sympathy and a true awareness of human nature; his idealism is wanting in that other tendency of charity which is compassion.

Overpowered by this awareness of evil in man, Jesus begins to fight his growing despair by asserting the purity of his ideals with an increasing force. He succumbs to that most terrible of temptations: the moral urge to establish order in life, which is unconsciously an ambitious desire to vindicate himself as the perfect realisation of that order. To submit is to fall through one's own strength and do the right deed for the wrong reason. Like an Old-Testament prophet, Jesus comes to equate love of God with a righteous scorn for this world. Human and material affections he chastises with malignant hate:

> . . . this world and the world to come were not one thing but twain. And whosoever chooses this world must remain satisfied

with its fleshly indulgences and its cares and its laws and responsibilities, and whosoever chooses the Kingdom of Heaven must
cast this world far from him, must pluck it, as it were, out of his
heart and throw it away, bidding it depart; for it is but a ghost.[39]

His first exhortations that 'if we would love God, we must abandon
father, mother, wife and children, for there is not room in our
hearts for two loves'[40] have hardened through opposition: 'to love
God a man must learn to hate his father'.[41] What began as a warning not to allow human affection to become idolatrous and as such
a rival to worship has changed to a commandment to scorn all
ties and responsibilities to material existence: not to give everything is as if to give nothing, for this world is but ashes. Through
a tragic loss of perspective, Jesus has come to enforce the literal
meaning of his doctrine and robbed it of its comprehensive humane
relevance; the poetry has given way to harsh abstractions.

Hatred of the manifest human evil that taints the blessedness
that is purity of heart drives Jesus to preach destruction in the
name of love. The Temple's corrupt authority must be destroyed,
but his ideal religion of the heart, as experience has taught him,
would not be free of similar contamination:

> . . . with a concentrated hate he spoke of the Temple as a resort
> of thieves and of the priests as the despoilers of widows and
> orphans, saying that the law must be abrogated and the Temple
> destroyed. . . . the one-time reformer sees clearly that the Temple
> must go . . . he was uncertain if the old foundations could be
> used. The old spirits of lust, and blood, and money would haunt
> the walls, and as fast as we raised up a new Temple the spirits
> would pull it down and rebuild it as it was before. We are for-
> bidden by the law of Moses to create any graven image. . . .
> Would that Moses had added: Build no walls, for as soon as
> there are walls priests will enter in and set themselves upon
> thrones. The priests have taken the place of God. . . .[42]

With visionary power, he wills chaos to come again and the natural
order to cease, that in the purging fire he may create and perfect
his ideal:

> All the world as ye know it must be burnt up like stubble, for
> a new world to rise up in its place. In the beginning I spoke
> sweet words of peace, and they were of no avail to stay the sins

that were committed in every house: so now I speak no more sweet words to anybody, but words that shall divide father from son, and mother from daughter, and wife from husband. There is no other way to cure the evil. What say I, he cried, cure! There is none. The evil must be cut down and thrown upon the fire, and whosoever would be saved from the fire must follow me. . . . I am the word, the truth, and the life. . . . Yes, he cried, we are nearing the springtime when life shall begin again in the world. But I say to thee that this springtime shall never come to pass. Never again shall the fig ripen on the wall and the wheat be cut down in the fields.[43]

But the people confuse his New Jerusalem with the coming of the Soldier-Messiah; divine intervention, they believe, is to establish the Jews in political authority. Again the figurative and moral Utopia is perverted to a gross material counterpart and the contradiction calls forth all Jesus's powers of self-assertion. Generating the fury is a terrible despair at the sheer power of rhetoric to force him into a line of action that is the very antithesis of his imagined ideal. Mathias's religion of the intellect had seemed to Joseph nothing but words; so Jesus's imaginative ideals are gradually emptied of any felt knowledge of the heart. The conflict between his imagination and the restricting power of rhetoric has contracted his consciousness to the point of spiritual death:

> He speaks with a strange, bitter energy, like one that has lost control of his words; he is hardly aware of them, nor does he retain any memory of them. They are as the wind, rising we know not why, and going its way unbidden.[44]

The change in his soul has its physical counterpart; to Joseph, Jesus now seems deformed, 'like a diseased panther'. His own words finally betray him to death, for the misrepresentation of his doctrine by the disciples invites political intervention from the Sanhedrin and Pilate.

> But when Jesus was crucified
> Then was perfected His galling pride.[45]

Moore's unidealized portrait of Joseph's family life at the opening of the novel provides the reader with material against which to test Jesus's criticism of human responsibilities. The opposition as offered is not a simple one. Joseph's upbringing has in part determined the weaknesses of his character; he has suffered and is suffering as a consequence of his father's ambitions for his future. Dan's affection is jealous and makes unnecessary demands on Joseph. But Joseph has a deep respect for Dan; it is one of the few enduring pieties of his life. The episodes where Joseph observes Jesus's ministry alternate with constant visits to his ageing father whom he nurses through a seizure with tender solicitude. That Dan responds to such generosity by exacting Joseph's promise not to become one of Jesus's disciples is cruel but understandable, knowing as we do how urgently as he approaches death he wishes to see Joseph married and settled in the family business and how sincerely he wishes he could ease the spiritual anguish he recognises in his son. The reader's sympathy ebbs and flows as Dan's motives, now selfish, now altruistic, influence his expressions of love. Jesus's ideas are perceptive of a certain truth but in seeking to eradicate men's selfishness he would stifle their sincere impulses too and so destroy their capacity to discriminate. Joseph is numbed with shock when, after tending his father, he is publicly cast out by Jesus from the Christian community and accused of betraying the divine cause for petty human considerations. Joseph has renounced much to comfort his father, and willingly so; irrespective of whether or not Dan has the right to be so exacting, Joseph's action cannot be dismissed as petty. Joseph's absence and return to the community enables Moore skilfully and rapidly to achieve radical developments in Jesus's character and to communicate the enormity of his new puritanical zeal in terms of the bewilderment of his followers. Joseph is horrified at his dismissal but with characteristic generosity he refuses to forget the persuasive initial impact of Jesus's mysticism and as the political crisis approaches can feel nothing but pity for the way Jesus has become the victim of circumstance. And Joseph controls the reader's response for he can discriminate: though his acute critical faculties, as we have seen, have fostered his inner restlessness they have their positive attributes too. Idea and experience, philosophy and temperament are sustained by Moore scrupulously in a state of fruitful tension to give the inner debate of the novel a provocative energy.

Moore's portrayal of Jesus bears a marked resemblance at first to Wagner's conception of Christ:

When I considered the epoch and the general life-conditions in which so loving and so love-athirst a soul, as that of Jesus, unfolded itself, nothing seemed to me more natural than that this *solitary* One – who, fronted with a materialism so honourless, so hollow and so pitiful as that of the Roman world and still more of the world subjected to the Romans, could not demolish it and build upon its wrack an order answering to his soul's desire; should straight way long from out of that world, from out that wider world at large, towards a better land Beyond – toward Death.[46]

But with that final evaluative statement Moore parts company with Wagner, for to Moore it is Jesus's dream 'of the world redeemed from the powers of evil and given over to the love of God' that brings him to the point of insane delirium.[47] As Pilate remarks to Joseph of the Jews in general and so ironically of Jesus's career: always 'your love of God resolves itself into hatred of men'.[48] Accepting the truth of this and that it leads to spiritual death is the first stage of Jesus's resurrection.

Taken down prematurely from the cross, Jesus is found by Joseph to be in a seemingly lifeless coma: as the Roman soldier remarks, 'Those that haven't been on the cross more than two days are brought back frequently, but the third day ends them'.[49] Again Joseph becomes the patient nurse; helped by his old cook, Esora, he heals the torn limbs and painstakingly restores Jesus's consciousness to sanity – an act of profound courage in view of the political danger to himself that gives the lie to Jesus's former teaching as Jesus now learns what it is to be utterly dependent on others' humanity and solicitude and discovers he has a life and identity others believe unquestioningly to be worth saving. He is returned secretly by Joseph to the Essene cenoby which he left to begin his ministry and again becomes their shepherd. The experience of death and the slow painstaking recovery make his appreciation of the fact of living the more acute. The *sensed* rhythm of the blood-pulse affects a wondering interest in nature, which keeps Jesus's mind centred on immediate actuality and prevents for a time the intrusion of painful memories of the past which might tend to madness. The familiar is seen with a new astonishing clarity and the precise individuality of things is what most impresses; to *discriminate* becomes for Jesus a new joy; and this is an apposite development of what is one of the most moving features of the Gospels, namely Jesus's poetic use in his parables of natural, human even mundane facts drawn from his immediate rural situation to show how, as Moore similarly believes, the visible world is sacred.

The pattern of the convalescence is the same as with Gogarty and Evelyn Innes, but the central incident here (Jesus in quest of a ram for his depleted flock protects and cherishes the life of a stray lamb, inventing ways of feeding it with milk till it is strong enough for him to carry back to the fold) is a felicitous redeployment of what is perhaps the most representative parable of the Christian faith, though Moore does not force the analogy on the reader. The incident could easily encourage a sentimental treatment but Moore concentrates the reader's attention throughout on the precise physical details of Jesus's husbandry and allows the placing of the story in the total narrative to make the reader aware of its psychological implications. Once again style and narrative method are rendering the state of mind. Jesus is now the focal consciousness of the novel and all his consciousness at this stage of his recovery is centred on physical activity which is partly a delight in his own renewed strength and partly the means whereby his psyche gains stamina to begin the process of recall. His memory is entirely preoccupied with rediscovering the techniques of his craft. Only in retrospect will Jesus appreciate the value of this period in his return to sanity.

Jesus's growing sympathy that this episode with the young ram illustrates is matched by new attitudes: 'No man . . . is wise but he who would learn, and none is foolish but he who would teach'.[50] On such humility he founds a new personal creed; it is his understanding of the motive for Joseph's care and the truth of his own feeling for life, born of an unconscious will to survive, that give him eventually the strength to face up to the reality of his former evil and confidently judge that moral failure in the light of his present experience. Only through suffering and in the face of death has he learnt to value life; and, as for Job, this becomes his new magnificat: 'Blessed be the Lord, because He chastizeth me'.

Jesus had spoken to Joseph in Galilee of the God that is in nature; having experienced the resurgence of life in his own consciousness he can return to his original mysticism with a conviction supported by all his faculties:

. . . to see and hear God, we have only to open our eyes and ears. God is always about us. We hear him in the breeze, and we find

him in the flower . . . he had come to comprehend that the world
of nature was a manifestation of the God he knew in himself.[51]

The world was right to defend itself against him who would destroy
it, for if every created thing is God, then to despise the world is
an act of blasphemy. Desire to attain Paradise is a more dangerous
form of covetousness than material greed:

> . . . we must despise nothing, for all things come from him, and
> return to him. I used, he said, to despise the air I breathed, and
> long for the airs of paradise, but what did these longings bring
> me? – grief. God bade us live on earth and we bring unhappiness
> upon ourselves by desiring heaven.[52]

God is infinite, beyond definition; and the symbols under which
he is worshipped as religion all too easily become images of the
gratified wishes of the celebrants:

> Rites and observances, all that comes under the name of
> religion, estranges us from God. . . . but shall we gather the
> universal will into an image and call it God? – for by doing this
> do we not drift back to the starting-point of all our misery?
> We again become the dupes of illusion and desire. . . .[53]

Such a god is a figment of the human mind and man's moral
enemy. His desire for spiritual satisfaction in Paradise was essentially scorn for his human condition: 'He who would escape from
God flees from himself'.[54] His sin 'was not to have loved men
enough'.[55]

Unlike Adam, Jesus does not seek to hide from the knowledge
of his own evil; by constant meditation on it in the light of his
new-found energy he comes to deduce from it a personal faith:
not our intelligence, as Mathias would argue, but our capacity to
become aware of the distinction of good and evil which is the
acquisition of conscience is 'a token of our divine nature'. With
this recognition comes mental harmony and an awareness that
such total self-knowledge is its own guard against repeated moral
failure:

> But I cannot fear God, for I love God, he said; my God neither
> forgives nor punishes, and if we repent it should be for our own
> sakes and not please God. Moreover, it must be well not to

waste too much time in repentance, for it is surely better to understand than to repent. We learn through our sins.[56]

Properly and fully to apprehend the instinct for life, he decides, is to acquire the finest gauge of moral conduct. It is to find joy in being, but a joy different in kind from Joseph's childhood innocence because it encompasses a careful enhancing respect for the integrity of other life.

This theme is presented first in Jesus's mastery of his craft as a shepherd, his recall of its traditional lore and the recovery of his expertise and later in his training of the shepherd-boy, Jacob, to be his successor with the cenoby's flock after Jacob had been dismissed by the local shepherd community for foolhardiness, which Jesus appreciates was occasioned not by the lad's stupidity but by his over-zealous ambition to succeed. Jesus's insight and trust restore Jacob's lost faith in himself. The evolving idea is matched always with a new pattern of behaviour. Jesus's attitude now is not simply one of passive contentment; in old age he confesses his past life on impulse to Hazael and the very terms of his self-condemnation here show a new compassionate understanding of the nature of responsibility:

> But my passion was so great in those days that I did not see that my teaching was not less than blasphemy against God, for God has created the world for us to live in it, and he has put love of parents into our hearts because he wishes us to love our parents, and if he has put into the heart of man love of woman, and into the heart of woman love of man, it is because he wishes both to enjoy that love. . . . I strayed beyond myself and lost myself in the love of God, a thing a man may do if he love not his fellows.[57]

As we see from Jesus's shrewd and humorous insight into young Jacob and his silent reverence for his old mentor, Hazael, his love is wholly free of bias or selfish intent. It is perhaps unfortunate that Moore chose not to give more extensive treatment to these two ideal father-son relationships to counterbalance the earlier scenes between Joseph and Dan; instead he offsets Jesus's self-knowledge and piety against a wholly different kind of religious sensibility by confronting him with St Paul *en route* in his missionary travels to Rome.

Paul is a parody of Jesus's former self, in both motive and deed, the more vicious in that the pride is here consciously assumed: 'there did not seem to be on earth a true Christian but myself'.[58] To free himself from his fear of his own powerful impulses and from his overwhelming sense of guilt in merely living, Paul has to believe in a miraculous divine intervention in human affairs. He believes in the miracle of the resurrection because it allows him to set his heart so irretrievably on the promise of an eternity that this life no longer holds material temptations for him: 'Freed from the bondage of the law and concupiscence by grace we are saved through faith in our Lord Jesus Christ from damnation'.[59] (The ecclesiastical tone and phrasing are, as we shall see, deliberate.) Paul can gain control over himself only by believing in grace as the special and scrupulous concern of the Almighty for him individually. When Jesus finds him in a deep swoon on the hillside Paul refuses to accept Jesus's explanation that he was drawn to the spot when his attention was aroused by a bird that 'turned aside abruptly from the rock on which he was about to alight';[60] he prefers to think Jesus was directed thither by an angel. There is no poetry for Paul as there is for Jesus in the reality that is nature. Again it is characteristic of the man that when he is asked by the Essenes to state his doctrine he chooses rather to give them an account of his own good works, all the sacrifices of the flesh which his confident spirit has allowed him to exercise and all his miraculous escapades which must prove he is one of God's elect since the moment of his revelation on the road to Damascus. In a very witty adaptation here of the method of the novel, Paul's story *is* the man; but like all adventure narratives, though it is initially gripping, it becomes monotonous in tone and thin in texture. Cumulatively Paul's tale is shrill in its self-assertiveness: 'My work is my conscience made manifest'.[61] Lacking allusion, density of insight and range of observation beside Moore's presentation of Joseph's or Jesus's consciousness, Paul's very tale exposes the limitations of his understanding of conscience in man. Paul's theories of predestination anger Jesus to whom it seems unworthy to love virtue in hope of heaven rather than for its own sake. Paul has no real love for his fellow men as individuals as is evident in his wish to mould others in his own image by 'saving' them through his doctrines.

Challenged with Jesus's presence, Paul retreats behind his

paradoxes:

> Thou'rt Jesus of Nazareth, I deny it not, but the Jesus of
> Nazareth that I preach is of the spirit and not of the flesh, and
> it was the spirit and not the flesh that was raised from the
> dead . . . my Christ is not of this world.[62]

Jesus senses that if he were to try to persuade Paul otherwise, that
the miracle of the resurrection was different from his conception,
'his mind would snap', since 'he is rapt . . . in the Jesus of his
imagination'.[63] Without that image however illusory as Paul freely
acknowledges 'I should turn to the pleasures of this world'.[64]
Beside Jesus, Paul's 'goodness' is only relative; he cannot come to
terms with his own fear of death or his capacity for evil. He is
determined to preserve his belief as infallible, whatever the cost in
personal suffering; the tone of his speech exactly reflects his psychological condition; for Moore, Paul is literally and figuratively
bound for Rome. He is trapped within the circle of his own mind;
his passion for metaphysical certainty abrogates all imaginative
sympathy. Paul cannot appreciate Jesus's fearless compassion that
is so totally without bias:

> Paul, it is better to love the good than to hate the wicked. . . .
> if we would arrive at any reasonable conception of God, we
> must not put a stint upon him. And as I wandered with my sheep
> he became in my senses not without but within the universe, part
> and parcel, not only of the stars and the earth but of me, yea,
> even of my sheep on the hillside. All things are God, Paul: thou
> art God and I am God, but if I were to say thou art man and I
> am God, I should be the madman that thou believest me to
> be. . . . God did not design us to know him but through our
> consciousness of good and evil, only thus far may we know
> him. . . . But seek not to understand me. Thou canst not under-
> stand me and be thyself; but, Paul, I can comprehend thee, for
> once I was thou.[65]

The novel ends significantly with Paul travelling westwards and
Jesus to the East.

Moore's own term for the style of *The Brook Kerith*, 'melodic
narrative' is in some ways misleading. Some critics have seen it as
inviting montony, 'melodic' implying to them evenness of tone and
a lack of texture. Neither judgement is true to a careful reading of

the novel. As with Virginia Woolf's *The Waves*, there is a certain uniformity that impresses one at first, the better to concentrate one's attention on subtlety of technique. With Mrs Woolf's novel one observes the slow development and maturing of the idiosyncratic patterns of imagery which evoke rather than define the intimate, private selves of each of her six characters; with *The Brook Kerith* one attends as we have seen to styles of narrative and above all to the rhythms of the prose. A particular strength of *The Lake* lies in the way in a subjectively orientated novel a range of minor characters are firmly established with an independent 'voice' and identity within the predominant rhythm of Gogarty's self-communing: Catherine, his curious and wily housekeeper; Gogarty's two sisters, the practical Eliza, whose brusque efficiency is redeemed from coldness by her sense of humour and her genuine affection for her brother, and, in sharp contrast, the peevish, quixotic and self-centred Mary; and the guilt-stricken curate, Moran, ever-depressed and ever-depressing. Each lives in the reader's imagination as in Gogarty's memory because each has an idiosyncratic rhythm of speech which exactly captures his personality. Powerful dialogue has been a recurrent feature of Moore's work. With consummate technical assurance in *The Brook Kerith* Moore modulates the rhythms from the internal ruminative voices of Joseph or Jesus to characterize through speech the wealth of figures who impinge on their consciousness. Many are little more than vignettes but, however brief the portrait, the personality is realised with clarity. The range is impressive: various styles of preaching from the starkly prophetic to the neo-platonic; the members of particular communities – Jesus's disciples, his shepherd-companions, the monks in the Essene cenoby; two contrasting types of well-intentioned elderly nurses – the indulgent Rachel and the garrulous but methodical Esora, whose flow of chatter is virtually meaningless but of a tone to inspire patience and confidence in the invalid whom she tends; the Roman centurion, an old soldier with a keen eye for a bribe; and Pilate, sceptical, aloof and with a patrician indifference, who suddenly warms to Joseph when he recognises an intellect he can respect. In a novel so concerned with the sanctity of the individual life and with the need for imaginative sympathy the technique is a particularly apt complement to the theme. It is therefore noticeable and equally apt in contrast with the main narrative how lacking in such marks of distinction are the characters in Paul's account of his life; even figures like Timothy or Barnabas, his close friends, do not live in the reader's memory as more than names. Since he has no interest in common humanity, Paul's adventures in the telling are quite devoid of tension for the reader; the narrative is here deliberately cold, even rather repellent, to reflect a criticism of the teller.

There is subtle variety of tone and pace too within the overall pervading atmosphere of inner contemplation and discovery recording the fluctuating of Joseph and Jesus's moods under the impact of external circumstances. The last hundred pages or so of the novel afford a good example here. Jesus has returned to the cenoby; his appearance is welcomed by the aged Hazael; they sit contented together sharing memories of Jesus's youth but Christ's calm is disturbed by a growing impulse to tell Hazael of his ministry and crucifixion, which is given an external correlative in the mounting tension and excitement that accompany Paul's arrival. Paul's strident narrative follows and this convinces Jesus he must speak of his past. Paul's self-centred story gives place to Jesus's quiet but firm confession to Hazael, where the tone is humble but in no way 'umble (a difficult imaginative feat to sustain), for accepting his past has brought Jesus spiritual gains that make abasement and shame utterly pointless. The clear, frank tone, the lucid exposition, the measured rhythm beautifully substantiate the truth of Jesus's new philosophy: the voice speaks out of a unified and harmonious sensibility. Finally Jesus guides Paul over the hills to Caesarea; Paul is deeply disturbed by the encounter and his talk is by turns resentful and petty or just superficial chatter to avoid serious debate. Jesus is quiet, understanding, concerned only for their safety on the journey. His care calms Paul and Jesus, seeing Paul's complete dependence on his created philosophy, resists the temptation to assert his own identity and awareness for that would totally destroy Paul. Paul's recovery of his equilibrium is the measure of Jesus's compassion and sympathy. Tone and prose rhythm work always to transform narrative into an evocation, a correlative, of a mental state.

The technical excellences in *The Brook Kerith* are many. There is the skill with which the depicting of a historical subject is invested with both a semblance of authenticity (Moore researched the background carefully with Dujardin's help and journeyed through Palestine to achieve an accurate verisimilitude) and a time-less relevance: first-century Judea is a credible barbaric world but not an alien one as its inhabitants struggle through political upheaval in quest of private and social values. Moreover the con-temporaneity of the inner debate within the novel about the permanence of values is never insisted upon to the point where the argument becomes doctrinaire or the pattern of incidents alle-gorical. A meticulous balance is sustained. There is the deft hand-ling of plot as we have seen and the reworking of the familiar Gospel story from fresh perspectives with a thoroughgoing psy-chological plausibility. And Moore sets himself the further problem of telling that story three times over by Joseph, Paul and finally Jesus and must maintain the reader's interest on each occasion by devising a different motive and mood for the retelling. What impresses is that this technical assurance in the handling of dia-logue, pace, tone, description, plotting is in no way flamboyant but is everywhere subdued to the demands of Moore's psychological purpose. External facts and events are important only in the resonances they activate in the psyches of the three major characters. The greatest technical achievement of the novel is its disciplining of traditional skills to create a wholly new kind of narrative art which demands that Moore's own presence as author must not be consciously felt by the reader since the narrating voice is to be held here to be the voice of consciousness in Joseph, Jesus and Paul by turns. Different narrative styles are symbolic of differ-ent modes of perception and different states of being. Stylistically this is Moore's most original attempt at a stream-of-consciousness technique and it is a fine vehicle for exploring his moral contention that 'for the whole man to think the whole man must live'.[66]

The Brook Kerith is basically an analysis of contrasting types of religious experience: agnosticism, degrees of orthodoxy, forms of conscious and unconscious hypocrisy, all of which are evaluated against the yardstick of Jesus's developing and flexible humanism. While Joseph and Paul are perhaps only half-truths of their proto-types (like Moore's account of Pater's agnosticism in Joseph, Paul's doctrine is a simplification of his biblical counterpart's) they offer accurate observations of the dangers that can and do beset prac-tical attempts to live their respective creeds. Jesus's development also amplifies the central argument concerning the spirit and the letter of faith and completes in Moore's thinking a redefinition of

religion that began with the characterization of Alice Barton and
Esther Waters. There are statements in the Gospels which it is
difficult to interpret and to relate to a religion of love; in the darker
periods of the Church's history they have been dogmatically insisted upon even to the point of death; all too frequently, and this
is the significance of the meeting between Jesus and Paul, an
enthusiastic orthodoxy misses the essential spirit of Jesus's teaching, the compassion and the humility. Jesus's character has thus
symbolic relevance: the significance of his career is analogous to
the progress of Bunyan's Christian. Moore is engaged in the novel
on a quest for the Christ of the Gospels, as distinct from the imita-
tive but inferior creeds practised in His name. Both aspects of Jesus's
development can be closely related to the Gospels, particularly St
Matthew's, in dialogue and incident. If Moore has simplified, he
has done so with a deliberate moral purpose: to explore through
its educative effect on character why man needs to have faith and
why he needs to find a faith that informs his whole being.

In saying, as did Pilate, behold the man, Moore discovered all
the intricate refinement of mind and yet the simplicity and compassion of the preacher of the Sermon on the Mount, a completely
religious Jesus and a man wholly divine. This presentation of Jesus
bears an obvious resemblance to the work of Hennell and Strauss.[67]
Moore, however, explores the implications of their exegesis in
terms of personality, comparing and evaluating the resulting statement of faith with contemporary forms of belief and disbelief. He
is not concerned with theoretical distinctions, rather his is throughout the novelist's interest in the effect of particular personal beliefs
on human response and character; his subject is the creative possibilities of moral awareness. Whether Moore ultimately came to
accept Christ as God Incarnate is an open question; there could be
no finer summary of Moore's belief than John Stuart Mill's definition of the Religion of Humanity:

> Religion cannot be said to have made a bad choice in pitching
> on this man as the ideal representative and guide of
> humanity. . . . it remains a possibility that Christ actually was
> what he supposed himself to be – not God, . . . but a man charged
> with a special, express and unique commission from God to lead
> mankind to truth and virtue.[68]

(iv)

Moore's two remaining novels may be dealt with briefly. The success of *The Brook Kerith* lies in the completeness of the integration of the thematic debate with both the historical subject-matter and the character-studies of types of religious temperament. *Héloïse and Abélard*, however, has a disparity between surface action and inner purpose which is felt almost throughout. Fine though many parts of the novel are (the kaleidoscope of medieval France has that vital, *lived* quality that Moore brings to all his descriptive historical recreations) it lacks a properly worked out central argument to give coherence and tension: it is obviously the work of an ageing man, garrulous, diffuse. Much of the power of *The Brook Kerith* came from the liberties Moore took in the interests of his psychological explorations with a story well-known to the reader; though Héloïse and Abélard are familiar enough names to most readers as tragic lovers, their story is not widely known in its details; ironically Moore seemed less willing as a result to play variations on historical fact. Their story moreover does not readily admit moments of pause for reflexion through which Moore could disclose the private consciousness of each of his main characters, until its very late stages when the lovers are separated and Héloïse, now in a convent, awaits Abélard's return and with the loss of her child has no comfort but her memories of her youth and of Abélard's passion. Evoking character through particular processes of memory like this shows Moore's method and style at their best and one is left wondering why more of the novel was not presented as retrospective contemplation as in *The Brook Kerith*. Abélard in particular remains a shadowy figure because Moore devises few moments that allow him to characterize the philosopher through the idiosyncratic play of his mind in the process of recall.

To have designed a structure which offered the contrasted retelling of their past from each lover's point of view would have taxed Moore's power of invention (it would have required a careful distinguishing between male and female sexual consciousness, though that is within the scope of his abilities), but the different perspectives would have made it easier for Moore to develop a thematic debate which would give his narrative a much needed density of implication. Beside *The Brook Kerith, Héloïse and Abélard* lacks texture. Despite its many refinements Moore's narrative technique in these last three novels is so close by derivation to that of the story-teller that without the degree of control he exercised in *The Brook Kerith* it runs the danger of reverting to its original. Something akin to this happens in the first half of *Héloïse and Abélard* when Moore tries to sustain an interest in four main characters, the lovers, Canon Fulbert, Héloïse's uncle, and his housekeeper, Madelon. Had he wished to imitate the structure of *The Brook Kerith* exactly, the whole of this section could plausibly have been rendered from Fulbert's point of view but it may be that Moore wished to test how adaptable his new fictional manner was (he was always unwilling to repeat a proven formula) and see whether he could sustain interest in four quite distinct temperaments and modes of perception simultaneously in relation to a shared sequence of events. This was a logical step to take but in practice no one character's consciousness is dwelt in long enough by author and reader to be apprehended with any fullness or subtlety. The idea would only work if the narrative were deliberately fractured into short self-contained units, each recording a particular viewpoint as in Virginia Woolf's *The Years* or Faulkner's *As I Lay Dying*; such a technique of fragmentation would run counter of course to Moore's desire for an overall melodic flow. Moore hovers on the brink of a technical innovation yet is apprehensive about accepting the consequences. *Héloïse and Abélard* is disappointing at least in its opening sections because it is full of exciting technical and thematic possibilities that are suggested but left undeveloped.

Abélard teaches that 'the two poles of man's moral existence . . . are faith and reason . . . both are equal'.[69] Later, he applies the same terms to his love for Héloïse, but the transition is unsupported by any marked readjustment of values; although much play is made with the words throughout, they never achieve precise definition in terms of character-development and character-contrasts as the word 'faith' does in *The Brook Kerith*.

Moore's chief difficulty in portraying the tragic relationship was to suggest adequate reasons for its failure. Writing to Eglinton about his later works, he stated that in his view a man's ambition and idealism become evil if he attempts to project them on to another.[70] *Evelyn Innes, The Lake* and *The Brook Kerith* all develop this theme in some degree. It would appear that in *Héloïse and Abélard* Moore is attempting to analyse what Yeats called the 'spider's eye' of love:

> Maybe the bride-bed brings despair
> For each an imagined image brings
> And finds a real image there.[71]

Being a woman. Héloïse has no possible means of achieving any of the ambitions generated by her unique intellectual abilities, and so she seeks to sublimate them in planning and working for Abélard's renown. She makes his fame a condition of her love; she must be his partner in a high enterprise: 'I would prefer thee to be great for then I could watch and rejoice in thy triumphs. Thou art my triumph'.[72] She has shaped her passion 'to an idea that the man must be glorious for a woman to love him'.[73] But advancement is in their world possible only through the Church and a religion, for which she frankly admits having little interest or respect. Orthodoxy, she argues, enforces canons of behaviour, ostensibly for man's spiritual well-being, but in reality to bolster the Church's temporal authority. Her reading of classical literature has encouraged in her a different outlook, a 'sympathy with our life in this world'.[72]

> It was Virgil who opened her eyes and gave her sight to see the world. . . . If it had not been for Virgil, I should . . . have seen the world only in relics of the saints . . . greater than the gift of vision was Virgil's revelation of human love, love of woman for man and man for woman . . . the physical side of our nature was known to me in the convent, but of the spiritual I apprehended nothing.[74]

Within the context of Moore's whole thinking at this time, his idiosyncratic use of 'physical' and 'spiritual' is capable of explanation but, as with his play on the other antithesis of 'reason' and 'faith', the use is not here immediately self-justifying. Even accepting that love, as spiritual, means for Héloïse a total experience, the 'singing string', as she calls it, in a woman's life, this still poses difficulties of interpretation.

Héloïse finds fullness of experience with Abélard, whose troubadour songs relate their passion to the natural cycle. Later, when she is pregnant and they are journeying together to Brittany, Héloïse admits that her ambitions for Abélard's success in the Church were delusions in contrast with her fecund joy:

> It was for moments like these that we met, . . . it is for our love that we live, but it's only now that I begin to know love, for in the beginning, Abélard, I was not true to thee nor to myself. It was not thy manhood that I loved, but thy genius. Thy genius exalted me, compelled me, to throw myself at thy feet, but that was not love but vanity. Abélard, I would tell thee all things. I would have thee know me as God knows me; but words are vain. . . I would have thee love the woman that I am. . . . But now I would cast the learned girl out of myself and I would cast the philosopher out of thee, leaving naught but the woman and the man for each to love the other through eternity. . . . I am not dreaming, Abélard, I am feeling; and in this moment I am consonant with the tree above me and the stars above the tree; I am amid the roots of the hills.[75]

Incidents of this kind during a journey through carefully detailed landscape invariably in the later novels lead to a significant moral decision. Héloïse, however, on reaching Brittany quite rejects her new instinctive awareness of completeness and harmony and returns to her ambitious demands for Abélard's future, yet Moore offers no adequate reason for her change of heart. The contradictory elements in her personality are presented fully but Moore never pin-points the precise motive on which the duality and self-betrayal rests. The characterization lacks clarity and that robs her of tragic stature. At various points in the early chapters Moore comments on how there are 'two souls in one body, each striving for mastery'[76] – the idea is introduced through Héloïse's reading of *Medea*. This would suggest that Moore is toying with a new conception of character and personality as in no way consistent or stable, but as fluctuating between extremes in response to some inner conflict of forces within the psyche. What determines this conflict in Héloïse and stimulates her sudden reversals is never even intimated; as an explanation of her capricious behaviour it does not convince, for its treatment – the idea is simply reiterated several times – is so slight that it seems merely a convenience.

Similarly, Abélard defines love as 'an end in itself and not a means to an end';[77] he sees, after the years devoted to intellectual pursuits, a valuable point of rest in Héloïse's affection and welcomes their son as a 'divine gift'. The courts of Love, his former way of escape from the pressures of accepted social mores, seem to him by contrast with mother and child to be founded on perverse illusions: the troubadours cult of 'blessed adultery' is a dangerous moral inversion, while living like Gaucelm d'Arembert in an ecstasy of adoration of one's beloved with one's desires perpetually unsatisfied is to him pitiful and pernicious. Yet, despite that moral awareness, he cedes to Héloïse's demands that their relationship be sacrificed to the greater glory of his mind. If he is content that the world be well lost for the sake of his ambition, we must know the cause, however irrational; or we must sense Héloïse's power completely to bewitch Abélard's moral judgement. Moore obviously wishes to define the positive values of the instinctive life which the lovers are tragically to waste but accounting for their rejection of this felicity causes psychological complexities which his characterization cannot resolve; neither Héloïse's ambition nor Abélard's all-conquering passion is adequately dramatized.

Seeking to satisfy her ambition, Héloïse brings about Abélard's destruction as a man and as a philosopher. Advancement is possible only through the Church, but then, only to the orthodox believer. However true Abélard's reasoned enlightenment may be, the Church fears him and his philosophy as an attack upon its privilege and authority. Moreover the priesthood is open only to *whole* men. The revenge Canon Fulbert, Héloïse's uncle, takes on Abélard is horribly complete in rendering him impotent. The lovers' sacrifice is therefore wholly futile. Their tragedy springs from an initial error of judgement about Abélard's acceptability to the Church, but the force of this irony is not felt until Abélard's final account of his life to Héloïse, by which time its effect is considerably weakened. The trouble lies in the fact that the Church is not felt throughout to be the omnipotent controlling force, the figure of Destiny, that it was in medieval Europe. Fulbert, its representative throughout much of the novel, is worldly, grotesquely Epicurean, selfish but too comic in his devotion to sensual ease to convey adequately the sinister power of the clergy. There is as a result too little sense of tension in the first part of the book.

After its frustrating opening the novel gains considerably in strength in recounting the gradual spiritual dessication of Héloïse

after she has imprisoned herself in the convent at Argenteuil and
is left a prey to her illusions as she waits for news of Abélard's
philosophical triumphs. Had her sacrifice been total and deliberate
she might eventually have gained peace of mind, but her parting
from Abélard is a calculated trick to undermine ecclesiastical
authority, a lie consciously enacted to achieve a conscious end:
'But of what use is fealty if there be no reward for it?'[78] When
Abélard has used the Church to gain power and prestige they will
reunite. Her pious meditations are given over to ecstatic visions
of Abélard's triumph and to these illusory hopes she clings despite
his long silence. Her ambition is the god she worships, that alone
gives her life meaning and purpose:

> Abélard was the law that was over her, and were she to break
> this law the mainspring of her life would be broken. . .[79]

Despite the loss of her child, Abélard's inexplicable failure to
return and her own vacillating mind and growing discontent,
Héloïse perseveres in her hope, resolutely refusing to break her
pledge neither to communicate with her husband nor to trust
another's confidence:

> Her hope was that it might all have happened as she imagined
> it happening, and these hopes caused her almost dead life to
> quicken; but as her hopes faded her life became empty as a
> shell, and it often seemed to her that she was no more than a
> ghost, so detached was she from all worldly ties. . . . But would
> the hope help her to bear with the agony of living? . . . He must
> not think ill of me, and rather than that should happen I will
> endure this convent life still a little longer.[80]

Her courageous resilience in the face of her own despair has great
pathos; but the constant effort dries up the resources of her
imaginative strength. The slow atrophy of Héloïse's sensibility is
finely rendered, the prose slowly losing its colour, detail and rhythmic energy as her mind closes in on itself, resists the attraction
of external stimuli and concentrates with nagging insistence on
cerebral calculations about the future. Once Astrolabe, her son,
disappears her consciousness completely loses contact with immediate experience. Nothing, seemingly, will placate the god that
is her illusion; but the injustice which, from the depths of her

frustration, she cries out against in God is entirely of her own devising. Each returning spring brings ever more bitter memories of her youth with Abélard: 'for us there is no return, life will never summon us again. . . . My life is it over and done?'[81] Her determination at the last is grimly stoical; her hope lies in Abélard's continuing, though to her inexplicable, silence; from Abélard himself she learns the dreadful truth that his silence was shame: shame at his total impotence. By repressing their passion they have lost every vestige of faith in their lives and with that their quintessential humanity. Too late they realise that their blasphemy has been not to trust their early belief that 'our instincts as much as our souls are the will of God'.[82] Héloïse tries to kill herself but Abélard prevents her and bids her trust in heaven and practise that very religion which all along has afforded her little comfort. Hope holds no relief now for Héloïse; it was played her false for too long. But for Abélard's sake, because generously he never once accuses her, she agrees to live. It is her act of generosity and of atonement. Again they go their separate ways: 'He for God only, she for God in him'.

This last section is a fine portrayal of the maturing of a relationship under the pressure of time from passion to devotion, to affection and finally an austere implicit trust, a counter-movement that sustains the reader's sympathy and justifies the lovers' legendary status. Though each has caused the other to experience the worst of despair, each to go on living needs to know the other survives. This latter half of the novel is of an altogether different quality from the opening. Freed now of the constrictions of historical fact, Moore can concentrate on Héloïse's predicament and explore from within a mind helplessly set on its own destruction yet still finding beyond its collapse into despair a tenuous hold on sanity. The novel exemplifies the dangers and limitations of using historical material as a vehicle for depicting consciousness and by contrast highlights the remarkable achievement of *The Brook Kerith*. In *Héloïse and Abélard* the many individual virtues do not add up to a satisfying whole.

After the technical difficulties in *Héloïse and Abélard*, Moore's final work, *Aphrodite in Aulis*, offers a simple narrative line; though it is a historical novel the situation and characters are wholly imaginary. That being so, Moore is at liberty to pace the narrative to his liking; he can condense periods of time in the interests of his plot or enter a consciousness at a particular moment in time and treat it expansively. Compared with the opening chapters of *Héloïse and Abélard*, this novel is beautifully relaxed but not diffuse. It is a celebration of family life within a community where each generation is prepared to accept and learn from its predecessors; where toil is a means to better the lives of all; where personal grief or joy is an event for communal mourning or sport; and where (to quote Wagner, for it is very like Wagner's ideal future state) 'man's whole enfranchised energy proclaim[s] itself as . . . pure artistic impulse'.[83] Aulis is Moore's Utopia and so the narrative moves entirely at the bidding of his imagination.

As his last novel, it is a suitably fine display of the strengths of his artistry. Once again there is a lively recreation of a historical age, mainly by centring the characterization on the timeless problems of human nature: the stoical contentment of the aged Otanes, proud of his wisdom and his memories; the maturing of Kebren and Biote's marriage from sexual passion to affectionate companionship in middle age and of Biote's love for her sons, passing through a covert envy of her daughters-in-law to a new pride in her grandchildren.

This feeling for the inter-relationship of the generations and the way a couple and then a family create a corporate identity and balance of individualities is well expressed and so is Moore's depiction of the changes in response that accompany the passing of time, the anguish at the loss of particular skills and pleasures and the joyful discovery of new potentials in experience to bring contentment. As in Moore's account of Joseph's childhood at Magdala, the exactness of his rendering transforms patterns of ordinary living; the familiar is made strangely new in our awareness and the process of ageing for all its tragic and painful incidents is seen as a wonder in its slow unfolding of the many ways the human mind as it accepts change can create order and harmony within an individual sensibility. Moore has taken a popular subject, the family saga, and by concentrating his attention on the changing emotional atmosphere within the group shows how an individual's perception of the passage of time is balanced by a counter-movement within his consciousness of constant renewal and self-discovery. Moore's method of presentation here carefully prepares the ground for and substantiates his other principal concern in the novel which is to define the nature of the artist.

Kebren in his youth came to Aulis as an actor, reciting, criticising and interpreting Homer; intent on reviving through his expositions the ancient and largely forgotten cult of Helen, 'a young man's dream, a sterile dream, without fruition in this world'.[84] He married the practical-minded daughter of the merchant, Otanes; and their children inherit both Kebren's artistic imagination and Biote's commonsense. When the people of Aulis decide to build a temple it is dedicated to Aphrodite, the goddess of love, whom they worship as the first principle of being in the universe. Rhesos, Kebren's son, is required to make a statue of the goddess, and consults the local oracle for inspiration. Having performed its instructions he sees not the expected vision of the goddess but the girl who is to be his wife. Love of her beauty is his inspiration. His master, Phidias, criticises in Rhesos' statue the lack of that principle of unity which idealizes reality, as in his own work; but Rhesos refuses to make an alteration, for his statue is true to Earine's beauty: 'She is the pattern that the Goddess chose to send me. I see nothing to alter. . . . My art is my own. . .'[85] To communicate that love of life which is his inspiration is to be the artist's aim; such art will be an act of worship. These later sections of the novel concerning Rhesos are almost an allegorical statement of Moore's own concept of realism in art as he has come to understand it in composing these late novels after his numerous experiments with fictional techniques to find appropriate styles for consciousness. Tantalizingly most Utopias are situated like Prospero's ordered island 'ten leagues beyond man's life'; for Moore Utopia lies within: it is a mode of perception that if cultivated invites a particular conditon of being. *Aphrodite in Aulis* is a fitting apology for Moore's art and achievement.

Conclusion

'In my work I can only write tragedy and in life play nothing but light comedy.'[1] So Moore describes himself in *Hail and Farewell*. His personality, he claims, is split between a sober chivalrous self as author and a clownish *alter-ego*, a Sancho Panza-like individual, whom he christens Amico Moorini.[2] It is Moorini who disports himself merrily through the autobiographical works and Moorini, he decides, who is the culprit responsible for any blunders of taste or inconsistencies of style in the novels. Given Moorini's explosiveness and volubility, it is remarkable that Moore could ever keep him restrained when he was engaged in serious composition.[3] The reins do slacken occasionally as in the pointless farcical episode in *The Brook Kerith* where the Essenes discuss whether to marry to perpetuate their order. Such moments are irritating but in the sweep of his narrative quickly forgotten by the modern reader; not so however by Moore's contemporaries. Here speaking through the novel was a voice like the Moore they knew in public, the Moore who with a characteristically Irish sense of fun enjoyed being provocative, even outrageous. Moorini relished disconcerting people he deemed humbugs and deliberately set out to tease minds that appeared unliberated, prudish or subserviently orthodox. Moorini became something of a myth and Moore in old age could not resist playing up to expectations. Inevitably this damaged his reputation as a dedicated novelist. Arthur Symons questioning why Moore had 'narrowly escaped being a great writer' decided that the answer lay here in Moore's tendency to exhibit 'the incorrectness of a man who knows better, who is not careless, and yet who cannot help himself'.[4] Symons was writing in 1891 before the appearance of Moore's first masterpiece, *Esther Waters*, and when with the publication of *A Mere Accident*, *Spring Days* and *Mike Fletcher* Moore's status had entered a critical phase. But the judgement persists: Susan Mitchell voiced it again in 1916[5] (even though privately she delighted in Moorini's preposterousness and frequently made him the butt of her satirical verse).

The Moore-myth has steadily evaporated over the years with the demise of Moore himself and those of his young associates who fostered it because they liked to be thought daring. The *Confessions of a Young Man* no longer seems naughty; reading the book is not likely to arouse shivers of guilty pleasure; it can be taken for what it is: an affectionate portrayal of youth with its voracious appetite for enthusiasms and a source of valuable information about the taste of a particular era. The burlesque of *Hail and Farewell* can be enjoyed and its technique of disguising shrewd criticism in fantasy appreciated without its rousing partisan fervours to defend the Dublin intellectuals who are the object of Moore's satire. Now we can see that his judgements are valid and his comic approach not abusive, for his aim is to provoke his fellow-Irishmen into undertaking some necessary self-analysis. In the novels, given the more relaxed moral climate today, the reader is less likely to find Moorini's attitudes shocking or subversive, rather his intrusions, which in Moore's best works are very infrequent, will be seen in terms of technique as passing failures of the narrator's control over his material. The lapses are regrettable but they make one conscious of the discipline Moore exercises elsewhere in his dramatic realisations of different qualities of consciousness. Moore cannot rise to Henry James's feats of discipline but his method of processing his material so as to achieve a synthesis of the planes of narrative that focusses on the psychological life of his characters is inventive and, for the most part, scrupulous.

In his transitional work, *Sister Teresa*, Moore at one point has his heroine muse to herself:

> No one can lay before another the life that passes in her soul. . . . Words are ineffectual to explain it. With words you can tell the exterior facts of life, but you cannot tell the intense yet involuntary life of the soul – that intricate and unceasing life.[6]

Moore's career was devoted to finding a language, a style, a novel structure and a technique of narrative to surmount this obstacle to expression, to discovering the words whereby consciousness could tell of its condition or infer it. There is no denying it was an arduous quest (though his finest work has a notable ease of manner) but Moore persevered unwaveringly. To read his novels in chronological sequence is to watch in miniature the transformation of the novel itself as a *genre* from its typically nineteenth-century to its typically twentieth-century mould, as it sought increasingly to depict the life of the mind and had radically to overhaul its methods and realign and synthesise its traditional elements into new formations to do so. It is significant that (Henry James always excepted) Moore was the one novelist amongst his contemporaries who was held in continuing esteem by the first generation of 'new' novelists. They honoured his endeavour as exceptional.

Though he frequently joked about Moore in private, James Joyce was elaborately courteous when they met; he took pains that Moore should receive complimentary copies of *A Portrait of the Artist as a Young Man* and *Ulysses*; and was distressed when the wreath he sent to Moore's funeral by some oversight of the executors was not listed amongst the tokens of respect received. Writing about one of their meetings Moore remarked: 'We agreed that our careers were not altogether dissimilar.'[7] It is a modest understatement. Joyce borrowed from *Vain Fortune* for his conclusion to 'The Dead'. *A Portrait of the Artist* and *Ulysses* as studies of the plight of the Irish intellectual bear a strong thematic resemblance to *The Lake* and *Hail and Farewell*: both writers argue that the flourishing of the individual sensibility is possible in Ireland only through a studied resistance to the determining social pressures of life there; when Stephen Dedalus takes on himself the burden of martyrdom to reveal to his race its innermost conscience, he is following in the steps of Moore's Oliver Gogarty and of Moore himself, as he depicts his mission to the Irish in 'Vale'. If Joyce and after him Beckett use styles of narrative, often in parody or pastiche, to illustrate the quality of particular minds in their fiction or to define the play of certain forces within consciousness, they are imitating, even if carrying the device to more sophisticated levels, an innovation of Moore's.

For D. H. Lawrence too, Moore was an 'admired model'.[8] He sent Jessie Chambers copies of *Esther Waters* and *Evelyn Innes*. At the outset of his career Lawrence, as Emile Delavenay has shown, 'assimilated techniques and themes' from both these novels.[9] In *The White Peacock* he drew heavily on *Esther Waters* for background colour, some narrative incidents and details and for the

major image of the peacock itself. Through *Evelyn Innes* Lawrence
first absorbed some knowledge of Wagner and learned of possible
ways in which his theories could influence literature; the influence
bore fruit in his next novel, *The Trespasser*.[10] Later when he was
having trouble finding a publisher for *Women in Love* he was
greatly excited to hear 'indirectly that George Moore had read
the MS. . . . and praised it highly'.[11] Reinterpreting the resurrection
of Christ in *The Man Who Died* to illustrate in its most challenging form his personal philosophy, he was once again imitating
Moore's example.

Like Lawrence, Virginia Woolf was critical of Bennett, Wells
and Galsworthy, largely for their apathy in merely accepting the
form of the novel as it had been handed down to them from their
nineteenth-century predecessors; even worse, along with the form
they had been content to inherit related conceptions of character
too. Moore she admired because he 'has kept his freedom when
most of his contemporaries have long lost theirs'.[12] Moore's company she enjoyed for he was 'as fresh as a daisy'.[13] In conversation
with her as with Joyce, Moore saw no reason to play the fool; he
recognised in her a free spirit, another dedicated author, one whose
vision was not unlike his own. After meeting him she recorded in
her diary a parody of his style of talk which she thought a little
'out of date'; but she was patently captivated by his personality
'and perfect manners, as I consider them. That is to say he speaks
without fear or dominance; accepting me on my merits; everyone
on their merits. Still in spite of all, uncowed, unbeaten, lively,
shrewd'.[14] When she came to assess his work in one of her rare
articles about contemporary writers, she admitted to finding his
judgements as a critic 'whimsical', even 'ill-balanced, childish, and
egotistical';[15] referring to *Esther Waters, Evelyn Innes* and *The
Lake*, she questioned whether Moore was not perhaps deficient
in 'dramatic power', since his best character-portrayals were but
thinly disguised portraits of himself (ironically a crticism often
levelled aganst her own work); but his place in English literature is
assured, she concluded, for 'he has brought a new mind into the
world; he has given us a new way of feeling and seeing'. She saw
its expression accurately as a result of painstaking effort over many
years, but had no doubt as to its value. Where one would disagree
with her final assessment is in seeing Moore's innovation as limited
to *Hail and Farewell*. 'He has devised,' she writes, '. . . a means of

liquidating the capricious and volatile essence of himself and decanting it in these memoirs'.[16] That is true of the autobiography, but what her remark implies about the fastidiousness of Moore's technique and his insight into psychology is equally true of *The Lake* and *The Brook Kerith*, which were shaped by the same set of inspirational circumstances.

But if a novelist's work is to have an enduring appeal, its interest must be more than technical and historical, strong though Moore's claims to attention are on these counts. As Virginia Woolf's essay asserts, the value of Moore's work is in the way it marks a revolution in feeling, though its range in this is perhaps broader than Virginia Woolf allows. It is here that the element of the gauche in Moore is at a premium, that sense that he is using his writing in his early years as a novelist to come to terms with other writers' ways of seeing in order to discover insights into his own beliefs and responses so as to be able in time to create a personal style. Moore passes critically through the false antinomian values of contemporary fashions and aestheticisms, discards orthodox intellectual attitudes as generally inviting hypocrisy, and re-discovers the essential values conducive to a full life in the very will to live itself. Because Moore is using the novel in order to find truths out for himself, his moral analysis never becomes fixed or schematic nor his approach scientifically detached; both are flexible and creative since they derive from an excited curiosity. Except in *Hail and Farewell*, and even then he has his tongue very firmly in his cheek, Moore is never the preacher; he invites the reader to join him (most persuasively so with his later style) in his explorations of human identity; insights are a shared discovery on the journey and are the more informative for being so. Moore's enthusiasm and pertinacity have gone into the making of the novels and these become the guiding qualities of the reader's response too. Whatever the ideas the novels may promote they are invariably reached through experience and in that lies their freshness of appeal. His best novels are, to use his own term, *illuminations*.[17]

If Lawrence and Moore admired each other's work it was surely because they recognised in each other similar ambitions. Lawrence's is a more openly stated philosophy, but it is one to which Moore's novels also give assent; both knew that 'for man, the vast marvel is to be alive'[18] and that the individual's life can be shaped in one of two ways:

Either everything is created from the mind, downwards; or else everything proceeds from the creative quick, outwards into exfoliation and blossom. . . . The actual living quick itself is alone the creative reality.[19]

In his last three novels Moore carefully works out the significance of his beliefs in terms of faith, marital love and art; but coming to these conclusions so late in life he lacked the energy to effect a greater reorientation of values necessary to relate these fundamentally personal qualities to a more comprehensive social theory, such as Forster attempts in *Howard's End* or Lawrence in *Women in Love*. His choice of historical subjects, presumably under Wagner's influence, was perhaps a weakness in this respect. However his portrayal of the movement to self-sufficiency, or its tragic failure, in a range of individual lives is achieved with a delicate concern for the minutiae of psychological plausibility. If Moore's voyaging into consciousness and his depiction of the awakening of the particular soul to the beauty of naturalness is conducted for the most part with an elderly man's tranquillity rather than with Lawrence's feeling for dynamism, his vision is nonetheless free of that dogmatic aggressiveness that mars some of Lawrence's later work. Moore never invokes the 'Dark Gods' (except perhaps marginally and unconvincingly with Héloïse); he believed that the marvel of the mind was its power to heal itself. His achievement lies in relating the spontaneous flow of instinct to a moral and psychological harmony. The quest was always for a more humane moral order than Victorian decorums permitted. If he is convincing in his conclusions it is because as narrator he demonstrates the validity of his beliefs. Literature, Virginia Woolf conjectured, kept Moore 'sweet and sane'.[20] Moore aimed in life to acquire a complete shamelessness in the best sense of an openness to experience; his moral and emotional questing is quite without guilt; his voice as narrator is relaxed not insistent. Exploring another mind and identity is a source of wonder to him because he never ceases to be excited by what engaging with another personality reveals to him about himself. The utter fearlessness with which he presents himself in his autobiographies finds its complement in the novels in a curiosity which encourages not malice but appreciation and compassion. The shamelessness he seeks, as for Lawrence and Joyce, has to embrace reverence; the religious impulse is not to be quelled but cleansed.

It is fitting that Moore should have perfected his quest with his return to Ireland at the turn of the century. It activated in his experience a quality (anticipated in the cyclic structure of *Esther Waters*) that was to become a strength in his subsequent thinking and writing: he returned to the familiar, long taken for granted, and saw it with new eyes, saw it indeed as vision. Seeing a thing openly for what it was in itself became a wonder. The process was at once a purging and an enriching of perception. Significantly in this respect, as *Hail and Farewell* records, it was AE and Synge amongst the writers of the Irish Renaissance who impressed him most deeply and that because for both of them rapture was rooted in an intimate sense of place and both were men of integrity since they were unfailingly true to their inner responses. In Ireland the elements of Moore's artistry fell into a new relation to accommodate the new theme. This last enthusiasm had seized on an enduring value and Moore's dedication to the novel since those impoverished days in Cecil Street had found its reward.

> I return then to the question, please whom? or what? I answer, human nature, as it has been and ever will be. But where are we to find the best measure of this? I answer, from within; by stripping our own hearts naked, and by looking out of ourselves towards men who lead the simplest lives most according to nature, men who have never known false refinements, wayward and artificial desires, false criticisms, effeminate habits of thinking and feeling, or who, having known these things, have outgrown them. This latter class is the most to be depended upon, but it is very small in number.[21]

So wrote Wordsworth defining different types of artists. The nature of Moore's life and work places him firmly in that last category. There lies his true worth.

Notes

Introduction

1 *Flowers of Passion* (1878) and *Pagan Poems* (1881).

2 This was published in 1879; another play, *Worldliness*, a comedy in three acts, was apparently published earlier *circa* 1874, but all copies were lost to Moore's great relief.

3 Activities by the Land League in Mayo in 1879 drastically reduced Moore's income from the rents of his estates.

4 The letter 'To George Moore on his Eightieth Birthday' was printed in *The Times* on February 24, 1932. It is cited in full but without the list of signatures in J. M. Hone: *The Life of George Moore*. 1936. p. 437.

5 George Moore: *Confessions of a Young Man*. Ebury Edition, 1937. p. 67.

6 Ibid. p. 66.

7 Ibid. p. 118.

8 Ibid. p. 139.

9 Gustave Flaubert: *Madame Bovary*. Translated by A. Russell. Penguin Classics. Harmondsworth, 1950. p. 157.

10 *Selected Letters of Gustave Flaubert*. Translated and edited by F. Steegmuller. 1954. p. 133.

11 *Confessions of a Young Man*. p. 140.

12 Ibid. p. 143.

13 Henry James: *The Art of Fiction and Other Essays*. Introduced and edited by Morris Roberts. New York and Oxford, 1948. p. 114.

14 *Confessions of a Young Man*. p. 140.

15 Emile Zola: *The Rush for the Spoil (La Curée)*. Introduced by George Moore. 1886. p. 107.

16 *Selected Letters of Gustave Flaubert*. p. 234.

17 *The Art of Fiction and Other Essays*. p. 156.

18 See *The Life of George Moore*, p. 93, where Hone publishes a letter from Moore to Zola asking if he would be acceptable as a translator.

19 See for example the sensuous description of the fruit shop in *La Vente de Paris*, which is likened to a seraglio; and the orgiastic beauty of Albine's garden in *La Faute de l'Abbé Mouret* and of Renée Saccard's conservatory, which excite their occupants to promiscuity. Money, vegetation and fruit are seen in interrelation with sexuality and the terms of reference as interchangeable between them. It is an endowing of environment with a psychological significance exemplary of the characters under analysis and as such a poetic rendering of Zola's theme of determinism.

20 *Confessions of a Young Man*. p. 119.

243

21   Ibid. p. 140.
22   *The Art of Fiction and Other Essays.* p. 30. This break in narrative and stylistic unity is apparent in *La Vente de Paris* and *Pot Bouille*, where impressionistic fantasies alternate with lengthy passages of mechanically observed and enumerated fact.
23   *Confessions of a Young Man.* p. 60.
24   These are Yelena's reflections after the death of her husband, Insarov, in *On The Eve.* (Translated by G. Gardiner. Penguin Classics. Harmondsworth, 1967. p. 227.)
25   ' "Love unites also – but not the love you're thirsting for now: not love the pleasure, but love the sacrifice." Shubin frowned.
     ". . . But I want love for myself: I want to be number one."
     "Number one," Bersyenev repeated. "Whereas I feel that one's whole destiny in life should be to make oneself number two." ' (*On The Eve.* p. 30.)
26   *On The Eve.* p. 28.
27   Ivan Turgenev: *Rudin.* Translated by C. Garnett. 1894. p. 87.
28   Henry James: 'Turgenev and Tolstoy, 1897', *The House of Fiction.* Edited by Leon Edel. 1957. p. 174.
29   George Moore: 'Turgueneff', *The Fortnightly Review.* 1888. pp. 237-51. The quotation is from p. 240.
30   Ibid. p. 245: 'Who among the many who have thought of turning the troubles of Ireland to literary account has not thought of an Irish Bazaroff . . . a soul so vital and so knowable. . . ?'

NOTE: Although the *Confessions,* as is pointed out in Chapter 5, are not wholly reliable in matters of autobiography, the work has been quoted here to illustrate many of Moore's literary views but only such as became settled opinions that were expressed again in his later critical writings, particularly in *Impressions and Opinions* and *Avowals.* Their setting forth in the *Confessions* has been chosen for quotation for being most nearly contemporaneous (1888) with the composing of the early novels which led to the formulation of these judgements.

Chapter One: *A Modern Lover*

1   George Moore: *Lewis Seymour and Some Women.* 1917. p. v.
2   Ibid. p. v.
3   George Moore: *A Modern Lover.* Vizetelly's One-Volume Novels. 1886. p. 26. This was the third edition and it incorporated many textual improvements of a local kind; it is also more accessible than the first edition in three volumes, to which, however, references are given in brackets, as in this instance. (I. p. 41.)
4   Ibid. p. 293. (III. p. 152.)
5   Ibid. p. 311. (III. p. 192.)
6   Of Manet, Moore wrote: 'Painting was one of the ways his nature manifested itself. . . . Never was an artist's inner nature in more direct

conformity with his work'. (*Modern Painting*. 1893. p. 31.) Whistler's
Nocturnes are described in the same volume as 'the outcome of a highly
strung, bloodless nature whetted on the whetstone of its own weakness
to an exasperated sense of volatile colour and evanescent light'. (Ibid.
p. 6.) In a less serious but nonetheless perceptive mood he said of the
same artist: 'A few pounds more of flesh and muscle and we should
have had another Velasquez'. (Ibid. p. 7.)

7   *A Modern Lover*. p. 216. (II. p. 216.)
8   Ibid. p. 156. (II. pp. 83-4.)
9   Ibid. p. 39. (I. p. 72.)
10 'We do not always choose what you call unpleasant subjects, but we
    try to go to the roots of things; and the basis of life, being material and
    not spiritual, the analyst inevitably finds himself, sooner or later, hand-
    ling what this sentimental age calls coarse. . . . If your stomach will not
    stand the crudities of the moral dissecting room read verse; but don't
    try to distort an art into something it is not, and cannot be. The novel,
    if it be anything, is contemporary history, an exact and complete repro-
    duction of social surroundings of the age we live in.' (Ibid. pp. 41-2; or
    I. pp. 77-8.) Compare Zola: 'Nous ne cherchons pas ce qui est répugn-
    ant, nous le trouvons; et si nous voulons le cacher, il faut mentir, ou
    tout au moins rester incomplet.' (*Le Roman Expérimental*.)
11 *A Modern Lover*. p. 60. (I. p. 118.) This is also the theme of Baudelaire's
    essay on Guys, *The Painter of Modern Life*.
12 *A Modern Lover*. p. 38. (I. p. 70.)
13 Ibid. p. 13. (I. p. 13.)
14 Ibid. p. 49. (I. p. 94.)
15 See Joseph Hone: *The Life of George Moore*. 1936. p. 51.
16 *A Modern Lover*. p. 316. (III. p. 204).
17 Ibid. pp. 12-14; 117; and chapter xx, Mrs Bentham's ball. (I. pp. 12-4;
    II. pp. 9-10). Many of these passages resemble Saccard's visions of Paris
    in *La Curée*; Moore wrote an introduction for Vizetelly's English tran-
    slation of this particular novel, published in 1886.
18 *A Modern Lover*. pp. 13-14. (I. pp. 13-14.)
19 See the opening of chapter xx, p. 177. (II. p. 123.)
20 Maxime Saccard is the one character in Zola who is as will-less and
    effeminate as Seymour, but there the effect is intentional in the pattern
    of symbolism. As Moore himself wrote of Maxime in his preface to
    Vizetelly's translation of *La Curée*: 'he is the son of the capitalist; he
    is the weed sprung from, but not the intelligence that has built up, the
    gold heap, and he festers and rots like a weed in an overpoweringly
    rich soil.'
21 Novels such as *Le Rêve*, where Zola attempts to write about moral
    goodness are cloyingly sentimental; they are virtually fairy stories.
22 Guy de Maupassant: *Bel Ami*. Translated by H. N. P. Sloman. Penguin
    Classics. Harmondsworth, 1961. p. 192.
23 Ibid. p. 191.
24 Henry James: 'Guy de Maupassant', *The House of Fiction*. Edited by
    Leon Edel. 1957. p. 161.
25 Ibid. p. 161.

26 *Lewis Seymour and Some Women*. p. vi.

27 Ibid. p. 296.

28 A similar ambiguity clouds the other major addition to the novel. The equating of Lewis's imagination and his amorous relationships in *A Modern Lover* with the amorality of rococo art is here considerably reduced; and in its place is described a visit by Mrs Bentham and Seymour first to the Petit Trianon and then to Fontainebleau, where they meet the poet, Mallarmé. Just as Marie Antoinette had played at being a milkmaid, he – a nineteenth-century scholar and poet – seeks to ape the life of an eighteenth-century peasant. For him the freshness of art lies not in its relevance to, and power to illuminate, life, but in its evocation of mystery. There is much to suggest that he is being presented as an example of the dangers to which the pursuit solely of pleasure may lead. Art is for him a means of easeful escape. The incident could have provided an excellent foil for the 'realists', Harding and Thompson, but careless authorial comments such as 'He [Mallarmé] was trying as we all are to escape from ourselves' make Moore's own position irritatingly ambiguous. There is a further discussion of this episode in chapter seven page 140.

Chapter Two : *A Mummer's Wife*

1 George Moore: *A Modern Lover*. 1886. p. 25. (I. p. 39.)

2 Ibid. p. 24. (I. p. 37.)

3 George Moore: *A Mummer's Wife*. Heinemann's edition, 1918. p. 68. (Ebury Edition, 1937. p. 54.) The text of the 1918 edition is substantially the same as that published by Vizetelly in 1885, but I have decided to use the later text for a number of reasons. Together with the Ebury Edition it is the more readily accessible. Also Moore made certain stylistic improvements and several additions to the novel over the years: the description of both the failure of Kate's marriage with Dick Lennox and of her mental and physical collapse is more detailed, stylistically simpler and, consequently, the more dramatic in the 1918 version. Mrs Forest's part in the action is greatly amplified here too; the significance of her character is thus the more deeply defined. Where possible in the following notes, references are given for all three editions.

4 Ibid. p. 69. (Ebury. pp. 54-5.)

5 Ibid. p. 71. (Ebury. p. 56; Vizetelly. p. 70.)

6 Ibid. p. 171 (Ebury. p. 135.)

7 Ibid. p. 174. (Ebury. p. 138; Vizetelly. p. 164.)

8 Ibid. p. 46. (Ebury. p. 36; Vizetelly. p. 51.)

9 Ibid. p. 47. (Ebury. p. 37; Vizetelly. p. 51.)

10 Ibid. pp. 7-8. (Ebury. p. 6; Vizetelly. p. 17.)

11 Ibid. p. 11. (Ebury. p. 9; Vizetelly. p. 22.)

12 Ibid. p. 58. (Ebury. p. 45; Vizetelly. p. 60.)

13 Ibid. p. 16. (Ebury. p. 13; Vizetelly. p. 27.)

14 Ibid. p. 415. (Ebury. pp. 329-30.)
15 Ibid. p. 447. (Ebury. p. 355; Vizetelly. p. 398.)
16 Quintessentially in *Hail and Farewell*. Moore, according to Gogarty and others, was in the habit of raising in conversations topics which he was currently engaged on writing about; he made mental notes of the ensuing debate and frequently made use of this copy, invariably appropriating all the best lines for himself. Hone relates in his biography of Moore (p. 98) that Glover used jokingly to claim that he was the real author of *A Mummer's Wife* since so many of the stories about touring companies included in the novel were ones he had related to Moore.
17 Kate's romantic illusions are frequently debunked by her assistant, Hender's crude gossip about theatre life, but Kate is emotionally too overwrought to be awake to the implications of this chatter. The passages finely establish the real nature of Lennox's life and the depth of Kate's illusions. See particularly pp. 106, 133, 150, 153.
18 *A Mummer's Wife*. pp. 87-90. (Ebury. pp. 69-71; Vizetelly. pp. 83-5.)
19 Ibid. p. 455. (Ebury. p. 361; Vizetelly. p. 404.)
20 Ibid. pp. 441-3. (Ebury. pp. 350-1; Vizetelly. pp. 392-4.)
21 A representative review is that in the *Spectator* of January 17, 1885 (LVIII. pp. 83-5), which expresses concern lest the innocent reader be contaminated 'by prolonged imaginative companionship with the very evil against which the moral warning is directed'.
22 *A Mummer's Wife*. pp. 503-4. (Ebury. p. 399; Vizetelly. p. 437.)
23 Ibid. p. 503. (Ebury. p. 398; Vizetelly. p. 436.)
24 Ibid. pp. 482-90. (Ebury. pp. 382-8; Vizetelly. pp. 424-9.)
25 There are several unfortunate faults of construction in the final chapters of the novel, suggesting an over-eagerness on Moore's part to finish the work. Montgomery is re-introduced without any preparation or pretext; and the sudden intrusion of Mrs Forest is casual to the point of absurdity. I have described my analysis of Mrs Forest's character and significance as taking the will for the deed: a comparison of the 1918 edition with Vizetelly's justifies that analysis by demonstrating how Moore revised his original sketch in order to develop the importance of her role. She is a more likeable and less absurd person in the later edition; Lennox is attracted to her for her personality and not as a patron, who though a crank is wealthy and therefore worth milking to finance his theatrical projects; and much more is made of her art and socialist ideas.
26 *A Mummer's Wife*. p. 501. (Ebury. p. 397; Vizetelly. p. 434.)
27 Ibid. p. 310. (Ebury. p. 246; Vizetelly. p. 286.)

Chapter Three : *A Drama in Muslin*

1 George Moore: *A Drama in Muslin*. 1886. pp. 203-4.
2 The truth of Moore's analysis of the debutante's position has been affirmed by both Susan Mitchell and Elizabeth Bowen (in *The Shel-*

bourne Hotel), and perhaps more movingly by the fact that none of his female friends and relations who were used as models for many of the characters took exception to the book.

3   *A Drama in Muslin.* p. 137.
4   There is much here that is reminiscent of Ibsen. Moore himself in his preface to *Muslin* writes of 'a hatred as lively as Ibsen's of the social conventions that drive women into the marriage market'. (*Muslin* 1915. p. viii.) Later in the preface he draws a parallel between Alice Barton and Nora of *A Doll's House*: both symbolize the belief 'that a woman is more than a domestic animal'. (Ibid. p. x.)
5   *A Drama in Muslin.* p. 169.
6   This was a situation aggravated by the 1881 Land Act, which destroyed the Landlords' power for good as well as their powers of malpractice. They could neither turn out indolent tenants nor put capital into their estates to improve the land with any certainty of a return.
7   *A Drama in Muslin.* p. 68.
8   Ibid. pp. 123-30.
9   Ibid. pp. 94-6.
10   Ibid. p. 226.
11   W. B. Yeats: 'My Descendants', *Collected Poems.* 1961. p. 229.
12   *A Drama in Muslin.* p. 27.
13   Ibid. p. 95.
14   Ibid. p. 71.
15   Ibid. p. 225.
16   W. B. Yeats: 'Nineteen Hundred and Nineteen', *Collected Poems.* 1961. p. 233.
17   *A Drama in Muslin.* p. 171.
18   George Henry Moore (1811-1870), the novelist's father, was elected M.P. for Mayo in 1847, when he supported most eloquently Gavin Duffy's tenant-rights movement, which alienated him from many of his own class. He was returned to Parliament again in 1868 and once more sought to protect the Mayo peasantry in his policies.
19   *A Drama in Muslin.* p. 71.
20   Ibid. p. 228.
21   Ibid. p. 69.
22   Ibid. p. 4.
23   Ibid. p. 300.
24   *Muslin.* p. viii.
25   'He sought Alice Barton's heart. . . . I fell to wondering how it was that the critics of the 'eighties could have been blind enough to dub him an imitator of Zola. "A soul-searcher, if ever there was one." ' (The elderly Moore is contemplating the younger self who wrote *A Drama in Muslin.*) See *Muslin.* p. viii.
26   A detailed account of Moore's growing interest in Huysmans' novels and style follows in Chapter Five, pp. 102-5. At first Huysmans' influence, as in *A Drama in Muslin*, was simply stylistic, following Moore's ecstatic review of *A Rebours* in 1884.
27   Susan Mitchell: *George Moore.* Dublin, 1916. p. 30.
28   *A Drama in Muslin.* pp. 172-3. See also Chapter 5, note 4, pp. 251-2.

29 In a letter to T. Fisher Unwin, January 14, 1902. Cited in *George Moore In Transition: Letters to T. Fisher Unwin and Lena Milman, 1894-1910.* Edited by H. E. Gerber. Detroit, 1968. p. 245.
30 *Muslin.* p. xii.

Chapter Four : *Esther Waters*

1   Cited in Asa Briggs : *Victorian People.* Pelican Edition. Harmondsworth, 1965. p. 102.
2   George Moore : *Confessions of a Young Man.* Ebury Edition, 1937. p. 108. See too footnote 35 below.
3   'Il nous est venu la curiosité de savoir si cette forme conventionelle d'une littérature oubliée et d'une société disparue, la Tragédie, était définitivement morte; si dans un pays sans caste et sans aristocratie légale, les misères des petits et des pauvres parleraient à l'intérêt, à l'émotion, à la pitié, aussi haut que les misères des grands et des riches. . . . que le Roman ait cette religion que le siècle passé appelait de ce large et vaste nom : Humanité; — il lui suffit de cette conscience : son droit est là.' Les Goncourts : Preface to *Gierminie Lacerteux.* Paris 1864.
4   George Moore : *Esther Waters.* Ebury Edition, 1937. p. 167.
5   The review of *Esther Waters* in *The Bookman*, May 1894, p. 53.
6   *Esther Waters.* p. 176.
7   Margaret Dalziel : *Popular Fiction 100 Years Ago.* 1957. p. 95.
8   Ibid. p. 95. Cited from 'Left to Themselves' in *Cassell's Illustrated Family Paper*, 1860.
9   Mrs Gaskell : *Ruth.* Everyman Edition, 1967. p. 118. Note the effect here of Benson's tutoring of his sister, Faith, into a knowledge of her true Christian duty.
10 Ibid. p. 119.
11 I have deliberately avoided a comparison here with Hardy's *Tess of the D'Urbervilles*, though Moore said he consciously modelled his narrative on Hardy's while allowing Esther to take exactly the opposite decision to Tess in each of her dilemmas of choice. Apart from Hardy's challenge in claiming Tess as 'A Pure Woman', he subordinates the more intimate details of her relations with Alec and the birth of her child, Sorrow, to his greater design of interpreting her fate as symbolic of the contemporary social destruction of the agrarian community of Wessex.
12 From a letter to Maurice Moore, cited in J. Hone : *The Life of George Moore.* 1936. p. 187.
13 *Esther Waters.* p. 161.
14 Ibid. p. 97.
15 Ibid. p. 95.
16 Ibid. p. 97.
17 Ibid. p. 104.
18 Ibid. p. 150.
19 Ibid. p. 150.

20 Ibid. p. 257.
21 '. . . Fifteen pun to 'alf a quid! as much as I'd earn in three months slaving eight and ten hours a day, a pint-pot on 'and and about them blooming engines.' Ibid. p. 100.
22 Ibid. p. 63.
23 Ibid. pp. 45-6.
24 Ibid. p. 53.
25 Ibid. p. 39.
26 Ibid. p. 324.
27 Ibid. p. 296.
28 Ibid. pp. 317 and 320.
29 Katherine Mansfield: *Novels and Novelists*. 1930. pp. 234-7. Moore's 'scrupulous method' and the 'even flow of narrative', she argues, have not 'the faintest stirring of the breath of life'; the attention to factual accuracy robs the novel of creative emotion. *Esther Waters*, she concludes, is an insult to her intelligence.
30 *Esther Waters*. pp. 156-69.
31 Ibid. p. 156.
32 Ibid. p. 158.
33 Ibid. p. 160.
34 Ibid. p. 161. This is given in full at the start of section (iii) of this chapter.
35 R. A. Gettmann: 'George Moore's Revisions of *The Lake, The Wild Goose* and *Esther Waters*.' *P.M.L.A.* LIX. June, 1944. pp. 540-55.
    During the composition of the novel Moore published draft-versions of chapters XX to XXIX with a summary of the early part of the story as a serial entitled 'Pages from the Life of a Workgirl' in the *Pall Mall Gazette* from 2nd till 14th October, 1893. Of special interest here is an episode describing Esther's infatuation for a Mr Bryant to whom she acts as laundress-cleaner in Norman's Inn, which bears a marked similarity to the encounter between G.M. and the housemaid, Emma, in *Confessions of a Young Man* quoted above (see footnote 2). The writing is trite and sentimental and Moore was right to omit it from the published novel. The revision is a good example of his maturing imaginative involvement with his subject.
36 *Esther Waters*. p. 6.
37 Ibid. p. 77.
38 Ibid. pp. 42-3.
39 Ibid. p. 325.
40 Ibid. p. 235.
41 Ibid. pp. 296-7.
42 Ibid. pp. 185-6.
43 Ibid. p. 190.
44 Ibid. p. 84.
45 Ibid. pp. 185 and 292.
46 Ibid. pp. 183-4.
47 Ibid. p. 32.
48 Ibid. p. 151.
49 Ibid. p. 122.
50 Ibid. p. 236.

51 Ibid. p. 293.

52 Ibid. p. 298.

53 Ibid. p. 348.

54 Ibid. p. 40.

55 Ibid. p. 210.

56 Ibid. p. 73.

57 Ibid. p. 377.

58 Ibid. p. 375.

59 Ibid. p. 364.

60 Ibid. p. 298.

61 See footnote 29 above.

62 *Esther Waters*. p. 151.

63 Ibid. p. 70.

64 Ibid. p. 86.

65 Ibid. p. 49.

66 Ibid. pp. 230-1.

67 I. Gregor and B. Nicholas: 'The Case of Esther Waters', *The Moral and the Story*. 1962. pp. 98-122. They see Moore's novel as melodramatic, religiose and *fin-de-siècle*.

68 Ibid. p. 121. My italics.

69 Ibid. p. 121.

70 *George Moore In Transition: Letters to T. Fisher Unwin and Lena Milman 1894-1910*. Edited by H. E. Gerber. Detroit, 1968. p. 71.

71 *The Moral and The Story*. p. 121.

72 'Mr George Moore is perhaps the most prominent exponent of what we may perhaps term the "colourless' theory of fiction.' Wells was here reviewing Bennett's *The Paying Guest* in the *Saturday Review*, April 18, 1896.

73 *Esther Waters*. pp. 365 and 146.

74 Ibid. p. 372.

Chapter Five: New Influences – New Problems

1 George Moore: *Muslin*. 1915. p. xii.

2 George Moore: *Mike Fletcher*. 1889. p. 295.

3 George Moore: *The Lake*. Revised edition, 1921. pp. ix-x.

4 George Moore: 'A Curious Book', *St James's Gazette*. September 2, 1884. pp. 6-7. (Both Gilcher in his bibliography of Moore's work and Hone in his biography describe this article inaccurately as published in the *Pall Mall Gazette*.) Moore sees *A Rebours* as 'neither more nor less than a catalogue of the whimsical fantasies of this product of over-civilization. . . . three hundred pages are filled, and admirably, with matter it is true of little interest, but with graces of fancy, imagination, and caprice that never fail to delight the literary *gourmet*'. (Ibid. p. 6.) This bears an obvious relation to the manner Moore adopted for *A Mere Accident, Mike Fletcher* and *Evelyn Innes*; also the article anticipates

many of the purple passages to be found in *A Drama in Muslin* (1886). Compare, for example, the following (where Moore is himself improvising in the Huysmanesque style while describing the episode of Des Esseintes's games with the scent-organ) with the passage quoted from *A Drama in Muslin* on page 67: '. . . the orchestration of odours is thoroughly gone into. Atkinson's white rose sings like violins, Ess. Bouquet like violoncellos, stephanotis like clarionets, mignonette like the tinkling of harps in the distance.' (Ibid. p. 6.)

5 Arthur Symons: *The Symbolist Movement in Literature*. 1899. p. 145.

6 These were very much the terms in which Moore promoted Gaelic studies on behalf of the Gaelic League at this time.

7 This new enthusiasm of Moore's dates from the day Yeats and Martyn came to seek Moore's help in finding English actors to play the two works with which they hoped to launch the Irish Literary Theatre Society some time in the spring of 1899. *The Countess Cathleen* was performed in Dublin on May 8th of that year and *The Heather Field* on May 9th. Almost immediately afterwards Moore became involved with helping Martyn finish his next play *The Tale of a Town* which was scheduled for performance the following February. In the event Moore took the play over completely and re-wrote it as *The Bending of the Bough*. By the summer of 1900 he was busy collaborating with Yeats on a dramatized version of *Diarmuid and Grania*. His literary ventures at the turn of the century became increasingly involved with furthering the Irish cause.

8 Virtually from the start of his career Moore waged a battle with Mudie's and Smith's lending libraries over his works. *A Mummer's Wife* received favourable notices but copies did not sell well since the libraries refused to carry the novel because of its affinities with Flaubert and Zola. On Wednesday December 10, 1884, Moore sent a long letter to the *Pall Mall Gazette* (it was published under the heading 'A New Censorship of Literature') which questioned the authority of the libraries to set themselves up as literary critics. He followed this up with a more powerful attack in 1885, 'Literature at Nurse or Circulating Morals'. Thereafter, largely on Zola's advice, he began encouraging young authors to publish their works in a single-volume format, as opposed to the more traditional set of three volumes, which would make the purchase of a new novel considerably cheaper to readers and so might encourage them to rely less on libraries.

9 William Gaunt: *The Aesthetic Adventure*. 1945. Constantly throughout his book Gaunt refers to Moore in relation with Wilde which is rather preposterous as they were never associates and had little in common but for their Irish childhood and an interest in French literature. A similar but inaccurate view of Moore has been promoted too by M. Elwin in *Old Gods Falling* (1939. chs. ii-iii.) and by Professor Graham Hough in *Image and Experience* (1960. chs. vi-vii.)

10 George Moore: *Confessions of a Young Man*. Ebury Edition, 1937. p. 38.

11 *The Aesthetic Adventure*. p. 117; and also *Confessions of a Young Man*. p. 94.

12 *Letters from George Moore to Edouard Dujardin, 1886-1922.* Translated
    by 'John Eglinton'. New York, 1929. p. 27. (The letter is dated March
    11, 1888.) Hone in his biography of Moore quotes Dujardin: 'The tran-
    slation of the *Confessions* was done by a man whose name I have for-
    gotten and who did not belong to our circle. Everyone agreed that it
    was very bad, and we decided to revise it before it was printed as a book
    by Savine. I did the revision, keeping throughout in touch with Moore,
    who was well satisfied with the result'. (J. M. Hone: *The Life of George
    Moore.* 1936. p. 139.) Given Moore's remarks here, it seems particu-
    larly odd of Gaunt to suggest immediately after commenting on the
    hero of Huysmans' *A Rebours* that Moore 'saw himself in this light – as
    one who lived an exciting inward life, pulsating with adventure and
    ecstasy of a purely mental kind'. Gaunt takes Moore's playful poses far
    too seriously; there is a section where Moore imitates Huysmans' novel
    but the episode is a fantasy designed to expose his youthful pretensions.
    The views Moore expresses are in no way consistent; one could counter
    Gaunt's remarks about Moore's cerebral delights with Moore's claim
    that 'contact with the world is in me the generating force; without this
    what invention I have is thin and sterile, and it grows thinner rapidly,
    until it dies away utterly'. (*Confessions of a Young Man.* p. 68) Gaunt
    ignores too the conclusion where the author fondly dismisses his youth-
    ful self: 'The feast is over for me, I yield my place'. (*Confessions.*
    p. 181.)
13 Pater's remark was made in a letter to Moore thanking him for a
    complimentary copy of the *Confessions*; it was dated March 4, 1888.
    Moore subsequently included it in full in his preface to the revised
    edition of the work published in 1904 and in all later editions.
14 *The Aesthetic Adventure.* p. 191.
15 Holbrook Jackson: *The Eighteen-Nineties.* 1913. pp. 75-6.
16 *George Moore In Transition: Letters to T. Fisher Unwin and Lena
    Milman, 1894-1910.* Edited by H. E. Gerber. Detroit, 1968. p. 56. In 'My
    Impressions of Zola' which he contributed to the *English Illustrated
    Magazine* in February 1894, Moore also describes in some detail his aim
    with the *Confessions*; it was, he writes, 'an attempt to reduce to words
    the fugitive imaginings of my mind, its intimate workings, . . . its shift-
    ing colours'. (op. cit. pp. 480-1.)
17 Frank Escott begins to assume this role at times in *Mike Fletcher* but
    he does not serve this function consistently throughout the novel. See
    chapter 6, page 125 and footnote 20, page 255.
18 Aldous Huxley: *Point Counter Point.* 1928. p. 440.
19 Review of *Vain Fortune* in *Athenaeum*. No. 3341. November 7, 1891.
    pp. 613-4.
20 George Moore: 'Turgueneff', *Fortnightly Review*. 1888. pp. 237-51. The
    general analysis from which these quotations are drawn is to be found
    on pages 241-2; the discussion of *Virgin Soil* follows on pages 245-6.
21 See *Mike Fletcher*, p. 37; or *Evelyn Innes* (1898) pp. 65-6, where after
    several pages giving Owen Asher's musing about women and religion
    he reaches the conclusion that 'he was deficient in the religious instinct'.
    Then follows the authorial comment: 'Awaking from his reverie, he

raised himself from the mantlepiece against which he was leaning. Never had he thought so brilliantly, and he regretted that no magical stenographer should be there to register his thoughts as they passed.'

22   Robert Liddell: *A Treatise on the Novel*. 1947. p. 105.
23   Henry James: *The Tragic Muse*. (A reprint of the 1890 edition) 1948. pp. 432-3.
24   George Moore: *Avowals*. Ebury Edition, 1936. pp. 1-96.
25   George Moore: *A Mere Accident*. 1887. p. 215.
26   There is a more detailed discussion of this episode in chapter 8, pages 150-1.
27   Review of *Sister Teresa* in *The Academy*. Vol. 61. July 20, 1901. p. 53.

Chapter Six : Four Novellas

1   George Moore: *A Mere Accident*. 1887. p. 282.
2   Moore treated Martyn's relationship with his mother more openly but with a similar compassionate understanding in *Hail and Farewell*; the relationship is tragic because it is based on a 'fatality of temperament which irrevocably separates two people bound together by the closest natural ties', who 'must go through life together without any hope that they will ever understand each other better'. (*Hail and Farewell*. Edited by Richard Cave. Gerrards Cross, 1976. p. 186.)
3   *A Mere Accident*. p. 28.
4   Ibid. p. 54.
5   Ibid. p. 103.
6   Ibid. p. 175.
7   Some years later Moore revised *A Mere Accident* as a short story for the collection, *Celibates* (1895). This is more successful than the novel, as he excised the long conversations between Norton and the Revd Hare about church-architecture, the Jesuit order and various Aesthetic topics, which formerly made Moore's moral position towards Norton confusing; as a result Kitty emerges more fully as both the symbol in Norton's mind of his quest for spiritual perfection and as an embodiment of the physical vitality he seeks to suppress in life because he considers it gross.
8   George Moore: *Spring Days*. 1888. p. 356.
9   Reference to Jane Austen here and elsewhere in the discussion of *Spring Days* is not out of place: at the time of the publication of his novel Moore wrote to the Marquise Clara Lanza of his great admiration for Miss Austen's work: 'I said to myself, "I will recreate Jane Austen's method. . . ." It was an attempt not to continue, but to recreate *Pride and Prejudice, Emma,* etc.' Moore had the grace to add: 'Apparently I have failed horribly.' The letter, dated September 9, 1888, is cited in J. M. Hone: *The Life of George Moore*. 1936. p. 148.
10   *Spring Days*. p. 225.
11   George Moore: *Mike Fletcher*. 1889. p. 29.
12   Ibid. pp. 80-3.
13   Ibid. p. 15.

14 Ibid. p. 16.
15 Ibid. p. 15.
16 Ibid. p. 90.
17 Ibid. p. 218.
18 T. S. Eliot: 'Baudelaire', *Selected Essays*. Reprinted 1961. p. 429. 'It is true to say that the glory of man is his capacity for salvation; it is also true to say that his glory is his capacity for damnation.' This applies in many ways to William Golding's heroes in *Pincher Martin* and *The Spire*.
19 There is a slight lapse into sentimentality (p. 108) when the pair decide finally to wed and start calling each other 'little wifie' and 'little husband' but this is redeemed almost immediately by the account of the wedding itself in which Moore sustains a mood of grim farce as Frank's revulsion at the coarseness of the proceeding poses a serious challenge to his determination to go through the ceremony for Lizzie's sake.
20 When for example Fletcher announces his intention of writing a prose poem about Lady Helen's suicide since he was inspired by the 'pictures-queness of the room – the Venetian blinds', Frank retaliates: 'If that's the way you are going to treat it, I would sooner not have it – the face in the glass, a lot of repetitions of words, sentences beginning with 'And', then a mention of shoes and silk stockings. If you can't write feelingly about her, you had better not write at all.' (*Mike Fletcher*. p. 101.) It is a pity that Moore did not develop this aspect of Frank so that he consistently served the function of criticising Fletcher, deflating his pretensions and exposing his bombast; the novel would have been the better for it. The deliberate contrasting of their careers as a structural parallel, a fairly traditional device in fiction, would have made for a more comfortable relationship between author and reader.
21 *Mike Fletcher*. p. 263.
22 George Moore: *Vain Fortune*. Revised edition, 1895. pp. vi-vii. Moore himself preferred this version of the novel and certainly the writing, though not greatly altered in the main episodes, is generally sharper for the revision.
23 Ibid. p. 166.
24 Ibid. pp. 254-5.
25 Ibid. pp. 270-2.
26 James Joyce: 'The Day of the Rabblement'. Cited in Richard Ellmann: *James Joyce*. New York, 1959. p. 260.
27 *James Joyce*. pp. 259-60.
28 See a letter from Moore to Edward Marsh: about *Dubliners* Moore wrote that 'the last story . . . seemed to me perfection whilst I read it! I regretted that I was not the author of it.' (Cited in *James Joyce*. pp. 418-9.) Even when Moore was adversely critical of Joyce's later work, always 'he allowed there was merit in "The Dead".' (Ibid. pp. 543-4.)
29 *James Joyce*. p. 260.
30 Samuel Beckett: *Eh Joe and Other Writings*. 1967. pp. 20-1.

Chapter Seven: Wagner and the Novel

1   George Moore: 'Since the Elizabethans', *Cosmopolis*. October, 1896. pp. 42-58. The phrases quoted in this paragraph are all taken from p. 57.

2   Ibid. p. 56.

3   George Moore: *Mike Fletcher*. 1889. p. 95.

4   Ibid. p. 96.

5   See above notes 1 and 2.

6   *Letters from George Moore to Ed. Dujardin, 1886-1922*. Translated and edited by 'John Eglinton'. New York, 1929. pp. 79-80.

7   'Balzac and Wagner have exalted me; I have joined in the processional crowds and have carried a blowing banner.' (George Moore: *Avowals*. Ebury Edition, 1936. p. 130.)

8   Edwin Muir: *We Moderns*. 1918. pp. 188-9.

9   Moore's letters to Lady Cunard abound with references to Wagner and images drawn from the operas. She was a frequent visitor to Bayreuth and helped to finance Sir Thomas Beecham's opera seasons in London before the First World War. Martyn's enthusiasm for Wagner stands on record in *Hail and Farewell*, especially in 'Ave'; he was also the author of an article entitled 'Wagner's *Parsifal* or the Cult of Liturgical Aestheticism' (*The Irish Review*. No. 3. 1913-4. pp. 535-40). Miss Horniman was the friend and secretary of W. A. Ellis, who translated Wagner's works into English. (Yeats refers to this aspect of Miss Horniman's numerous artistic interests in a letter to Arthur Symons, *Letters of W. B. Yeats*. Edited by A. Wade. 1954. pp. 459-60.) Catulle Mendès, who introduced Moore to Zola, was an ardent Wagnerite; his wife, Judith Gautier, maintained a lengthy correspondence with the composer; both of them accompanied Villiers de l'Isle Adam on two occasions to Germany, where they became Wagner's guests. (See G. Jean-Aubrey: 'Villiers de l'Isle Adam and Music', *Music and Letters*. XIX. 1938. pp. 391-404; and 'Wagner and Judith Gautier', *Music and Letters*. XVIII. 1937, pp. 134-49.) Arthur Symons wrote several articles on Wagner, most notably 'Bayreuth: Notes on Wagner' (*The Dome*. IV. August, 1899. pp. 145-9.) and 'The Ideas of Richard Wagner' (later published in *Studies in Seven Arts*. 1906. pp. 225-98). He was also acquainted with the Wagnerites, Verlaine, Mallarmé, Huysmans and D'Annunzio and several of his plays were inspired by Wagnerian themes.

10   George Moore: *Conversations in Ebury Street*. Ebury Edition, 1936. pp. 182-3.

11   That with Martyn described in 'Ave'; another in 1908, referred to in his letters to Lady Cunard (*George Moore: Letters to Lady Cunard, 1895-1933*. Edited by Rupert Hart-Davis. 1957. pp. 62-7); and a third undertaken with Lady Cunard's party in 1910, during which they suffered a rather serious accident at Munich.

12   *The Musician* was a shortlived journal that ran for a dozen or so numbers in 1897. It is an interesting document of musical taste in the late Nineties. Though a periodical devoted to music generally, the

articles on Wagner's music, prose works and theories far out-number those on any other composer. Of particular interest to the student of the novel is the constant recurrence in these articles of discussions about Wagner's innovatory conceptions of psychology. Ernest Newman reviewing a translation of Wagner's study of Beethoven concentrates almost entirely on what Wagner says about the consciousness of the artist in the act of creativity rather than on Wagner's analysis of Beethoven's actual works and technique.

13 Richard Wagner: *Opera and Drama*. Translated by Edwin Evans. 1913. Vol. 2. pp. 582-3.

14 Richard Wagner: *A Communication to my Friends*. Translated by W. A. Ellis. Complete Works. Vol. 1. 1892. p. 286.

15 Edmund Wilson: *Axël's Castle*. Fontana Paperbacks, 1961. p. 24.

16 *La Revue Wagnérienne*. 2ᵉ Année. No. 5. June 8, 1886. p. 154. Another typical comment by de Wyzewa at this time was '. . . il faut au-dessus de ce monde des apparences habituelles profanés, bâtir le monde saint d'une meilleure vie: meilleure parce que nous le pouvons créer volontairement, et savoir que nous le créons. C'est la tâche même de l'Art.' (*La Revue Wagnérienne*. 2ᵉ Année. No. 4. May 8, 1886. p. 102.) This completely ignores a recurring theme in Wagner's prose that 'only from *Life* . . . can art obtain her *matter* and her *form*.' (*The Art-Work of the Future*. Translated by W. A. Ellis. Complete Works. Vol. 1. 1892. p. 86.) Always in Wagner's work we find a reverence for life as the mightiest impulse within every creature: 'that alone is true and living which is sentient' (Ibid. p. 72); and the best art is that which is 'the highest expression of activity of a race that has developed its physical beauty in unison with itself and Nature'. (*Art and Revolution*. Translated by W. A. Ellis. Complete Works. Vol. 1. 1892. p. 38.)

17 Cited in E. L. Duval: *Teodor de Wyzewa*. Geneva, 1961. p. 26. Duval then draws attention to de Wyzewa's analogous remark: 'Seul vit le Moi, et seule est sa tâche éternelle: créer.'

18 Cited in *Mallarme*. The Penguin Poets. Introduced by A. Hartley. Harmondsworth, 1965. p. xix.

19 Ibid. p. ix. See also Moore's *Confessions of a Young Man*: 'Not the idea itself but the idea of the thing evokes the idea. Schopenhauer was right; we do not want the thing. The thing is worthless . . . we want the idea drawn out of obscuring matter and this can best be done by the symbol. The symbol, or the thing itself, that is the great artistic question.' (Ebury Edition, 1937. p. 119.)

20 Cited in Arthur Symons: 'The Ideas of Richard Wagner', *Studies in Seven Arts*. 1906. p. 282.

21 George Moore: *Lewis Seymour and Some Women*. 1917. p. 132.

22 George Moore: *Modern Painting*. 1893. p. 188.

23 *Lewis Seymour and Some Women*. p. 300.

24 George Moore: *Confessions of a Young Man*. 1888. pp. 270-1. This passage was omitted from later revised editions.

25 Mrs Virginia Crawford: *Studies in Foreign Literature*. 1899. p. 193. Mrs Crawford contributed a translation of the *Tristan and Isolde* passage from the novel to *The Musician*, September 15 and 22, 1897.

26 Ibid. p. 218.
27 J. M. Hone: *The Life of George Moore.* 1936. p. 205.
28 'You speak about *The Triumph of Death* by D'Annunzio; I have just finished *L'Intrus*, another book by him. I think it quite wonderful. You know that I seldom praise a novel – well, I could write twenty pages about *L'Intrus*. . . . He is a little wanting in outline – but what wonderful writing!' (*George Moore: Letters to Lady Cunard, 1895-1933.* pp. 23-4.)
29 *Studies in Foreign Literature.* p. 190. Elsewhere she describes D'Annunzio as 'probably the most acute interpreter of the sex emotions of the century'. (Ibid. p. 187.)
30 Henry James: 'Gabriele d'Annunzio', *Notes on Novelists.* 1914. p. 231.
31 *Studies in Foreign Literature.* p. 199.
32 'Such externalities as D'Annunzio's are worthless.' (George Moore: 'The Nineness in the Oneness', *Century Magazine.* Vol. 99. November, 1919. pp. 63-6.) Even in 1897 one can detect a certain scepticism in some of Moore's comments on the Italian novelist. In 'Mr Moore on Music and Literature' (*The Musician.* September, 1897. pp. 392-4), while Moore praises D'Annunzio's 'exquisite fluidity of . . . execution' and his intensity, he adds rather wrily that like physical gratification the intensity of style is curiously 'unrememberable' (p. 393) and continues: 'His art consists largely in the ceaseless chatter of the soul, the little egotistical soul that never ceases to bemoan its own sorrows, to exult in its own joys, to view the world from its tiny eyelit-hole [sic].' One wonders whether the choice of words was infelicitous in the heat of the interview or quite deliberate to intimate he had some serious reservations about D'Annunzio's work. Commenting finally on D'Annunzio's 'attempt to write by means of motives' in imitation of Wagner, he admits the technique always runs the danger of lapsing into 'artifice', which perhaps reflects some of his own difficulties with composition at this time.
33 'The Nineness in the Oneness'. p. 63.
34 This is explored more fully in the following chapter, pages 160-1.
35 *Studies in Foreign Literature.* p. 93.

Chapter Eight: *Evelyn Innes* and *Sister Teresa*

1 George Moore: *Sister Teresa.* 1901. p. 53.
2 George Moore: *Evelyn Innes.* 1898. p. 69. There is a difficulty with page-references for this novel. Two editions of the first version came out in quick succession in June and September, 1898. For the second of these Moore made an addition of two pages at the beginning of Chapter XII, which means that references in some copies dated 1898 will differ slightly from others. Elsewhere, the two editions are identical. I give references to the second edition in brackets where it is necessary.
3 *Evelyn Innes.* p. 160. (p. 162.)

4   Ibid. pp. 210-11. (pp. 212-3.)
5   Ibid. p. 211. (p. 213.)
6   Ibid. p. 391. (p. 393.)
7   Ibid. p. 335. (p. 336.)
8   Ibid. p. 333. (p. 335.)
9   Ibid. p. 467. (p. 469.)
10 Shortly after the first edition had appeared Moore wrote to Fisher Unwin the publisher and admitted: 'The worst part of *Evelyn Innes* ... is Ulick Dean; the character was not assimilated'. (*George Moore In Transition: Letters to T. Fisher Unwin and Lena Milman, 1894-1910.* Edited by H. E. Gerber. Detroit, 1968. p. 169.)
11 *Evelyn Innes.* p. 238. (p. 240.)
12 *Sister Teresa.* p. 24.
13 Ibid. p. 140.
14 *The Life of Saint Teresa.* Translated by J. M. Cohen. Penguin Classics. Harmondsworth, 1957. p. 85. Moore is known to have read this work in preparation for the novel.
15 St Teresa. Cited in William James: *The Varieties of Religious Experience.* Fontana Books, 1963. p. 41.
16 *Sister Teresa.* p. 217.
17 Ibid. p. 207.
18 Ibid. p. 129.
19 Ibid. p. 199.
20 Ibid. p. 200.
21 Ibid. p. 218.
22 Ibid. p. 221.
23 Ibid. pp. 232-3.
24 *The Varieties of Religious Experience.* pp. 247-8.
25 See the review in *Athenaeum.* No. 3849. August 3, 1901. pp. 150-1.
26 *Sister Teresa.* p. 234.
27 Ibid. p. 235.
28 Ibid. p. 235.
29 The 1909 version is decidedly weaker than the original. The convent-scenes are simplified but much that is valuable is excised in the process. The chief addition, apart from the revised ending, is a detailed account of Asher's life after Evelyn has entered the convent. This allows Moore some set-piece descriptions about hunting game in the Sahara Desert, but there is little development in Asher's character of any significance. His meeting with Evelyn again and the renewal of their friendship on a purely platonic level successfully avoids too excessive a sentimentality.
30 Making his heroine offer such a challenge exposed Shaw to criticism from Catholics who considered he had turned Joan of Arc into a Protestant martyr and saint.
31 *Evelyn Innes.* p. 383. (p. 385.)
32 The *Athenaeum* review cited above, note 25.
33 During the composition of the novel Moore was interviewed by a reporter from *The Musician* (an account of the meeting was published in the magazine on Wednesday September 29, 1897, pp. 392-4, under

the title, 'Mr George Moore on Music and Literature') to whom he related the anecdote which had inspired him: 'May Robinson, Madame Darmstetter, told me of a little actress who had scruples of conscience about her lovers and had gone into a convent. She could not stop there because the nuns were all so childlike'. The *donné* appears to have tyrannised over Moore's imagination with the last-mentioned detail, while the rest is quite transformed by his treatment. None of the patronising jocularity of tone evident in the telling of the anecdote has survived in Moore's handling of Evelyn or her suitors but an ungenerous superiority is directed at times towards the nuns.

34   In a letter of June, 1903, cited in J. M. Hone: *The Life of George Moore.* 1936. p. 245.

35   In a letter to the *Irish Times* that was published on Thursday September 24, 1903. Unfortunately the seriousness of his avowal was undermined for his Irish audience by the fact that the letter also included some satirical barbs at the expense of certain dignitaries of the Catholic Church who, despite their stated Nationalist sympathies, had recently and in public been remarkably obsequious to King Edward VII during his State Visit to Ireland. Despite his zeal for the Nationalist cause, he should have restrained himself from uniting the public and private issues in his statement. AE and Gogarty both advised Moore against doing so; the whole tone of the letter seemed to them inappropriately facetious. Moore would have his way and too late realised that his impetuousness had got the better of him. *The Lake, Hail and Farewell* and *The Brook Kerith* were all in some sense attempts to recover some of the esteem he lost through his flippancy. His decision was not an idle one but based on a carefully evolved philosophy, one which his late works propound with increasing assurance.

36   T. S. Eliot: *East Coker.* 1940. p. 14.

Chapter Nine: *The Lake* – The Wagnerian Novel Perfected

1   George Moore: 'My Impressions of Zola'. *The English Illustrated Magazine.* February, 1894, pp. 477-89. The article is recalling a visit Moore paid to Zola in 1888 to try and defend himself for the many criticisms he made of the French novelist and his technique in *Confessions of a Young Man*. A revised version of this article retitled 'A Visit to Médan' was included in the 1904 edition of *Confessions*. The article itself differs markedly from another account Moore wrote of Zola's working methods at the height of his enthusiasm for the master of Médan, 'My New Novel. By Monsieur Zola'. (*Pall Mall Gazette.* May 3, 1884. p. 6.)

2   See the closing chapters of 'Ave' in *Hail and Farewell* and J. O. Baylen's article, 'George Moore, W. T. Stead and the Boer War'. (*Studies in English.* III. 1962-3.)

3 Moore appears to have quarrelled with Lady Cunard during the summer of 1900. There is a lengthy gap in their published correspondence at this date. Moore renewed his friendship with her in October 1904, when Clara Christian, his companion during the first years of his stay in Ireland, went to spend several weeks at Rapallo in Italy prior to her marriage in January of the following year to Charles MacCarthy, the City Architect of Dublin.

4 These date from the spring of 1899.

5 For a more detailed account of this relationship and its effect on Moore's work see my article, 'George Moore's "Stella".' (*Review of English Studies*. New Series, Vol. XXVIII. Number 110. May, 1977. pp. 181-8.)

6 Russell, Meyer, Synge and Clara Christian alone among the major figures who appear in *Hail and Farewell* are treated consistently with respect.

7 'Salve', *Hail and Farewell*. Uniform Edition, 1933. p. 124.

8 Ibid. p. 124.

9 In a series of reviews and articles published in *The Speaker*, which were subsequently collected into the volume, *Modern Painting* (1893). See also 'Vale' chapter VI.

10 Edouard Dujardin: *Le Monologue Intérieur*. Paris, 1931. p. 55.

11 George Moore: *The Lake*. Revised edition, 1921. Preface, pp. viii-ix. (Ebury edition. p. viii.) I have in this chapter made use of the later revised text of the novel; not only is this more accessible than the first edition of 1905, but it includes much revised material which makes it a superior work. My reasons for using this particular text are given in detail in the course of the chapter. The Ebury edition (1936) and the 1921 edition are identical; and I give references to both.

12 Ibid. p. 145. (Ebury. p. 109.)

13 Ibid. p. 262. (Ebury. p. 194.)

14 Ibid. pp. 28-9. (Ebury. pp. 21-2.)

15 George Eliot: *The Mill on the Floss*. World's Classics edition, 1961. Book Fourth, Chapter III. p. 311. The same pattern is of course repeated in the life of Dorothea Brooke in *Middlemarch*. Interestingly both George Eliot and Moore make a reading of Thomas à Kempis a turning-point in their characters' lives of renunciation.

16 *The Lake*. p. 81. (Ebury. p. 59.)

17 Ibid. p. 110. (Ebury. p. 82.)

18 Ibid. pp. 140-1. (Ebury. pp. 104-5.)

19 Ibid. p. 151. (Ebury. p. 113.)

20 Ibid. p. 153. (Ebury. p. 115.)

21 Ibid. pp. 172-3. (Ebury. p. 129.)

22 Ibid. p. 195. (Ebury. pp. 144-5.)

23 Ibid. pp. 197 and 199. (Ebury. pp. 146 and 148.)

24 Ibid. p. 220. (Ebury. p. 163.)

25 Ibid. p. 219. (Ebury. p. 162.)

26 Ibid. p. 230. (Ebury. p. 170.)

27 Ibid. p. 204. (Ebury. p. 152.)

28 M. J. Brown: *George Moore – A Reconsideration*. Seattle, 1955. pp.

167-8. Though this is perhaps not Brown's stated conclusion, it is strongly implied. He seeks in his study to champion Moore's work but throughout presents a view of him as entrapped within late nineteenth-century forms of Aestheticism and not breaking through to new ground. He offers a curt synopsis of *The Lake* which describes Gogarty as embracing hedonism in response to the heroine's aestheticizing and concludes that the novel is a return 'to the position he had occupied twenty years before in *Confessions of a Young Man*'. There is no discussion of the style or structure.

29 Zola's novel was published in 1875.

30 Emile Zola: *The Sin of Abbé Mouret (La Faute de l'Abbé Mouret)*. Translated by M. Smyth. 1904. p. 37.

31 *The Lake*. p. 154. (Ebury. pp. 115-6.)

32 Ibid. p. 216. (Ebury. p. 160.)

33 James Joyce: *A Portrait of the Artist as a Young Man*. 1917. pp. 200 and 299.

34 *The Lake*. p. 238. (Ebury. p. 176.)

35 Ibid. p. 239. (Ebury. p. 176.)

36 Ibid. pp. 240-1. (Ebury. pp. 177-8.)

37 Ibid. p. 241. (Ebury. p. 178.)

38 *George Moore: Letters to Lady Cunard, 1895-1933*. Edited by Rupert Hart-Davis. 1957. p. 36. This was in a letter dated October 22, 1904; in July he was still expressing fears whether he would be able to complete the novel (Ibid. p. 41.); but by mid-August he was correcting the proofs in Paris. His pride in the work later was because of the great technical difficulties which he had overcome.

39 *The Lake*. p. 265. (Ebury. p. 196.)

40 Ibid. p. 265. (Ebury. p. 196.)

41 Ibid. p. 266. (Ebury. p. 197.)

42 Ibid. p. 268. (Ebury. p. 198.)

43 Ibid. p. 268. (Ebury. p. 198.)

44 Ibid. p. 268. (Ebury. p. 198.)

45 Ibid. p. 269. (Ebury. p. 199.)

46 Ibid. p. 264. (Ebury. p. 196.)

47 Ibid. p. 269. (Ebury. pp. 198-9.) There is generally a coarsening of Moore's vision and attitude in the final chapter. When Gogarty in his meditation assesses his maturer experience in rational terms, Moore resorts to the naive and the anecdotal: Nora is 'a cure for religion' and Gogarty 'doubted if the reading of the Scriptures would have taught him as much as Nora's beauty'. (Ibid. p. 260. Ebury. p. 192.) Such statements merely belittle the careful definition of the instinctive life as a controlled but spontaneous imaginative growth which the novel makes elsewhere.

48 Ibid. p. 206. (Ebury. p. 153.)

49 Ibid. p. 154. (Ebury. p. 115.)

50 It is here that Moore most closely approaches Turgenev's method as outlined in the introduction to this study, pp. 19-20.

51 *The Lake*. p. 58. (Ebury. p. 42.)

52 Ibid. pp. 37-9. (Ebury. pp. 27-29.)

53 Ibid. p. 273. (Ebury. p. 202.)
54 Edouard Dujardin: *Les Lauriers Sont Coupés*. Paris, 1888. pp. 31-2.
55 *The Lake*. p. 72. (Ebury. p. 53.)

Chapter Ten: *The Brook Kerith*
and the Late Historical Novels

1 For a more detailed examination of the structure of *Hail and Farewell* see the introduction to my edition of the autobiography (Gerrards Cross, 1976). pp. 31-5.
2 Arthur Symons: 'Bayreuth: Notes on Wagner', *The Dome*. IV. August, 1899. pp. 147-8.
3 George Moore: 'The Nineness in the Oneness', *Century Magazine*. Vol. 99. November, 1919. pp. 63-6.
4 George Moore: *Héloïse and Abélard*. Ebury Edition, 1936. p. 180.
5 George Moore: *The Brook Kerith*. Ebury Edition, 1937. pp. 354-5.
6 A. N. Jeffares: 'George Moore.' *Writers and Their Work*. No. 180. 1965. p. 31.
7 George Moore: *Mike Fletcher*. 1889. p. 127.
8 George Moore: 'Wagner's *Jesus of Nazareth*', *The Musician*. Wednesday May 12, 1897. pp. 8-9.
9 'The washing of the hands is the symbol of a man's last horror of a deed of blood, which he would avert if he could. The washing of the hands is the act not of a weak but of a strong man who is overborne by circumstances.' (Ibid. p. 9.)
10 Some of Wagner's notes for themes in his opera anticipate fully worked through conceptions in Moore's novel such as 'So Jesus frees our human nature, when he abrogates the law which makes that nature appear sinful to itself through its restrictions, – when he proclaims the divine law of Love, in whose envelopment our whole being is justified.' ('Jesus of Nazareth', *Prose Works*. Vol. VIII. Translated by W. A. Ellis. 1889. p. 303.)
11 The latter half of 'Salve', where Moore sets out to prove that no Catholic has ever written a good book is the one *longueur* in the trilogy as Moore becomes every bit as fanatical as the Irish clerics he wishes to expose. He quite loses touch with his real aim in the work which is to criticise through ridicule.
12 George Moore: *The Apostle*. Dublin, 1911. p. 100.
13 Ibid. p. 88.
14 *The Brook Kerith*. p. 33.
15 Ibid. pp. 2-3.
16 Ibid. pp. 30-1.
17 Ibid. p. 25.
18 Ibid. p. 27.
19 Ibid. p. 27.

20   Ibid. p. 110.
21   Ibid. pp. 123-5.
22   The terms of Coleridge's 'Dejection Ode' seem peculiarly appropriate here; his visual perception was remarkably acute and yet, as with Joseph, the sense of beauty in nature rarely invited a sustained inner peace.
23   *The Brook Kerith.* p. 61.
24   Ibid. p. 62.
25   Ibid. p. 81.
26   Ibid. p. 87.
27   Ibid. p. 85.
28   Ibid. p. 123.
29   Ibid. p. 195.
30   Walter Pater: *Plato and Platonism.* 1883. p. 177.
31   Walter Pater: *Studies in the History of the Renaissance.* 1873. p. 210.
32   *The Brook Kerith.* pp. 227-8.
33   Ibid. p. 144.
34   Ibid. p. 143.
35   Ibid. p. 158.
36   Ibid. pp. 145-6.
37   Ibid. p. 195.
38   Ibid. p. 160.
39   Ibid. p. 183.
40   Ibid. p. 184.
41   Ibid. p. 181.
42   Ibid. p. 220.
43   Ibid. p. 221.
44   Ibid. p. 222.
45   William Blake: *The Everlasting Gospel.*
46   Richard Wagner: *A Communication to My Friends.* Translated by W. A. Ellis. 1892. pp. 378-9.
47   *The Brook Kerith.* p. 231.
48   Ibid. p. 232.
49   Ibid. p. 261.
50   Ibid. p. 280.
51   Ibid. pp. 342 and 344.
52   Ibid. p. 354.
53   Ibid. p. 355.
54   Ibid. p. 360.
55   Ibid. p. 438.
56   Ibid. p. 342.
57   Ibid. pp. 432-3 and 438. Dostoievsky's Father Zossima takes a similar view:
'He who does not believe in God, will never believe in God's people. But he who has faith in God's people, will also behold his Glory, though he had not believed in it till then. . . . Nature is beautiful and without sin, and we, we alone, are godless and foolish and we don't understand that life is paradise, for we have only to want to understand and it will at once come in all its beauty and we shall embrace

and weep.' (*The Brothers Karamazov.* Translated by D. Magarshack. Penguin Classics. Harmondsworth, 1958. pp. 345 and 352.)

58 *The Brook Kerith.* p. 395. (Interestingly, this is almost a word-for-word echo of Bunyan's first and illusory conversion : 'I thought there was no man in England that pleased God better than I.')

59 Ibid. p. 423.

60 Ibid. p. 442.

61 Ibid. p. 458.

62 Ibid. pp. 458-9.

63 Ibid. p. 459.

64 Ibid. p. 457.

65 Ibid. pp. 461-3.

66 George Moore : *The Lake.* 1921 edition. p. 218. (Ebury Edition. p. 162.)

67 Man, according to Hennell, will discover 'in the Universe itself a Son which tells us of a Father, and in all the natural beauty and moral excellence which meet us in the world an ever-present Logos, which reveals the grace and truth of its invisible source.' Strauss adds a complementary gloss: 'we nowhere find him (Hennell) deriving religion from priestcraft, but from the tendencies and want of human nature'. The same could be said of Moore. (The quotations from Hennell and Strauss are cited in Basil Willey: *Nineteenth Century Studies.* 1949. pp. 217 and 219 respectively. I am indebted to Professor Willey's book for the formation of many ideas expressed in this chapter.)

68 J. S. Mill: *Three Essays.* 1874. p. 255. Cited in *Nineteenth Century Studies.* p. 186.

69 George Moore: *Héloïse and Abélard.* Ebury Edition, 1937. p. 80.

70 *Letters of George Moore.* Edited with an introduction by 'John Eglinton'. Bournemouth, 1942. See particularly the letter dated December 18, 1915. p. 29.

71 W. B. Yeats: 'Solomon and the Witch'. *Collected Poems.* 1961. p. 199.

72 *Héloïse and Abélard.* p. 145.

73 Ibid. p. 146.

74 Ibid. pp. 44-5.

75 Ibid. pp. 175-6.

76 Ibid. p. 72.

77 Ibid. p. 146.

78 Ibid. p. 388.

79 Ibid. p. 334.

80 Ibid. pp. 427 and 429.

81 Ibid. pp. 389-90.

82 Ibid. p. 424.

83 Richard Wagner: *Art and Revolution.* Complete Prose Works. Translated by W. A. Ellis. 1892. Vol. 1, p. 57.

84 George Moore: *Aphrodite in Aulis.* Ebury Edition, 1937. p. 60.

85 Ibid. p. 257.

Conclusion

1   George Moore: 'Ave'. *Hail and Farewell*. Ebury Edition, 1937. p. 84.
2   George Moore: *The Lake*. 1921. p.x.
3   J. M. Hone cites an occasion when in conversation Moore remarked: 'It is so very easy to be facetious (that's one of the things that's wrong with Bennett) and I have great difficulty in cutting out the smart sentences and humorous passages from my own work. Pater knew better than that. He knew what was right and what was futile and frivolous.' (*The Life of George Moore*. 1936. p. 374.)
4   From a review of Moore's *Impressions and Opinions* by Arthur Symons in *The Academy*. March 21, 1891. Vol. 39. pp. 274-5.
5   'Is there a little devil in Mr Moore that makes him want to annoy?' (Susan Mitchell: *George Moore*. Dublin, 1916. p. 30.)
6   George Moore: *Sister Teresa*. 1901. p. 207.
7   Cited in Richard Ellmann: *James Joyce*. New York, 1959. p. 630.
8   Emile Delavenay: *D. H. Lawrence: The Man and His Work*. 1972. p. 58.
9   Ibid. p. 476.
10 Ibid. p. 93.
11 Letter to J. B. Pinker, dated December 18, 1917. *The Collected Letters of D. H. Lawrence*. Edited by H. T. Moore. 1962. Vol. 1. p. 534.
12 Virginia Woolf: 'George Moore'. *Collected Essays*. 1966. Vol. 1. p. 341.
13 *The Letters of Virginia Woolf*. Vol. III: 'A Change of Perspective'. Edited by N. Nicolson and J. Trautmann. 1977. p. 249.
14 Virginia Woolf: *A Writer's Diary*. Edited by Leonard Woolf. 1953. pp. 86-7. (The entry is for March 9, 1926.)
15 Virginia Woolf: *Collected Essays*. Vol. 1. p. 338.
16 Ibid. p. 341.
17 See the letter to Dujardin cited in chapter 7, page 136. The term was noticeably a favourite with Virginia Woolf too.
18 D. H. Lawrence: *Apocalypse*. 1932. p. 222.
19 D. H. Lawrence: 'Democracy'. *Selected Essays*. Penguin Books. Harmondsworth, 1966. p. 88.
20 *A Writer's Diary*. p. 86.
21 *The Letters of William and Dorothy Wordsworth*. Edited by Selincourt and Shaver. Oxford, 1967. Vol. 1. p. 355. (The letter is dated June 7, 1802.)

Index

267